Grace in Mombasa

My heartfelt thanks go to Nigel, who was the most perfect
writing companion anyone could ask for. Thank you so
much for all your hours of hard work in helping perfect
this story.

Thanks also to Piers Tilbury, who donated the wonderful
book cover, and to Storm who did the blurb.

"Not all of us can do great things. But we can do small things
with great love."
Mother Teresa

This story was inspired by and is dedicated to…

Moira Smith

A woman who lived her life by Matthew 25:35
I was hungry and you gave me food to eat. I was thirsty and you
gave me a drink. I was a stranger and you welcomed me.

Acknowledgments

Wendy H Jones
Author and member/webmaster Association of Christian Writers

Tracy Traynor's writing transports you from World War 1 and 2 England to the courts of heaven, via Mombasa. With characters which pop off the page and straight into your heart, this is a book you will remember for a long time.

Sean McIntyre
Missionary with Barnabas and minister at AOG Colchester

The story of Grace captures the experience of many others who, though quite ordinary by themselves, find that the love of God propels them towards quite extraordinary endeavours. Tracy is the author of Grace's story but the inspiration was Moira Smith and the author of her story was none other than God himself, described in the Bible as the 'author and finisher of our faith'. I commend Tracy's book "Grace in Mombasa" to you in the hope that, inspired by the story of Grace and Moira, you will become hungry for a story of your own and that you will turn to the great author of all our lives. He already has a story prepared for you!

Table of Contents

Part One
Newton Le Willows, England

With puzzle-filled, hazel eyes, under frowning eyebrows she looked up at her father.

"But if someone has lost their faith, can't we help them find it?"

Chapter 1

By the Grace of God
November 1912

"You need to prepare yourself, if she survives the night it will only be by the grace of God." The doctor stood tall and straight, he appeared aloof and certainly could have given the news in a gentler fashion, but he was exhausted and barely had the energy to stand, let alone offer words of solace and compassion. His working day started over twelve hours before and the midwife should not have called him, because there was nothing he could have done for the poor woman, and she surely would have known that.

The gentleman to whom he spoke so harshly appeared crushed, and with good cause, for the master joiner and his son had recently carried out the man's dead wife and now he'd been given the news that his new-born daughter was knocking on death's door. Unable to offer comfort, the doctor picked up his medical bag and hastened out of the once quaint bedroom. With black-timber ceiling beams and whitewashed walls, and with a pretty, woollen carpet in the middle of the room, this had been a tranquil bedroom, but now it was tarnished with blood and grief. *A sad affair to be sure.* He inclined his head towards the weary midwife on the stairs as she headed back up to help the vicar care for his dying child.

"Good night, Mrs Brown."

"Good night, Doctor."

Elsa stood in the bedroom doorway for a moment as the doctor made his own way out of the house. Her old, lined face was heavy with sadness as she stared at the back of the vicar's head. He'd hardly moved since his wife had passed and she imagined his knees must be hurting something awful. His hands, that had held Annie's hand until she'd been taken away, were now clasped so tightly his knuckles had turned white. Praying, and apparently with no answer. She needed to get him downstairs so she could strip the bed before the smell took an irremovable hold.

"Eclampsia be a God-awful thing," she said without thinking. He looked at her blankly. "Oh," she said, clasping her hand over her mouth. "I be awfully remorseful at the utterance that falls out of my big stupid mouth, Vicar."

"It's all right, Mrs Brown. I agree with you, tis a God-awful thing." All at once, the realisation that God hadn't stepped in to save his Annie hit him like the thud of a bullet. The pain in his chest crushed him and he moaned, dropping his head onto the bed, finally giving way to an inconsolable flood of tears.

Elsa had been a midwife for the last twenty years and was well used to the deaths of both mothers and infants, but somehow, looking at the vicar, it seemed worse, for surely he must feel as if his God had let him down? Tears trickled down her ruby cheeks as she picked up the tiny, premature baby and started gently wiping away the remains of afterbirth. The child lay limp and lifeless in her arms and she wished she would cry.

"What will you call her, Vicar?" Elsa enquired, wrapping a clean cloth around the baby.

He looked up, his eyes bloodshot and black-ringed with sorrow. "We haven't chosen a name. We were going to wait to see if it was a girl or a boy and then proceed with the first name that came to us. That was Annie's idea. I can't give her a name yet."

Elsa offered the child to him, and for a moment it seemed he wouldn't take her. Then slowly, shakily, he got up and put out his arms.

"Why don't you take her downstairs? The fire is lit in the kitchen and tis mighty warm in there."

He nodded, and with unstable steps made his way out of the bedroom and down the creaky wooden stairs. Sitting in his comfortable chair by the fire, he gazed down at the tiny bundle in his arms.

"Would you take both of them away from me, God?" Even as he uttered the words, he felt shallow and lacking in faith. Annie would never have questioned God, never have doubted that in all things, He works for the good of everyone. He was the one who wore the dog collar and yet he longed for half the faith his wife once had. "Oh Annie, what am I to do without you?" As he cradled the tiny bundle close to his chest, a tear dropped onto her face.

"Lord, I promise to dedicate the life of this child to You, if you would only grant that she may have life." Looking down at her tiny face, he marvelled at her little squashed nose and tiny wisps of blonde hair. "Please God. What say You?"

Suddenly, the baby startled in his arms and began a sorrowful whisper of a cry. For a moment Richard looked down at her in shock, and then he heard the midwife's footfall as she came charging out of the bedroom and down the stairs.

"She's crying, Lord above, she's crying." Mrs Brown entered the kitchen with whirlwind speed. She charged over the stone-tiled floor, her shoes clip-clopping as she came to a breathless stop by the vicar and looked down at the infant. When she looked up again she was smiling.

"I'll be right back, Vicar. I'll just go and fetch a wet nurse for you."

"A wet nurse?"

"Yes, sir. It seems she will want feeding."

Against all odds, the petite, premature baby made it through the night. The wet nurse had managed to get her to suckle a few times before going home to get some sleep herself in the early hours of the morning.

Richard didn't want to wake, but a constant tapping was penetrating his tender dream of dancing with Annie. Peeling his eyes open he spotted the midwife waving frantically at him through the kitchen window. He pushed his tired, aching body out of the chair and winced as memories of the previous day flooded back, prompting him to glance at his sleeping daughter and automatically send up a prayer of thanks.

"Good morning, Vicar," she chirped with the largest of smiles. "I've been down to see Mrs Willows. She has six daughters, you know? *Very* busy woman. Her sons all work out on Telford's farms, but the girls... well, what to do? Not so many young men around these days to marry them off to, now is there? I had a good chat with her, and she's *more than* happy for her eldest, Millie, to come and be your live-in. She'll be along shortly. I'm sure you'll get on with her right-grand, tis a good lass she is."

"A live-in?" said Richard, when the midwife finally paused for breath.

"Yes, of course. You will need someone to both keep house and look after your daughter now, won't you?"

Richard froze as he looked at her, wondering what was wrong with the woman. He hadn't even buried his wife yet.

The midwife screwed her face up and stood on tiptoes to peer into his eyes. "Are you feelin' all right, Vicar?" Before he could answer, her hand sprang forward and landed on his forehead with a slap. "You not be feelin' hot like?"

"No, no I'm fine." He batted her hand away from his head.

"Good, so that's settled then." She nodded, then went to the hearth and threw a few logs onto the embers. "Might as well keep it stoked," she chirped merrily. "The little 'un should be kept as warm as possible, what with her having no meat on her. Poor little mite."

"About the live-in," said Richard, trying to get the situation back under control.

"Millie? Yes, lovely sweet girl, she'll be a blessing to you she will. She'll need ten shillings a month and every other Sunday off to give her mum a rest." The midwife paused and turned to look at him, as if just realising he wasn't happy with the situation. "The little 'un will need looking after, and your house will need cleaning, unless you're thinking of giving up your job and entering the poor house?"

"Of course I won't be giving up my job. It's not a job anyway, it's a calling."

"Good. Then you'll be wanting Millie to start right away."

He gave in and went back to his chair. Of course, he would need help, and the church had recently informed him that now he had his own vicarage he could have a live-in maid. He didn't know why he was resisting. Closing his eyes he laid his head back and sighed.

"So what's her name, then?" Elsa asked, picking up the infant.

Richard groaned and opened his eyes. The midwife was holding the baby and coochy-cooing her.

"What's your name?"

"Me? Well, I'm Mrs Brown, of course."

Richard smiled. "No, I know that. I mean what's your first name?"

"Why, I'm Elsa, sir. Oh dearie me, don't tell me you're thinking of naming her after me? Heavens above, Vicar, don't do that!"

"Why not? I think Elsa is a lovely name and my mind is a blank."

"Firstly, there happen to be three little Elsas in town already and secondly, hadn't you better pray about it? Ain't that what you always say on Sunday mornings?" Elsa paused to stand straight and mimic the vicar. "We very rarely have the answers to anything, but *praise* the Lord, He knows everything," she said in the deepest voice she could muster.

Richard couldn't help it and the briefest smile fluttered at the corners of his mouth. "Well, Lord, what is it to be?" In a flash, the doctor's words came back to him, 'only by the grace of God will she survive.'

"Grace."

"What's that, Vicar?"

"Grace. Her name is Grace."

"Oh, that's mighty sweet, sure your Annie would approve."

Richard felt like a spinning top, his emotions chasing each other around inside him, both sadness and joy. Joy and sadness. Grace. He had a daughter and her name was Grace.

"Let me hold her," he said, holding out his arms.

Elsa gave Grace to him and smiled softly up at him. "Millie'll be here soon, Vicar. I've got to get on, Mrs Rushton went into labour during the night and it must be almost her time now." She reached over and touched his arm. "You'll be all right, Vicar. We'll all be right here beside you."

Richard felt choked with gratitude for her consideration. "Thank you."

The midwife closed the door quietly behind her as she left, and Richard was left gazing down at his daughter's face. She was fidgeting and obviously getting ready to feed again. He leant down and kissed her forehead.

"Lord, I promise thee that I will raise her to know and love you." Richard reached across to the table and picked up Annie's King James Bible.

"In the beginning God created the heaven and the earth. And the earth was without form, and void; and darkness was upon the face of the deep. And the Spirit of God moved upon the face of the waters. And God said, Let there be light: and there was light. And God saw the light, that it was good: and God divided the light from the darkness. And God called the light Day, and the darkness he called Night. And the evening and the morning were the first day."

*****

From that day forward Richard would read the Bible aloud to his daughter whenever he could, but without fail, he read it to her before she fell asleep at the end of each day. He kept Annie's Bible solely for this purpose, and when he got to the end he would simply go back to Genesis, and start all over again. So it was that from an infant, Grace was soaked in the word of God.

*****

Millie stood by the kitchen window and waited for the vicar to stop reading before gently tapping on the door.

"Come in, it's open," he called, hoping it was the wet nurse as Grace was definitely becoming agitated.

Millie popped her head around the door and looked across at him with huge brown doe-like eyes. Her eyelashes fluttered and she gulped before whispering, "Me Ma sent me to come help 'ee."

"Ah, Millie, come along in, Mrs Brown has just told me all about you."

Slowly Millie emerged from behind the door. Tall and skinny, with freckles and a massive mop of brown hair, Millie was wearing an unfashionably long plain tunic style dress that almost reached her ankles. Her brown lace-up boots showed their age and use and displayed a hole, through which Richard could see her big toe.

"Why on earth haven't you got a coat on, Millie? Come on inside for goodness sake, and shut the door quickly before we all freeze to death."

"Oh, I'm sorry, sir. I'm that used to the cold I forget sometimes to shut the door. Me Ma's always saying I should live in the barn and that I'd forget my head if it weren't screwed on tight, like."

Richard studied her, slightly bemused, wondering how anyone so skinny didn't feel the cold. "They say it will be freezing this evening and you forgot to bring your coat?"

"Oh no, sir. I didn't forget it. We only have one between us, me Ma and me, and she's off to town like, so she took the coat with her."

He didn't know what to say, but made a mental note to give her Annie's coat later on. "Did you by chance see the wet nurse on your way here?"

"I don't rightly know who that be, sir."

"Well you obviously know Mrs Brown, do you know where she is? Could you go and ask her about the wet nurse?"

"Yes sir, I can do that," Millie answered with a broad smile.

Just then, however, there was a knock on the door. Millie jumped, and her eyes opened wide in shock.

"Answer the door, Millie," Richard said when she showed no signs of moving.

She jumped again. "Yes sir, of course."

Richard sighed; this was going to take some getting used to.

Millie opened the door and Margaret, the wet nurse, came in.

Richard sighed again, this time in relief, and stood up straight away. "Ladies, I am very glad you are both here, but you will excuse me please, I need to go and see my Annie now."

Margaret shrugged off her long coat and hung it on the nail on the back of the door, before coming to take the baby from him.

"We've called her Grace," Richard said, placing the baby in her arms.

Richard walked across town as quickly as he could. He needed to see Annie, somehow needing proof that she had gone. Mr Stephenson, the joiner come undertaker, lived on the outskirts of town, and by the time he arrived there Richard was cold through and through. He reached up to touch the big brass knocker but paused a moment, staring at his shaking hand. He lifted the ring and knocked it down with no enthusiasm, no longer sure how he would feel when he saw his wife. As soon as he knocked the door sprang open, and he found himself face to face with Mrs Tigins, the joiner's assistant. He guessed she must have been peeking out from behind the curtains as he approached the house. Huge, robust, with a mop of red curly hair and ruddy cheeks, she stepped back and indicated for him to come in. The smell of a coal fire burning permeated the house, creating a feeling of comfort, while the scent of baking from the kitchen almost disguised what lay within.

As Richard had been there many a time before he knew the way to the cool cellar below, which served as both work room and holding place of the dead.

"Would you like me to come with you, Vicar?"

Richard shook his head and descended the tiny stone steps alone.

To disguise the smell of dead bodies that sometimes rested in the cellar, Mr Stephenson always had two large buckets of vinegar on the floor. These broadly absorbed most of the smell but to be doubly sure, Mrs Tigins put pinecones on the fire to fill the house with the smell of the forest. Normally the smell would be noticeable whenever Richard entered, but today he was unaware of everything, except the body that lay beneath the white cover. With a shaking hand, he pulled back the sheet and beheld the still face of his beautiful Annie, who looked serene and peaceful, as if in a tranquil sleep. A lump formed in his throat and tears fell unchecked as he reached out and stroked her face. For the first time since he was five years old, he couldn't hold his emotions in check. His father had taught him well – that men don't cry or show their emotions – but this was too raw and painful and needed to be expressed.

"Oh, Annie love, our time together was far too short." He bent down and kissed her on the lips.

"We have a little girl, Annie, I've called her Grace. Do you like it?" Richard looked at her as if expecting an answer. "She is the spit of you, my darling, and as long as she is by my side you will always be with me." He kissed her again, then slowly went down on his knees and prayed for her soul's safe deliverance into Heaven.

*****

Richard wasn't too sure how he got through the funeral. Michael, his friend from the Liverpool Diocese, had taken the service. Richard had little input to most of it and was feeling lost and dazed. Mr Stephenson had made the coffin with care, sealing the joints with melted pitch and even taking the time to engrave Annie's initials onto the side. So many people had come; all offered him words of comfort and firm handshakes, but the oddity of being on this side of a funeral left him feeling bewildered.

Millie followed him around for most of the day, always holding Grace in her arms, ever waiting and watchful for the moment he would need to take hold of his daughter and remember why it was that he still went on. Funny, after only a week of having the nervous girl in his house, Richard felt as if she belonged. *Annie would like you,* he thought as he watched her hovering, ever close, but always at a respectful distance.

Everyone, except Michael and Millie, had finally left and he let out a sigh of relief.

Michael crossed the room, making his way towards his friend. "It's been a long day for you, Richard. I'll take myself off to bed and give you some space."

"Don't go yet, stay and have a whiskey with me."

"Of course, shall we go into the sitting room?"

"No, the fire is almost out in there and this one's still burning bright, let's stay here. Millie?"

"Yes sir?" Millie said coming over to him.

"You should get yourself off to bed now, you must be exhausted."

"Oh, I'm all right sir, tis used to 'ard work I am. Grace is asleep now, so I'll just put all this food away before I go up."

"People are so kind," said Richard, looking at the leftover food, all of which had been given to him by his parishioners. Far too much food for a wake, and he knew it was their way of making sure he would eat well for the next week. He watched Millie as she started wrapping the cooked meats in linen cloths. "I don't know what I would have done without you," he said and he meant it. She had become this all-helpful, do everything person, who seemed to know exactly what he needed before he requested it.

"I wish you could have met Annie, you know. She would have loved you."

"Oh, I did meet her sir, several times in the market. Lovely lady she was, right lovely, always smiling and always a kind word on her lips. I do hope little Grace grows up to be like her."

"So do I." Richard picked up the decanter and two glasses from the dresser. After pouring two good measures, he passed one to Michael and sat down.

"To Annie," said Michael.

"To Annie," Richard answered, then knocked the drink back in one and immediately poured himself another.

"What will you do now?" Michael enquired, rolling his whiskey around his glass.

"The bishop was here yesterday, he's confirmed that I can stay on at St John's and remain in the vicarage. They would prefer a married couple to run things, but he has granted me some time to see how I manage on my own. He indicated that after a suitable amount of time it would be better to find myself a new wife who could take up the duties of a vicar's wife."

"I'm sure he didn't mean to be disrespectful, Richard, I know the diocese thought highly of Annie, though I think maybe he might have waited some time before having this conversation with you."

"I think he believed that being matter-of-fact about it all would make me feel better; of course it didn't. I don't believe I will ever marry again, Michael, Annie was my one true love."

"We don't know what's around the corner, and ever is a very long time, don't you think?"

Richard just umm'ed.

Chapter 2

The Bells
Monday 12th November 1918

All morning the town had been quiet. The cold north wind rushed through the High Street and people scurried, heads bent and covered, with no time for friendly banter. Four and a half years of death and hardship had taken its toll on everyone, during the war.

Most people still hoped an end was in sight, and that it would come swiftly, before anyone else they loved was lost to the unfathomable horrors of war. They were in this together, patriotism ran high and the town's folk emanated it with pride; good would win out. But how many of them would die before it did?

Into this dismal grey day, the beautiful ding-dong of the church bell rang clear. For a fleeting moment, everyone was shocked into motionless statues. The bell had been silent for over four years. By the third peal of the bell, people were pouring into the High Street, their tasks abandoned as they gathered together with hysterical hopefulness.

"It's over," yelled the Postmaster, waving a telegram as he charged out of the church and up the street. His first port of call had been the Vicar to get the bells ringing; now he needed to shout the news for all to hear. A slow rumble built up and then erupted into deafening cheers as the news passed from person to person.

"Come on, Grace." Richard grabbed her hand and started hurrying through the church.

"Daddy?" Worry etched her face as she tried to keep up.

"It's over, Grace. It's finally over." They charged up the street to join the throngs of people who were jumping up and down in sheer excitement.

"My lad will be coming home," blurted out Mrs Green, throwing her arms around the vicar. "Praise be to God, oh, praise be." She simultaneously burst into tears and laughter.

"It's wonderful news," said Richard, disentangling himself from Mrs Green's arms and dusting off a layer of flour that fluttered from her apron.

Richard received a thump on the back and turned around to find Henry, the church curate, grinning at him.

Grace watched the event in awe. She could only remember people being quiet and serious. Now there was a riot of noise, an unforgettable blend of shouting, laughing and crying. She wasn't a hundred percent sure what had happened, but the emotion of the town's folk caught in her chest and she burst into tears. And just like always, as she needed her Millie appeared, gathering her up in her arms and smothering her head in kisses.

"It's a great day," said Millie, wiping the tears off Grace's face.

The next few days were confusing to Grace. Things were the same, and yet different. Today, she was sitting in the corner of the front room quietly drawing, hoping no one would notice her, as she listened to the grown-ups' conversations. Things were being said that wouldn't normally interest her, but there was a tension in the air. Loud voices engaged in heated discussion. Whoever David was, he certainly was the biggest part of the debate. The passion in her father's voice enthralled her, and she sneaked a look at him from under her overly long fringe.

"He'll never allow this to happen again, he's an honourable man. He'll keep his promise and call an election, you'll see."

"Richard, he's going to give women the right to vote. They won't let that happen, someone will do for him, mark my words." Thomas Brown, the foreman at the Vulcan Foundry, scratched his balding head as he paced up and down.

"And so he should," said Henry. "Women have kept that locomotive factory of yours running all through the war, you would have shut down without them."

Thomas stopped his pacing to glare at Henry. "They made shells, not locomotives."

"Shells, five tank engines and numerous Burnley Sweeps, to be accurate. You're outrageous, Thomas, next you'll be saying poor men shouldn't be getting the vote either."

"Well," said Thomas pointing his finger at Henry, "there is a good argument that says if you can't read and write you probably don't know what's best for the country."

Henry jumped to his feet, his fists clenched at his sides.

Before Henry had a chance to spurt his rage, Richard stood up and gave a gentle cough.

"Gentlemen, please, we are all friends here. You've been quiet today, Seth. Not like you to have nothing to say."

The old man scrunched up his wrinkled face and chewed his lower lip before answering. "When the river bank floods, there is no stopping it. You have to let the water take its course until the force of it subsides. My wife, God bless 'er soul, would have been mortified at the way women behave today. Sure, she would rather have died than worn a pair of trousers. But these 'ere woman of today, well, they be a different kettle of fish. Times change, people change. We either go with the current or we drown."

"But now the war is over the men will be coming home and they'll want their jobs back, women will have to return to their kitchens and parlours, it's just the way it is. Giving them the vote will make them think they have choices." Thomas flopped down in a chair, he had spoken matter-of-factly and everyone knew he was genuinely worried for everyone.

"God says there is a time for everything under the sun."

The five men in the room all turned to look at Grace, who had stood up. Lifting up her mother's Bible and clasping it to her chest, she continued, "God wouldn't let us drown, and couldn't we wear trousers, if we want to?" Grace slipped her left hand behind her back and crossed her fingers; she had been asking her father for a long time for a pair of breeches.

There was a short silence and then Richard started laughing.

Seth chuckled. "She obviously spends too much time shadowing you, Richard. Maybe you should let her take the sermon this Sunday, aye?"

Grace's eyes lit up, she daydreamed all the time about speaking at the front of church.

Richard came over and ruffled her hair. "We might be moving forward, and building, but bless me, we'll *never* see the day when women take the pulpit... not even my darling six year old daughter." The light in Grace's eyes diminished. Richard gave her a gentle nudge towards the door. "Go on now, go and play with your dolls whilst you still can. You'll be grown up fast enough and can carry the weight of the world on your shoulders then."

"Women in the pulpit," said Henry with a shudder. "Heaven forbid."

"There's a time for everything under the sun," Grace called over her shoulder before running into the kitchen.

Richard quietly closed the front room door.

"What's up with your face?" quizzed Millie, gently knocking Grace's chin. Grace climbed onto her stool so she could sit at the table where Millie was preparing dinner.

"Do you ever dream, Millie?"

"It's probably best not to dream, that way you won't be disappointed when it doesn't come true. Here," she said, pushing a bowl of peas towards Grace, "shell these for me whilst I peel the spuds."

"I dream all the time."

"Really?" said Millie raising her eyebrow at Grace. "And what might you dream of?"

"Being God's little helper."

Millie smiled. "That's a good dream, I'm sure He will appreciate all the help you give Him."

Grace scrutinized Millie to check if she was making fun of her. Millie's face was serious. "Do you want to know how I'm going to help Him?"

"Indeed I do."

"I'm going to tell everyone in the whole wide world, all about Him. I am going to stand at the front of church and teach about the Bible."

Millie stopped mid-stroke of peeling a potato and looked at Grace with loving concern. "Women will never be able to stand in the pulpit, Gracie. I think you should find another way to help God."

Grace's chin wobbled as she tried to hold back tears of frustration. "Just because women don't talk in church today, doesn't mean they can't. I know God wants me to tell people about Jesus, I just know He does."

"You don't need to stand at the front of church to tell people about Jesus, Gracie. You can stand in the gutter and tell people if you want. The pulpit is just a wooden box, you don't need a wooden box to talk about God. That is an easy job, because people come to you to listen. It is much harder to go out into the world and find people to talk to."

Grace mulled the thought over for a while as she shelled peas and filled the pan. "Where should I go to tell people about Jesus, then?"

Millie smiled at her. "Anywhere that God tells you to go."

Grace pulled a sullen face as she stared at Millie. God didn't talk anymore, everyone knew that. So how was God to tell her where to go? She was going to give it some serious thought.

Chapter 3

Good & Bad News
Sunday 3rd September 1939

Grace finished straightening up the Bibles in the pews and took a minute to sit down and gaze at the images in the stained-glass windows. The sunlight poured through, bringing them to life, and filled the church with colour. Although she had seen them nearly every Sunday for the last twenty-seven years, the beauty of them never lessened. As always, the images pulled her into heart-felt prayers. Her knuckles whitened as she clenched her hands and bowed her head, as words flowed from her like an unstoppable waterfall.

"I think when I get to Heaven I am going to give the Father some muffs for His ears, for truly, child, you must give Him earache."

Grace ignored him, even when he came and sat in the pew next to her.

"Sometimes, Grace, less is more."

She continued her mutterings for another two minutes, before the silent presence of her father became too much, and she brought her prayers to a halt. Before sitting up straight, she sneaked a quick sideways glance at him. He was leaning back against the pew, eyes closed, worry lines etched into his forehead. For all his making fun of her, she knew he was praying. She leant back and waited for him to finish.

"There's no stopping it, then?" Grace asked, although she knew the answer.

Richard reached over and gripped her hand tightly. "They've announced that there's to be a broadcast from Downing Street at eleven o'clock. Let's go home, my little love."

They locked up the church together and walked the short distance up the hill to the vicarage. As they turned into the path, they saw about twenty people standing by the front door. There was no reason to ask why they were there; everyone would want to hear the wireless broadcast. Richard unlocked the door and the solemn group headed into the lounge. Richard sat in his favourite chair by the hearth whilst everyone else piled in and found somewhere to stand or sit. Grace turned the wireless on, and after a moment or two of tuning in, the melodic sound of the Glenn Miller Orchestra filled the room. Grace sat herself on the floor by her father's chair.

There was no chatter as they waited until 11:15 am, when it was announced that Neville Chamberlain would be speaking to the country from 10 Downing Street. Grace closed her eyes. *Please God, let it be good news.*

"This morning the British Ambassador in Berlin handed the German Government a final Note stating that, unless we heard from them by 11 o'clock that they were prepared at once to withdraw their troops from Poland, a state of war would exist between us."

Grace's heart was beating so fast she thought she was going to faint. As if knowing she needed him, Richard dropped his hand onto her shoulder and gently squeezed it.

"I have to tell you now that no such undertaking
has been received, and that consequently this
country is at war with Germany."

The whole room gasped, and Grace dropped her head as tears
came. She knew she should be listening to what the Prime
Minister had to say, but when she finally got control back he
was on his last sentence.

"Now may God bless you all. May He defend the
right. It is the evil things that we shall be fighting
against - brute force, bad faith, injustice, oppression
and persecution - and against them I am certain that
the right will prevail."

"I never thought I would ever see a war again," sobbed Mrs
Thackeray, "'tis dreadful, absolutely dreadful."
Not knowing what else to do, and with it being obvious that
no one was about to leave, Grace went into the kitchen to make
tea for everyone.
The whistling of the kettle brought Mrs Thackeray bustling
into the kitchen, giving a last sniff before stuffing her
handkerchief into her pocket. "Have you got the teapot heating
up, ducky? Ruins a tea it does, if you pop the water into a cold
pot. Ah, I see you have the tray and cups ready. Good girl.

Don't suppose you have any cake to go with the tea, do you? You know how good food is for calming everyone down."

Grace smiled to herself as she went into the larder and came back out with a large, round tin. It didn't matter how old she was, she would always be the vicar's little girl.

"Happen to have made a sultana and almond cake, yesterday. I'm sure if we slice it thinly it will go around just nicely."

"I'll do that for you, lovely. You take the first tray of cups through, I'm sure everyone is longing for a good cuppa after that awful news."

"I tell you, if there was any way Chamberlain could have prevented this war, he would have done. You can hear in his voice that the thought of young men dying sickens him just as much as it does us," her father said, leaning forward and tapping his pipe against the fireplace to empty it, before sitting back down.

"That's true, Richard. We all feel the same. To be honest, it doesn't feel so long ago that we were celebrating the end of the Great War, and to be entering into another war now, so soon… well it doesn't bear thinking about. Having said that, I for one do not want to sit by and do nothing while some dictating, completely crackers despot sweeps across Europe in some narcissistic way," responded Fred.

Grace put the tray gently down on the table, and then left to fetch the pot of tea. As she went, there were murmurs of agreement from most of the people in the room in answer to Fred's statement.

"Yes, but surely peace talks would be the best option," replied Richard.

Grace halted in the doorway and turned around. "Not for those who have been oppressed by the tyrant. It is too late for the people who have died by his orders, and for those who are still suffering under Herr Hitler's rule. I am so worked up inside over the injustice of it all, that I would happily sign up and go to war myself."

"Less theatrics please, Grace," said Richard, stuffing his pipe with fresh tobacco.

Grace loved her father very much, but just then she could have happily shaken him for his dismissiveness. She turned around before the desire worked its way out of her, and headed back to the kitchen.

Mrs Thackeray had finished slicing the cake so they returned to the lounge with cake and tea.

"Cup of tea, everyone?" said Mrs Thackeray, pouring tea into the first cup. Slices of cake on tiny, delicate, flower-patterned china plates were passed around the room.

"I always said they made that Treaty of Versailles too harsh and it would come back and bite us on the backside," said Mrs Tigins, before sipping her tea.

"Tasty cake," William whispered behind Grace's shoulder.

She turned around, her eyes sparkling with pleasure at his compliment. "It's the ground almonds, they keep the cake moist."

"I need to talk with you, Grace. Come on outside with me for a moment."

Grace nodded and put her cup down on the table.

As soon as they left the house, he took Grace's hand tightly as they walked down to the cemetery. They meandered through the graves and went to their favourite bench that looked across at Newton Brook. For a while, they sat in silence, William absentmindedly stroking Grace's hand. Grace felt uncomfortable as she imagined all the worst possible things he could be about to say. William had mentioned several times that the army posters kept pulling his attention.

The autumnal sun sprinkled them with warmth and bounced off the gold and brown leaves still clinging onto the branches in a vain attempt to retain the last vestige of summer; this was Grace's favourite time of year. The water gurgled and splashed over the rocks in the brook, and sparrows and blue-tits tweeted melodically.

Finally, William shifted slightly on the bench so he could look at her. He was shaking. "I love you, Grace. Will you marry me?"

Grace was completely shocked, that wasn't what she thought he was going to say. She stared at him, horrified, as he opened a small red box and offered her a ring. With shaking hands and an extremely puzzled heart, Grace lifted up the ring to look at it, emotions running riot over her face. It was a small gold band, with a square face holding a small round sapphire.

"I don't understand," she finally said.

"Don't you want to marry me, Grace? I thought you loved me?"

"I do. I have loved you for years, you're my best friend."

"Then please marry me, Grace."

"But… but… you don't like women that way."

William let go of Grace's hand and dropped his head. "How do you know?"

Grace took hold of William's hand and gave it a gentle squeeze. "I saw you looking at Simon one day, a couple of years back now, and in that moment I just knew that you loved him."

William looked up at her, tears pooling in his eyes. "You never said anything?"

"What was there to say? I dreamt for a long time that you would ask me to marry you, I must admit. I used to spend hours torturing myself as to which of the horrible things about me kept you from falling in love with me. I mostly decided it was because I am a right plain-Jane and a religious nut to boot. Somehow, realising that you never fell in love with me because you had a preference that lay in another direction, well that kind of made it easier for me."

"You don't have anything horrible about you, you are a wonderful, kind and caring person and I really *do* love you."

"Yes, I know, just not in the way that a married couple should like each other. So…" Grace lifted up the ring and tilted it towards him. "What's all this about then, Mr Shelby?"

"Don't hate me, Grace."

"I could never hate you, William." She squeezed his hand tightly. "So?" She raised the ring up again.

"I've signed up."

"Oh, William." This had been the news she'd both expected and dreaded. Tears sprang forth instantly, ushering in a wave of grief.

William, always the gentleman, pulled a huge white handkerchief out of his pocket and passed it to her. "I've been saving. I opened a bank account years ago. I was going to ask you to marry me when I had enough money to set us up somewhere."

Grace looked into his clear blue eyes and saw his sadness. "You were?"

"Yes, I've always thought, if you didn't fall in love with someone else, that we could be happy together. We could genuinely be good companions and care for each other. I know it is not very romantic, and not the reason why any young woman would want to get married, but I do believe in my heart that I could make you happy. I wouldn't ask you otherwise."

"You never even hinted about it to me, why now? And be honest."

William chewed his lip nervously, then looking down at the ground he explained, "I'm frightened. Only last month, Trevor was nearly left for dead after a gang jumped on him, all because he defended pansies and they thought he must be one. I've joined up, I have to, it's my duty. But what if they find out about me? I am more frightened of my regiment finding *that* out, than I am of facing the Nazis."

"All right then, I think I would like to be Mrs Shelby, very much."

"Are you sure?" He looked at her, his light blue eyes full of hope.

"Yes. Better to be married to my best friend than to be left an old maid, hey?"

"We're doing this then? We'll let everyone know we're engaged and in love? It's just, I think, if I can send letters home to my fiancée and sweetheart no one will ever guess the truth."

A little of the happiness that Grace had felt a moment before ebbed away with the realisation that William was only proposing because he was going to war and was afraid of the future. She brushed the thought away quickly. She would be frightened if she were going to war. With the Great War so recently gone by, the knowledge of the atrocities that war created lay heavily on everyone. She blinked in an effort to shake off the gloom threatening her spirit and forming a tight, uncomfortable ball in her throat.

William cupped Grace's face with his large, gentle hands. "I promise I'll be good to you, and we'll live happy ever after, you wait and see." He took the ring from her and slipped it on her finger.

"It's very pretty."

"I have to confess that the ring is second-hand, I got it from the pawn shop. I've only recently finished my apprenticeship at the Vulcan, as you know, so I haven't been able to save up as much as I would have liked. What I do have in the bank is for our future. You don't mind, do you?"

"Of course not, it is so pretty. I love old things, it adds to the charm."

Happy tears trickled down Grace's cheeks.

Although this wasn't the proposal she had dreamt of in her younger years, she was still happy at the thought of sharing her life with William. He was the sweetest, kindest man she knew, and truth be told, she had loved him since leaving school.

The conundrum was, how could a day be both dreadful and wonderful at the same time?

Grace fidgeted with her buttons, an act of nervousness that was not missed by Richard.

"Sir," started William, which he instantly followed with a dry cough. "I would like your permission to marry your daughter." William squared his shoulders and looked Richard in the eye. William didn't know why he was nervous; he knew the vicar liked him.

Richard looked at the pair for a moment, and then started laughing. "About time, William Shelby, thought you were never going to make an honest woman of my little angel, young man."

Grace threw herself at her father and clung onto his neck, happy and sad tears once again wetting her face. She had never once held back the truth from her father and she felt that she was deceiving him. She knew he wouldn't understand why she was marrying if he knew the full truth, and decided that sometimes not revealing the whole truth was simply the best for everyone. Richard held her back a bit so he could look at her.

"No need to ask if you're happy. I am sincerely glad for you both, and you certainly get my blessing, William. So, have you thought about a date? With things the way they are I guess we should do it as quickly as possible?"

Grace stepped back from her father and took hold of William's hand. "We're going to have to wait, Dad. William has enlisted and goes away the day after tomorrow. We're going to wait until he returns."

"Are you sure?" Richard scrutinized his daughter's face.

"I've waited an awfully long time, I don't mind waiting a little bit longer."

"Enlisting means he will be away for four years," said Richard, trying to convey his concern without imposing his will.

"I feel strongly about protecting both Britain and the people I love, sir. I enlisted the moment they announced Hitler had invaded Poland," said William. "We are so much more prepared and surely we have more advanced weapons than anyone else. It might not be over in months, but I need to help to get it finished as soon as possible. You do understand, don't you?"

Richard didn't hold out the same hope, but he was loath to take away his daughter's happiness. "So, marriage when you get back then. Can we at least have an engagement party?"

"Sounds like a jolly good idea to me, sir."

"Here, there's no need for that, I'm going to be your father-in-law, Richard, will do."

"I'll try sir, but that might take a bit of getting used to."

Despite the day's awful news, Grace found her heart full of mixed emotions, but the strongest by far was love. The future was uncertain, but her happy-ever-after wasn't. She would

marry William, as soon as he came back, and they would start a
family, for he had assured her that despite his interest in men he
would perform his husbandly duties. She knew he wouldn't
want to share a bed with her except for these moments, but she
was also convinced that so long as she had a child, she wouldn't
mind.

"So, shall we combine Sunday supper with an engagement
party?" Grace asked.

"Good idea. I have some money in my shoe polish tin,
Grace, take that and use it to buy some tasty things."

"Thank you, Dad," she said with a sigh of happiness.

Grace had never liked looking at herself in the mirror. She
considered herself downright plain, someone you could look at
and never remember you saw them. With her shoulder length,
brown, slightly curly hair, her plain features and the fact that she
was only five foot, one inch tall, she appeared, to herself, to be
most unattractive. Today, she stood in front of the mirror and
had a good hard look. She was thankful William had proposed,
she was fairly certain no one else would notice her. Moreover,
William was handsome and that gave their children a good
chance of being better looking than herself. She felt heat in her
cheeks as she thought of him; and how close they would have to
get to have children.

Most of her clothes were plain and brown but her father had
persuaded her to buy something 'pretty' for the party. She
brushed her hair with a hundred strokes to make it shine,
pinched her cheeks to add colour, and bit down on her lips for so
long to make them plump and red that they now hurt. But she
smiled. The soft blue dress she wore fitted her perfectly. It
hugged her waist and complemented her slender figure. The

short sleeves and dove neckline added to the image of party. She could honestly say, she'd never thought she'd look as nice as she did today. But it was time to move away from the mirror and go downstairs, for Sunday evening had finally arrived.

The vicarage was overflowing with people, although Grace was sceptical about whether they came to wish them congratulations or whether they heard that farmer Tom had given half a pig to put on the spit roast in celebration. But her happiness was infectious and people smiled at her wherever she went. Despite the constant talk of war people enjoyed the occasion with much merriment. So many had donated food to the event, that Grace had spent hardly any of her father's money, which she was very glad about.

A few people came bearing gifts, and Grace was overwhelmed by their generosity and love. Mrs Tilbury, from the grand house up Southward Road, handed William a beautiful oak case. Grace peered over his shoulder as he opened it and gasped in appreciation when she saw the cutlery set inside.

"Now before you get too excited, it isn't silver and it isn't new, as you've probably guessed from the box. However, it is I think a very pretty little set."

Grace gave her a tight hug. "Thank you, that is so very generous of you, I can hardly believe it."

Mrs Tilbury literally expanded with joy at the thanks she received from Grace. "It has just been sitting in the cupboard for years now, but I am glad that you like it."

William put the box on the dresser next to the assortment of trinkets given by other people.

Despite only purchasing one bottle of cheap Port, Grace was amused to find that several people were getting merry. She glanced around the room with a smile, wondering who the culprit was, and wasn't surprised to find Millie filling glasses with the bottle of cooking Sherry.

"You sure that's a good idea?" she challenged, reaching out and putting her hand over William's glass before Millie could top it up.

"It's just one for the road, Grace. The lads are coming to pick me up soon."

Millie gave the pair a sad look and moved over to Mrs Tilbury, who despite her airs seemed rather fond of cheap Sherry.

"It's gone far too quickly." Grace ground her teeth together in an effort to stop the lump in her throat from choking her. William put his glass down, took Grace's hand, and led her into the hallway. The pair sat on the stairs and William put his arm around her shoulders and pulled her in close for a gentle kiss.

"The war will be over before we know it, Grace. I don't want you to worry about me. When I come home we'll go house-hunting and make all the plans for our future come true." He pulled a crisp, white handkerchief out of his shirt pocket and gently dabbed at the tears trickling down her cheeks. "You don't regret waiting to get married until I get back, do you?"

Grace shook her head, then blew her nose loudly, angry at herself for crying yet again when she had vowed not to. "Not at all. I have plenty of time now to make a dress and get a trousseau prepared."

"You mean you haven't got it ready? I was sure you would be ready to fly out the door on the day I asked you to marry me."

"Hey!" Grace elbowed him in the ribs.

"Oww."

"You deserved that. What made you so sure I would say yes?"

"Ah Grace, I know you've loved me since you were fifteen."

"You do? How dreadful."

"Your beautiful hazel eyes always sought me out on Sundays, and they sparkled every time I looked at you. Your love is plain to see, for all who care to notice."

"Oh Lord. Really? What must people think?"

"People love you, Grace, look at everyone who is here tonight. They're all so pleased for you."

"For us."

"Yes, for us, but mostly for you. You spend your life helping everyone, you always go out of your way to help and encourage. You are my little ray of sunshine and have always been."

"Why have you waited so long then?" Grace didn't have to elaborate, he knew what she meant.

"I waited to see if you would find someone else first, I needed to be sure I was doing the right thing by you. Plus, I wanted to offer you a home, not just a two-up, two down. A proper home like you have here, er, well, maybe not as big as here."

"I would have lived in a shed with you, William."

He hugged her tight, pulling her against his chest and planting a kiss on the top of her head. "I want something better for you. I want to give you a home you'll be happy in always.

"Grace…" William paused to move her away a bit so he could look into her eyes. "I have been in for a meeting with Mr Campbell at the bank today. I have left a will with him. If anything happens to me and I don't return, he is to give you the money. It isn't enough to buy a house yet, but it is a fair amount and it would help you in whatever you decided to do."

Grace's chin started wobbling. "You're coming back, William. I know you are. I am going to pray every day until you return, asking for your safe keeping. God will bring you home, I know He will."

"I'm sure He will Grace, but if he doesn't, the money is yours."

Mixed emotions tore at her, happy to be marrying the man she had fallen in love with years ago, yet sad that he so obviously wanted to make up for not loving her the way a husband should, that he was driven to making her happy in other ways.

Just then, there was a hefty bang on the front-door knocker.

"That'll be the lads. We're leaving together."

Grace crossed the hallway and opened the door whilst William pulled on his huge trench coat. Richard came into the hallway followed by most of the guests.

"You take care of yourself, young man," he said offering his hand.

William took it and shook it firmly.

The guests piled in around William, the men shaking his hand and the women crowding in to hug him. As Grace watched she was overcome with emotion. Previously, she had thought she would be okay, but now she couldn't hold back the tears and her shoulders shook as she lost control. William saw her out of the corner of his eye and in a moment he had pulled himself away from the well-wishers and pulled Grace into his arms.

"Don't cry, my girl, don't cry." However, there was no stopping now she had started and Grace sobbed on William's chest.

A hush fell over everyone and before long most of the females there were crying.

"Come along now. Let him go before you soak him." Richard gently prised Grace off William and she reluctantly let him go.

"You come back to me, do you hear?"

William leant in and gave Grace a last kiss on her cheek. "I promise, Grace."

"We've got his back, Grace. We'll all watch out for each other."

Grace took the dry handkerchief her father passed her and looked at the three young lads standing on the path. "You better had, Jake."

The young man with his freckled face and ginger hair grinned back at her.

"We've signed up before conscription starts. We'll get the better pay as warrant officers and the comfy jobs to boot. Don't worry about us, Grace, we'll be fine."

"God speed to you all, young men," said Richard.

"Thank you, sir," they all replied.

"Come on, we'll miss the train if we're not quick," said the ultra-skinny Simon.

Only Graham hadn't spoken. He stood straight, his crisp new uniform hanging off him like clothes on a washing-line. His large brown eyes seemed full of fear and Grace suddenly felt sick. She took a step towards him, reaching out her hand as if to touch his arm but he took a step backwards and set off down the street.

"Bye, Grace," called William, blowing her a kiss. "Write to me as often as you can."

"I will," she said, but her voice was croaky and she wasn't sure he heard her. She stood on the path for a long moment after they had gone, until Millie appeared by her side.

"Help me with the clearing up?"

Grace nodded. She would have to keep busy now, every moment of every day, until William came back to her.

Chapter 4

The Letter
Tuesday 17th October 1939

There was no mistaking the postman, in his shiny blue suit with the gold GPO badge on the front of his smart hat, and as soon as Grace caught sight of him coming up the path she went tearing through the house and yanked open the front door before he could even knock.

"Here it is, Grace," he grinned as he handed over a tiny white envelope.

She took it with trembling fingers and gazed lovingly at the spidery writing. She looked up, full of happiness. "How is your wife?"

Joe took a breath and let out a slow sigh. "Still taken to her bed, I'm afraid. Since our Graham took off there's no consoling her, she's convinced she'll never see him again."

"Oh, I am sorry, Joe." Grace reached out and touched his arm.

"I thought," said Joe, nodding towards the letter she held, "that maybe your William might have mentioned how our Graham is doing?" He looked at her full of hope, and despite her longing to read her precious first letter on her own, she didn't have the heart to turn him away.

"Come in. I'll put the kettle on then we'll see what William has to say."

A grateful grin spread across his face. "Thanks, Grace, it will mean an awful lot to Betty if William should happen to mention our Graham."

They went into the kitchen and Grace gently put the envelope on the wooden table. She filled the large metal kettle and placed it onto the stove.

After lighting the cooker with a match, she stuck her head into the hallway and called out, "Dad, I'm making a brew, do you want one? Joe's visiting."

A chair scraped on the floor before Richard called back, "Coming." Richard came into the kitchen, smartly dressed in a suit, his crisp white dog collar around his neck, as always.

"Looking very dapper there, Vicar. Where you off to?" asked Joe.

"I have a diocesan meeting in Liverpool this afternoon. And what brings you in for a cuppa with us today?"

"Grace has got her first letter," Joe said nodding at the envelope. "I'm hoping like, as our Graham doesn't write so good, that William might have mentioned him. Be able to tell me Betty then, that the lad's doing good."

Richard took a seat at the table next to Joe. "How is Betty today?"

"Quite awful, actually. Still won't be fetched out of 'er bed. Says her body's dying like, with the emptiness she feels inside."

Richard couldn't help but raise an eyebrow. "To my knowledge he's still in training, is he not?"

"Oh, I know. Tis mighty melodramatic she is, 'er mother always said she should be on the stage. She's blaming me, but I've told her over and over I never had anything to do with it."

Grace hadn't long ago boiled the kettle and it started whistling before she'd even finished putting the tea cups on the table. She lifted the kettle up using the towel to protect her hands and poured steaming water into the pot over a fresh batch of tea leaves. After putting the kettle back, she came and sat at the table. Her fingers trembled a little as she picked up the envelope.

"Would you rather be on your own, Grace?" her father asked.

"No, it's quite all right." Grace ran a knife along the top of the envelope to open it. As soon as she saw William's writing her face lit up.

"Dearest Grace," she read aloud. "Firstly, I must apologise for the delay in writing. I received your two lovely letters and have been eager to write back to you, but basic training has been long and hard." Grace paused slightly as she watched her father fill their cups with tea.

"Both Jake and I have passed our Corporal's exams, which you can imagine we are highly delighted about. Unfortunately, both Simon and Graham failed them. Simon was a bag of nerves and fell apart, poor sod, and Graham, well, unfortunately his grammar wasn't up to scratch." Grace stopped and looked over the table at Joe.

"Tis all right lass, we knew he wouldn't pass, bit surprised he went for it to be honest. Carry on."

Grace smiled at Joe and looked back down at the letter. "Being some of the first chaps here has given us the advantage of being able to choose what we want to do. Simon has volunteered for the aircraft unit and he will be going to

Weymouth tomorrow. When Graham discovered that the cooks earn a ton more than privates, he signed up for that on the spot."

Joe laughed. "Tis just like Graham that, can't wait to tell me Betty. Sorry, sorry. Keep going."

Grace smiled at Joe and her father with laughing eyes and returned to the letter. "I wanted to send home all my earnings to you for our savings account, but something fishy is going on and we've been told we can only send a proportion of it home. The sergeant in charge of our quarters has also deducted huge amounts for damages in the barracks. It's outrageous, Grace, the stuff was like this when we arrived. We have all contested it and found ourselves with extra duties for doing so. We're learning to keep quiet, but the injustice of it can eat at a man. My suspicion is that the government is running out of money, and we haven't even started war manoeuvres as yet. Still, enough of my moans. We're in this together, and all the men are of the same mind. For King and for Country, no matter what. I sincerely hope that I am able to write to you each Sunday, and I eagerly await news about you and the goings on in Newton Le Willows. I miss the freedom of walking wherever I want, and I miss the k…" Grace blushed and looked up.

"He just says goodbye after that." She reached for her cup and took a gulp of tea.

Joe stood up. "I've got to go home. I can't wait to tell Betty. Thank you so very much for sharing your letter with us, Grace."

"You're quite welcome, Joe," said Grace standing up too. "I'll see you out."

Back in the kitchen, her father stood near the stove that was slowly cooking a casserole on a low light.

"That was very gracious of you, sweetheart."

"I felt a bit funny at first, I have to say. However, I know if William couldn't write to me I would be longing for news of him some way or another, so I understand. Anyway, you had best be going so you're not late for your meeting. If you're home late I will just leave your dinner in the oven on tick-over."

"Thank you. I hope that I won't be too late, awfully tiresome some of these diocesan meetings and it's dreadfully hard to stay awake sometimes. Thankfully I have Michael to give me a kick under the table if my head nods."

They walked into the hallway and Grace lifted down Richard's coat from the stand and helped him into it.

"The last train will be leaving Lime Street at 3:45 pm, please don't miss it. You know I worry about you." Grace wrapped a woollen scarf around his neck. "Please be home before it gets dark, the roads are dreadfully unsafe at night."

"Stop fussing about me, child. I am very capable of looking out for myself."

"It's not you I'm worried about. It's those lunatics who still insist on driving when it's dark. You know someone gets knocked over nearly every other day, it's just terrible."

"I can just as easily fall down the stairs and break my neck. You have to stop worrying so much."

"Don't you worry about me when I go out?"

"No, not at all."

"Dad!"

"Well I know the Lord looks after his little chatter-box," said Richard, before leaning forward and kissing Grace on the forehead.

Back in the kitchen, Grace was glad to be on her own for a while. She picked up the letter and read it again. She read the ending (that she hadn't shared with the others) ten times.

Grace, how I've missed you. I long for your company and to hear your laugh. I miss your common sense and your way of looking at things. I wish we had wed before I left so that I could know you will always be looked after. I didn't realise that we would be sent away so quickly, so it is with regret and, to be honest a great deal of trepidation that I have learned we are to be shipped out directly. It doesn't seem to me that any of us are ready; most of us are still trying to get to grips with cleaning our guns let alone shooting them at men.

I wish I had married you, my sweet girl. Then you would have had your special moment and been made to feel like a queen for a day. I am filled with dread that you will find another, I don't know where this fear comes from because I know you have never loved anyone except me.

Promise me that you will never take off your engagement ring? Let me know that you will wear it always as a reminder of how fond of me you are.

I hope I will be able to write to you again soon, please write me often, tell me of home and most importantly, of your thoughts towards me.

Your loving William.

Ps. My letters will be censored if I send them through the forces, so as much I can I will seek to post mine to you through other channels.

Grace folded the letter carefully and placed it back in the envelope, then rushed out of the kitchen towards the door. She grabbed the huge metal ring that held the church keys and flung the door open.

Although the sun was out for a change, the freezing wind with its icy cold touch stopped Grace in her tracks and she turned around swiftly, grabbing her coat off the stand. She went running down the road, pulling her coat on as she went. She felt a tightness in her chest that caused pain to ripple through her. Her hand shook as she put the huge key into the church's south door. Inside there was still no slowing her as she raced towards the altar. Dropping to her knees she looked up at the coloured image of Jesus nailed to the cross in the window.

"Father," she cried in anguish; she meant to pray but instead she was wracked with the sobs of fear. Fear that had been in-between every line of William's letter, both his fear of dying and his fear of losing her, and her fear of losing him took an uncontrollable grip on her emotions. She felt short of breath and panic set in. She curled up into a ball and lay on the cold stone floor, the only prayer she could manage to call out 'Father'.

She didn't know how long she lay there; she lost all sense of time and reality. She felt cocooned in her fear and blackness. Lost and alone. Then she felt a touch of warmth on her face and opened her eyes, expecting to see the sun through the window. Looking up, she saw the light retreat and fade and shifted her eyes upwards to the window. Wooden slats nailed to the outside prevented the coloured glass from reflecting light against the night moon. No sunlight found its way into the church. Grace sat up. She should have been cold and stiff after lying on the stone floor, but she felt… warm and peaceful.

There are some things in life that you just *know*. Know, deep down inside of you, as truth, and whether someone else would believe you or not is not important.

Grace knew God had visited her. She knew, without a shadow of a doubt, that whatever happened in her life the Lord would be with her. She felt loved.

Chapter 5

The Lady from London
March 1940

The train pulled into Earlstown station at 5:30 pm precisely. Grace searched the faces of the people getting off, eager to catch her first glimpse of the Land-Army recruit. Eleanor was easy to spot in her jodhpurs uniform as she came striding towards the exit.

"You-hoo," Grace called, waving her arms high to catch Eleanor's attention. The young woman from London smiled broadly when she caught sight of Grace.

"You must be Grace." She dropped her suitcase and pushed her hand out towards her.

Grace took the hand, slightly surprised, but nevertheless shook it quite firmly. "How do you do?"

"Very well, thank you. And you?"

"Rather well actually, life goes on pretty much the same as always around here. I am most eager to hear about life in London. But come, let's go back to the vicarage before we get to know each other. Father will only be in for a short while before he starts his rounds, and I do so want you to meet him."

Laura was waiting on the street outside with the milk float.

"It's a squeeze I'm afraid, but better than having to walk home with a suitcase," said Grace, taking Eleanor's case off her and popping it on the back of the float. Once they were in the sturdy but slow vehicle Grace went into dialogue overload, pointing out every shop and person she saw on the route, determined, it seemed, to let the woman know the entire history of Newton Le Willows in the fifteen minutes it took to get back to the house.

"Thanks, Laura." Grace waved as the milk float pulled away and Laura put her hand out and waved as she made a dash for home before it got dark.

"Father," Grace yelled, opening the front door to the vicarage. "Eleanor is here."

Richard came out of the parlour, nodding and smiling. "It is very good of you to come," he said, reaching out to shake hands.

"It is both my pleasure and my duty." Eleanor smiled broadly whilst shaking the vicar's hand.

"Unfortunately, I have to go out now," said Richard, reaching for his duffle coat from the coat stand. "I need to start my rounds early tonight as London's 'Blackout Ripper' is causing tremendous fear amongst the ladies, most are frightened to go out on their own after dark now. Honestly, it is almost too much to bear; as if the war wasn't terrifying enough we have to have a mad man on the loose. I am praying diligently that this lunatic is caught very soon, for although he is in London, the extent of fear he radiates has reached the far corners of Britain, including Newton Le Willows."

Grace reached up and kissed him on his cheek. "Be careful, Father."

"Always am, my love. Always am."

Grace waved him goodbye as he set off up the High Street, before closing the door.

"He is a warden?"

"Yes, being a vicar meant he didn't have to sign up, but he wanted to do something, so when the Home Office gave out the call for Air Raid Precaution wardens he signed up straight away. He takes his role very seriously, as he does everything in life. Come into the kitchen, it's the warmest room in the house."

Grace flicked a match and put the kettle on. "Please take a seat. I have soup to warm up, it won't take long. Are you hungry?"

"Rather famished, actually. I did make some sandwiches for the journey, but this little chap just kept looking at me and I had no choice but to offer them to him. Never seen a child wolf down food so quickly."

Grace's eyes sparkled as she smiled at Eleanor, knowing instantly that they were going to get on like a house on fire. "It's only vegetable soup I'm afraid, but it's mighty hearty and I have plenty. Let's see if I can fill you up."

Eleanor gave a little snort. "Ha, you will have a hard job there. According to my mother, I have hollow legs."

Grace found herself laughing as she poured hot water into the teapot. "She'll be glad you've come to stay with us for a while then."

"Sure, she would be, if she was still here. She caught pneumonia a few months back, didn't make it."

"Oh, I'm dreadfully sorry."

"Hey, cheer up. It is okay. She had a good innings. She always said she had a happy life full of love. No regrets… well except for not seeing me get hitched, that is."

Grace picked up a cup and passed it to Eleanor. "Is there someone special in your life, then?"

"Good heavens, you mean, do I have a beau? Certainly not. I want to live a little before I get tied to the kitchen sink."

"There is more to marriage than washing dishes."

Eleanor looked at Grace to see if she was being serious. When Grace showed no signed of joking, it tickled Eleanor's funny side and she burst out laughing.

"You country girls do make me laugh," she said wiping her tears away with her sleeve. "I think when this war is over I should take you to London and show you how marvellous being single can be."

"I would quite like to see Buckingham Palace, but as for visiting London with no other reason than living it up, well I'll pass if you don't mind. I'm rather fond of the country, and I am very much looking forward to being tied to the kitchen sink, as you say."

"Aww, so you have a sweetheart. Come on then, tell me all about him. What is his name?"

The evening flew by as the two got to know each other. After dinner, Grace pulled blankets down over all the windows and switched on the paraffin lamp, which she hung from a hook in the ceiling over the table.

"Have you ever worked on a farm before?"

"Golly gosh, no. Nearest I have ever been to a cow is pouring myself a glass of milk." Eleanor laughed at her own wit. "Moreover, as for tilling the land, well, I do not even have a window box for flowers. I have to confess I do not have green fingers." She paused for a moment, fiddling with her hands. Then she looked up and grinned at Grace. "I am willing and able, though."

Grace caught a hint of sadness behind Eleanor's jolly words and wondered what her history held. "We have an early start tomorrow, shall we turn in?"

"Yes, I think that would be grand. I have enjoyed this evening very much, but I have to say all this talking has me quite exhausted."

Grace stood looking at the door, wondering what to do. She had tapped several times with no response. She didn't want to hammer on the door and wake her father, who had come home very late, but didn't want to open the door and frighten Eleanor to death either. In the end she decided giving Eleanor a little scare would be more favourable than waking her father. She tapped two more times for good measure, then turned the handle and slowly pushed the door open.

"Sorry," she whispered, as she reached out and touched Eleanor's shoulder.

Eleanor screamed and jumped out of bed, giving Grace a shock, who herself staggered backwards and banged into the wardrobe. A box on top of the wardrobe came crashing down next to Grace, making both women scream.

"I am not alone," Eleanor yelled, "you'd best get out of here before my husband gets to you."

"Eleanor? It's Grace. Grace Clifton. You're at the vicarage, in Newton Le Willows."

"What on earth's going on?" Richard came into the room tying his dressing gown.

"Oh Father, I gave Eleanor a scare, I'm sorry to have woken you."

"Right, okay then. If you're fine, I will take myself back to bed."

Grace waited for him to leave before turning on the light. After a moment of squinting, her eyes became accustomed to the bright light and she sought out Eleanor. Eleanor was standing with her back to the wall, still clearly in shock, her fingernails impaled into her hands.

"Eleanor, are you okay?" Grace moved across the room quickly and put her arm around the woman, who didn't answer. "Come and sit down for a moment. I'm so sorry to have frightened you like that, I'd never have come in if I realised it would cause you such stress."

Eleanor started crying. Her shoulders shook as a flood of fear-filled tears fell down her face.

"Oh, I'm so sorry," said Grace, squeezing Eleanor in the tightest of hugs.

It was a few minutes before Eleanor managed to compose herself again. "I am all right, sorry about that." Eleanor blew her nose loudly on a handkerchief that had been on the bedside table. "I guess my mother's death, on top of all the horrific things that are going on in London has taken its toll on me." Eleanor could tell by Grace's face that she didn't completely understand why she had been so scared. "My best friend was raped last week, by burglars. It is why I left London so quickly. I just had to get out of there."

"Oh no, that is dreadful. You'd think, with the horrors of war, and the bombing and everything, that would be enough to make people do the right thing. It's so hard to understand why everyday crime continues. I just don't get it. I'm so dreadfully sorry to hear about your friend, is she okay now?"

"Not really. Luckily, her mother has a sister in Dorset so they have gone to stay with her, to try to help Jane recover. I simply couldn't bear to stay in London on my own but they didn't have enough space for me to go with them. They have taken in five evacuees, apparently, doesn't leave them much space."

Grace dried her face with her sleeve. "Well, you're with us now. You don't have to be on your own any more, and I hope we can make you feel safe."

"Maybe I should look for an alarm clock today? So you don't have to wake me again?"

Both women chuckled.

"I think that would probably be a good idea."

Eleanor walked into the kitchen just as Grace was filling two bowls with porridge.

"It's still dark outside!"

Grace saw the indignant look on Eleanor's face and grinned. "You're lucky. Giles said I could break you in gently so we've missed the first round of chores. Tomorrow we will be getting up at five."

"Nooo…"

Grace got the giggles. "Oh, I'm going to enjoy having company." She put the pan back on the stove and came back to the table to sit opposite Eleanor, who was looking into her bowl in distress.

"There's nothing like a bowl of porridge to keep you full until lunch time." Grace offered Eleanor a small jar. "Honey on top helps wash it down."

Eleanor took the honey and poured a spoonful over her steaming breakfast. "You don't eat this every day, do you?"

"No. Only on good days." Grace heartily tucked into her porridge. When she was half way through, she noticed that Eleanor hadn't picked up her spoon and was still looking into her bowl. "It tastes better than it looks, honest."

Eleanor took the plunge and picked up a spoonful. Her eyebrows were high up her forehead as she ate. She nodded. "Not so bad, actually."

"It's even better with cream poured over it, but I've not had any cream since the rationing began."

Eleanor gulped down another spoonful. "That's dreadful, you mean we're going to work on a farm and we don't get any perks?"

"Absolutely not. Rationing is here for a very good reason. I wouldn't want to be seen as abusing the system by taking free issues off Giles. Besides, he would get into awful trouble if the police found out."

"How exactly would the police find out?"

"I don't know. Anyway, even if they didn't find out, God would know, and I won't do anything that I might be ashamed of facing up to when I stand before Him."

Eleanor choked on her last spoonful of porridge.

"Here," said Grace, passing her a cup of water.

When the coughing had stopped, Eleanor looked at Grace. "You're kidding me, right? You actually believe God would care if you took a jug of cream?"

Grace sat back in her chair and thought about how to answer. "I believe that God is concerned with every tiny aspect of my life, and yes, I think He would care if I broke the rules."

"Seriously? There is a war going on, men are killing each other. There is starvation around the world, people are doing dreadful things, and you think God would notice if you took some cream?"

"Yes."

"You're nuts." Eleanor picked up the bowls and went to the sink. Rolling up her sleeves, she poured some hot water from the kettle over the dishes and then started cleaning them. She was obviously bringing the conversation to a close and Grace wondered what to do. Not able to formulate a clever answer, Grace decided to leave it for another time.

The bike ride from the vicarage to the farm took them half an hour. By the time they arrived, the early morning mist was beginning to evaporate and the cool breeze left Eleanor feeling fresh, and very, very wide awake. Her eyes were sparkling when she propped her bike against the shed.

"Are the birds always that noisy in the morning?"

Grace laughed. "I'm afraid so. Come on, let's see if Giles is still in the cottage." They walked across the cobbles and before they reached the house, the door opened.

"Mornin', Grace. You must be Eleanor. Thanks for comin', we need all the 'elp we can get. Grace, I'm gonna 'elp the lads in the fields, can you show 'er around? After that, could you get started in the sheds?"

"Will do."

"Thanks chuck." Giles tipped his head at Eleanor, and then went striding across the cobbles, two Border Collies leading the way.

Grace glanced at Eleanor's slightly bemused face. "We don't go in for formal introductions around here. But trust me, Giles is mighty pleased you've come to help. There's a great emphasis on all farmers to produce more and more, and they can't do it without help. Since the German submarines have been targeting our food supply we've become fiercely reliant on our own farms. The pressure is great."

"No time for pleasantries, you're telling me."

"Afraid not. There'll be a chance to say hello properly at noon, when we gather together for something to eat. Come on, I'll give you a quick tour."

The first day flew by. By teatime, Eleanor's body was protesting, with aches and pains appearing in places she didn't know she had muscles. The bike ride back to the vicarage wasn't as bad as she thought it would be as the lanes were either sloping downwards or on the flat. Still, riding over the rough stony lanes was a battering too far for her backside, and she nearly collapsed when they got off their bikes.

"I think I may walk tomorrow, if it's all the same to you."

©ImperialWarMuseum

Chapter 6

A Blitz Too Close
20 December 1940

Life goes on… that's what they say, with good intentions. But Grace didn't feel like life was going on, she felt she was moving through each day in slow motion, like an old film sticking in the reel and begrudgingly jolting from scene to scene.

Her morning prayers were getting shorter by the day. It was hard to ask God to intervene, to keep them safe, whilst thousands of innocents died. She had beseeched the Lord so many times that He would show His hand and create a miracle that would cause this incomprehensible killing to end. There was no evidence that He heard her. There had been many times when she might have questioned her faith. Eleanor, for example, could see no reason to love a God that would allow such suffering and dismissed Grace's faith frequently. Yet, one thing glued Grace to her faith, the memory of the light in the church and knowing without a shadow of a doubt that He existed. Why He should remain silent through such horror she was unable to comprehend. She didn't know how to explain if anyone asked this question, and this left her feeling empty and bemused.

Eleanor's scorn of her faith was the only thorn in their friendship. They got on well, and surprisingly, found something to giggle about nearly every day. But, even after nine months of living in the vicarage, Eleanor was yet to take a single step inside the church. Nothing Grace or Richard said would convince her that God was real. She outright refused to learn anything about a God who would allow such suffering.

Richard had cautioned his daughter about trying too hard to convert her, reminding Grace that free will was the right of everyone. It was Grace's complete inability to get Eleanor to see the truth which made Grace reflect on the fact that she hadn't converted a single soul to the Lord. Day after day this piece of information began to eat away at her and a feeling of shame crept into her heart.

One evening, on a rare occasion when her father was home, Grace and Richard sat reading their Bibles in the lounge. No longer able to contain the burden of her failure, she found herself pouring out her feelings.

"Father, how many people do you think you have led to the Lord?"

"Umm, I'm not so sure. What makes you ask?"

"It has occurred to me that I haven't led a single person to Jesus. I… feel like a fraud. How can I love God and not be able to convince anyone about Him?"

Richard leant back in his chair and was silent for a few minutes. "Why do you want to lead people to Jesus, Grace?"

"That's a silly question. We are told to go and make disciples; it is my duty to tell people about Jesus. Unfortunately, for some reason it has only come to my mind in the last few months that I have never, in my entire life, converted anyone. I've let God down, I'm a failure. No wonder He doesn't answer my prayers."

"Oh dear, Grace."

"I know, it's awful isn't it. I have decided to make it my life's mission now to convert as many people as possible." Grace was looking intently at Richard but he had closed his eyes. She wanted him to reassure her that it didn't matter if she wasn't leading people to the Lord, that she filled her life with good deeds and this was enough. Plus, she still had time, didn't she?

After what felt like an eternal moment of agony, Richard opened his eyes and gazed at her with such love and tenderness. "The heart Grace, the heart."

Her forehead squished into lines as she stared at him, not understanding.

"From the first page of the Bible until the last, God tells us over and over again, it is about our heart. Not deeds or actions, but intentions and motivations. It would not matter one iota if you led someone to the Lord or not, so long as your heart is full of good intentions and your motivation for trying to enlighten someone is for the glory of God and not a score list you may be keeping."

Grace felt herself welling up. In the gentlest way, she felt rebuked. "But the Bible says we should lead people to Him."

"Exactly, Grace. You can lead a horse to water, but you cannot make him drink. Your duty is to reflect the Glory of God in your actions and to tell people about Him whenever you have opportunity, but it is between God and the individual as to whether they accept Him or not. If God wants to use you as a vessel to draw people to Him, don't you think He would do so? He only needs your heart to be open and your motivations to be pure, then He'll use you to evangelise. But Grace, you must remember, if someone chooses not to accept what you are sharing they have that right, and you are not to blame. I'm sure the Lord has Eleanor in the palm of His hand and He'll take care of her. Just love her for who she is."

Grace smiled. Of course her father would know where her worries were stemming from. "I do, Father, she is very dear to me. In fact, I feel like she's the sister I never had. I just want her to know the love of God and to feel His peace so badly."

"My ears are burning," said Eleanor coming into the room.

"So they should be, my dear, for we are constantly talking to God, about you."

Eleanor went over and dropped a kiss on Richard's forehead. "So long as you are talking to God about me, and not me about God, then I give you my blessing. Now, Grace, how do you think I look?"

Grace looked her up and down. Eleanor wore her favourite blue suit, tight pencil skirt and tightly fitted jacket over a soft white blouse with a huge collar. She wore her deep brown hair up, pinned curls that gleamed in the light. A bit of lipstick and a tiny touch of rouge, and Grace had to admit, she looked gorgeous.

"You look delightful. Where are you going?"

Eleanor pulled on her little white gloves and gave a feminine pose. "George Hamilton is taking me to see a film."

"He's a little bit old for you, isn't he dear?" said Richard.

"Maybe, but as all fit and able men are either married or gone to fight, pickings are rather slim. Besides, he can afford to take me to the pictures, and I'm simply dying to see 'Gone with the Wind', everyone is raving about it."

"I guess there is no harm in going to the pictures with someone. Make sure he walks you home, I don't want you coming down the High Street on your own when it's dark."

"I never knew a safer place than Newton Le Willows, Richard. I will be perfectly safe to walk home on my own. But thank you for worrying. Night, now. Don't wait up for me."

They waited a moment until they heard the front door bang closed.

"Wouldn't you like to go to the see the film, my dear?"

"It's four hours long. I don't have so much free time to waste sitting in a stuffy, smoky room when there are other things I could be doing."

"You are too hard on yourself, you can let your hair down sometimes, you know."

Grace didn't say what she was thinking, but Richard knew his daughter too well. "They say the government is organising all sorts of entertainers to visit the troops and lift their spirits. I've heard that young lass from London, what's her name… Vera, something."

"Vera Lynn."

"Yes, that's the one. They say she is going to visit the troops all over the world and sing to them. So, even the soldiers get a little rest sometimes."

"They deserve it. Although, from what I've heard she hasn't got an amazing voice and I'm not sure what all the fuss is about."

"I should imagine the popular artists wouldn't like to risk their lives."

Grace looked up at her father, aware of his rebuke.

Sunday 22nd December 1940
9 am

The church was packed. Dwindling numbers at the Sunday morning service meant they were surprised when people started flooding in through the doors as early as 8:00 am. The windows were boarded up with wood and the only light inside came from the dismal, grey light that seeped in through the door and numerous candles dotted around, most of which sat in front of the altar. People spoke in the quietest of whispers or sat in silence. Even the children felt the sombre atmosphere, and clutched their dolls or wooden cars as they sat quietly beside their parents. Not even a baby was crying.

It was eerie, and created a sense of foreboding gloom.

Grace closed the heavy wooden doors behind Mrs Humphries, who had come rushing, red-faced, up the path at the last moment. She nodded towards her father to let him know everyone was in, and then took a seat on the back pew.

Richard was quiet for a moment as his eyes scanned over the congregation; he spotted quite a few people who hadn't been to church in months. He nodded slightly, towards Joe and his wife Betty – this was definitely the first time she'd been to church since Graham had joined up.

Manchester was on high alert, the prospect of being bombed imminent, not maybe, but when. The German Luftwaffe had been bombing Liverpool since August, making it the most heavily bombed part of Britain outside of London. The death toll was rising daily, but because the government didn't want Germany knowing how much damage had been done to the port, news of the bombing was kept low key. Newton Le Willows, being half way between Liverpool and Manchester, knew what was going on, and a sadness-filled fear had spread throughout the town. Surely the Luftwaffe would bomb the Vulcan Foundry next? For everyone who worked there this was a real threat, one that had cast a shadow of utter dread over the town.

Richard's heart was heavy and he wished above all else, that right then he would be able to take away their fear and give them hope. He closed his eyes for the briefest moment and cried to God for help with his sermon.

"I have been reading Ephesians, and it seems to me that never has there been a time when this book is more relevant to us, than now."

Just then, the handle turned and the door creaked as it was pushed open. Richard waited to let the newcomer come in. Grace jumped up and went to greet whoever it was. She smiled in surprise as Eleanor popped her head tentatively around the corner. Grace offered her hand to Eleanor, who took it in relief. Grace quietly closed the door and led Eleanor to the back pew to sit with her.

"For our struggle is not against flesh and blood, but against the rulers, against the authorities, against the powers of this dark world and against the spiritual forces of evil in the heavenly realms. Therefore, take up the full armour of God, so that when the day of evil comes, you will be able to stand your ground, and having done everything, stand." Richard paused for a moment, earnestly connecting his gaze with as many people as possible.

"This might seem like a ridiculous thing to say, when we know our current enemy is Germany, and that the threat of the Luftwaffe's bombs is very likely to cut right through any shield of faith we may have, leaving us dead. But, my friends, it is now more than ever that we need to believe that *all things* work together for the good, for those who love Him. We should not fear, for fear is from the enemy and causes us to doubt the love of God. We should not fear, for we have a Father in Heaven who counts the hairs on our head and has had a plan for us since before time began. Who can destroy that plan? No one, I tell you. Not Adolf Hitler, not his soldiers, nor his bombs. Not the devil and his evil plans. No one can destroy us.

"For our bodies are of earth and will crumble in the ground, but our souls are heavenly, and will soar with the angels on the day we leave our bodies behind. Our hope is not in today, or tomorrow, but in eternity. So I say to you again, do not let fear steal your peace. Fear is from the enemy, and peace is from above. Our home on Earth is temporal, but our home in Heaven is eternal. This life we now live is but a fleeting part of our existence.

"We have not sung in this church since the war broke out, but today we are not going to let the fear of being heard prevent us from worshipping God. Today we are going to raise our voices and praise our Father in Heaven, who loves us, and loves us unconditionally and without measure. Come, come. Get to your feet. Let's rejoice in the love and peace we receive in knowing that when we leave here, we go home. A home full of the people we love who have gone before us."

There was movement throughout the church as the congregation stood.

"Mercy, where are you?"

"Here, Vicar," said an old woman waving her hand.

"Come and play the organ, Mercy."

"But we've been told not to," answered Mercy with surprise.

"Come on, Mercy, come and play *Onward Christian Soldiers* for us. Today we will fear nothing, not even being reported to the authorities."

Mercy didn't need asking again, she knocked her husband on the leg to indicate he should come to pump the organ, and rushed to the front to play, something she had missed doing so very much. Within moments, the church erupted into song, every word sung from the heart.

> *Onward Christian soldiers*
> *Marching as to war*
> *With the cross of Jesus*
> *Going on before*
>
> *Onward then, ye people*
> *Join our happy throng*

Blend with ours your voices
In our triumph song

Christ the royal master
Leads against the foe
Forward into battle
See His banners go

Crowns and Thrones may perish
Kingdoms rise and wane
But the cross of Jesus
Constant will remain

They sang the hymn three times before Richard waved his hand, indicating they should sit again.

"Let us pray." Heads instantly bowed, hands clenched.

"Lord, we thank you. We thank you for the Blood of Christ that was poured for us, so we should not die but have eternal life. Thank you, Lord, for the love and peace you give us so that we do not need to live in fear. Now I ask you Father, please bless every person here. Give them eyes to see you, ears to hear you, and a heart open to receive the Holy Spirit. Go with them, Father, I pray, and let them take your peace wherever they may go. In the name of our Lord Jesus Christ, I ask these things. Amen."

A resounding 'Amen' flooded the church.

"I will be staying in the church this morning to pray for the war to come to an end, and also for the people of Liverpool and Manchester to be brave and covered with God's grace. Please feel free to stay and join me if you wish."

Most people left the church, but they left feeling completely different to the way they had entered it. Their spirits had been lifted and their eyes turned once more to Heaven. Seven elderly people stayed behind to pray with Richard and they went into the first pew and knelt down side-by-side.

Grace went about the pews collecting the Bibles and hymnbooks and stacking them on the shelves at the back of church. Eleanor helped her. When they had finished Grace closed the door gently behind them and they went home. Although Grace was busting to ask Eleanor why she had decided to come to church today, she held herself back and waited to see if Eleanor wanted to talk about it.

Once home they went straight to the kitchen, where Grace immediately put the kettle on. She placed a few spoons of tea leaves into the pot and fetched two cups. Before she sat down, she opened the oven door and checked the pot roast. The smell of the roasting pork joint surrounded by vegetables instantly filled the kitchen.

"Oh quick, shut that door before I dive in there," said Eleanor.

Grace came and sat down at the table and shook the teapot a little to mix up the tea. She popped the cosy over the pot to keep it warm whilst it brewed.

"Why are we born?" Eleanor looked Grace right in the eye.

Grace was a little unprepared for this question, but out of nowhere, it seemed, the answer came to her and she started talking. "I believe that Earth is like a school. Just like we send children to school to learn, so God sends us to Earth, so that we can grow in love and in knowledge."

Eleanor scrunched up her nose as she digested this comment. "Why would He send us to a school where there is so much suffering? We'd never send children to a school if we knew they could get hurt there."

Tough, Grace thought, *this is tough.* She thought for a moment about trying to explain how sin entered the world and how Jesus had to sacrifice Himself to save us from ourselves, but she decided against it.

"I don't know the answer to that, Eleanor. I don't think anybody does, to be honest. I have thought about it in the past, especially recently, but I always come back to the same thing. I don't feel it is for me to understand the ways of God, or to judge why He does things the way He does. It is for me to accept that the ways of God are a mystery, and to trust that everything that happens is for a reason. I do believe that when I get to Heaven, He will allow me to ask these questions, but rather than let the things I don't know hold me down, I let the things I do know build me up."

"What do you mean?"

"I know that when I die I am going to Heaven and that I will meet my mum for the first time. That thought gives me so much joy. I know that God loves me and that He listens to my prayers and answers them according to His will. Knowing these things gives me peace."

"How can you know? What if he's not real?"

"If He isn't real, then what have I lost? Fear? But what if He is real? What have I gained? Eternal life, peace, hope and security for ever more. I win both ways, Eleanor. Wouldn't you like to take the chance that He's real and give your life to Him? If He isn't real, all that you've done is said a simple thing out loud, and if He does exist then you've just received forgiveness for your sins and a doorway into Heaven."

"You make it sound so simple."

"It is simple. God loves you and cares about you, and that really is all there is to it."

"Will you tell me what to say?"

1 pm

Grace turned the oven off and took the pot-roast out. Wearing her huge oven mittens, she brought it to the table.

"Just a very small amount for me please, Grace," said Richard.

"Me too," said Eleanor, "I'm not feeling very hungry."

Grace spooned small helpings onto three plates and sat down. They picked up their forks and without any enthusiasm, began to eat. Whether due to the small portions, or in recognition of Grace's hard work, everyone managed to finish.

Habits are hard to break, and in fact routine was often what kept them going, so after lunch Richard went to the drawing room to read the Sunday papers, whilst Grace and Eleanor washed the pots and cleaned up.

They were just hanging their aprons up on the back of the kitchen door when they heard Richard swear. They looked at each other in surprise and hurried into the drawing room.

"Damn and blast that bloody Lord Haw-Haw!"

"Father!"

"I'm sorry, but sometimes a man just has to let his frustrations out."

"What has he said now?" asked Eleanor, sitting on the sofa opposite.

"He's told the people of Manchester that buying their turkeys is a waste of time because they won't be cooking them. Blast that man, I wish someone would catch him."

"He deserves to be hung," said Eleanor.

"I'm afraid I agree," said Grace, sitting down next to Eleanor. "He fills people with such fear."

"I don't think ever a man walked the earth who was hated as much as Lord Haw-Haw." Richard folded his paper and dropped it in the paper box by the fire.

"I do think we hate Hitler just as much, Father."

"Do you? There is something about betraying your *own* people that is hard for even the most faith-filled to forgive."

Eleanor frowned. "Do you think they'll bomb the Vulcan Foundry?"

"The foundry and the village have been here since 1833, it's as sturdy as the steam locomotives it builds. I would be rather surprised if it didn't survive this war."

"I'm sure if the Germans knew that the foundry was making Matilda tanks they would target it in a shot."

"I'm sure they would, Grace. But we're in the middle of nowhere and Manchester is known for its industry. Unfortunately, Lord Haw-Haw's comment only confirms the fears that were already here, and that Manchester will be the next city to be blitzed."

They decided to take their minds off the inevitable and opted to play cards instead.

3:30 pm

"Anyone thirsty? I feel like making a fresh pot of tea," said Grace, standing up and stretching. Everyone wanted one and Grace went off to the kitchen and put the kettle on. She was just coming back into the drawing room carrying a tray with teapot and cups when a loud rumble started. She put the tray down on the coffee table and looked at Eleanor and her father. Both of them had stood up. The first rumble moved on but was quickly followed by another and then another. There hadn't been much bombing over the Warrington area since September and the return of the Luftwaffe filled them with dread.

"Quick," ordered Richard, "under the stairs, now!" They raced out of the room, down the corridor and into the cupboard under the staircase. They dived in one after the other and sat crossed-legged inside. The roar of the planes was great and seemingly never-ending.

Grace sat up straight. "Did we put the blackouts up over the kitchen window?"

Eleanor took Grace's hand and squeezed it tight. "We did."

"There's so many of them," whispered Grace.

"God help Manchester," said Richard in a croaky voice.

Grace smiled very briefly, as she lifted Eleanor's hand up off hers and placed it in Eleanor's lap. She bowed her head and clasped her hands in front of her. At 3:44 pm a strange sensation rippled through the earth, much like an earth-tremor, as the first bombs rained down.

"Lord, hear our prayers."

Chapter 7

The Only Gift that Matters
Christmas 1940

For two days the bombs fell on Manchester, blasting holes in streets and causing the city to burn. Albert Square, the Royal Exchange and buildings near the Cathedral were in flames within the first few hours. The first night was hell on earth. Twelve people died in one house in Gilda Brook Road where they had gathered to celebrate Christmas. Life goes on… so they say, carry on regardless, don't let Hitler determine how we live. Most of the children, thank heavens, had been evacuated in the previous weeks. But how could life go on?

The city centre wasn't the only place to get blasted. The surrounding areas of Stretford, Hulme, and Salford were also targeted on the first night. Six police officers died in East Union Street when a landmine fell on them; it was only 8:42 pm and the death toll was rising.

Anti-aircraft guns fired from around Manchester all night long, but the planes and the bombs kept coming.

In the early hours of Monday morning, a blast at Manchester Cathedral lifted the roof right off, but miraculously, it fell back in place. All the stained glass was blown out and the furniture caught up in the air and then dropped.

At 6:28 on Monday morning the air raid sirens declared that the raiders had passed. Germany immediately started broadcasting that important factories in Manchester had been targeted and put out of action.

Fire crews had been working all night without rest, but couldn't stop as the city continued to burn. A cry for help was sent out, and people flooded in from everywhere to help with the fires and the clearing of roads so that life could go on.

Grace, Eleanor, and Richard went on the black painted Charabanc with lots of people from Newton Le Willows, willing to do anything to help. By 11:30 am all the fires were extinguished, done with the help of four hundred fire engines that arrived from the surrounding areas.

Charabanc

They were completely black from the smoke, they were also thirsty and tired, and so when the police started informing everyone that the worst was over, they sank down on a patch of blackened grass to catch their breath.

"There's so many police around," said Grace.

A copper overhearing her paused and nodded. "We were drafted in ma'am, to help keep order like, but the Manchester people are conducting themselves admirably, like right honourable people. Dare say we'll need to stay alert, but really we're just helping with the clear up at the moment."

"You're doing a grand job, sir, and we're lucky to have you," said Richard.

"Seeing everyone pulling together like this, it makes you proud to be British, doesn't it, sir?"

"It does indeed, young man."

"There's a café just around the corner up there." The policemen pointed to the left. "The owners are giving everyone something to eat and drink for free, if you're thirsty?"

"Thank you," said Grace. Her throat was sore from coughing, a result of the smoke and ash.

"Gudday to you," said the officer touching his helmet.

"Girls, you go and get yourselves something to eat. I want to see if I can find Henry, I know he's supposed to be at All Saints near the university. I won't rest until I know he is okay. If I'm not back by the time the bus is ready to leave, go without me, I'll find somewhere to bed down for the night."

Grace jumped up. "No. No, you can't go off on your own. That's ridiculous; the planes might come back tonight. You can't put me through that, stay here with us."

"God is with me, Grace. I do not fear, nor should you. Now go and see if you can find something to eat, and remember, get on that bus whether I'm back or not. Eleanor, please?"

Eleanor got up and took Grace's hand. "Come on chuck, there's more work needs doing and we won't be fit for it if we can't find something to eat."

Grace threw her arms around her father's neck. "You be very, very careful. Do you hear me?"

"I will, my little love. Now let me be gone, for the quicker I'm gone the quicker I'll be back."

Grace stood and watched Richard until he turned a corner.

"He'll be back," said Eleanor.

"Of course he will."

Giles found them helping to clear out a shop near the station. "Come on girls, the bus is leaving. It's going to be dark in half an hour."

"But we were going to stay until 5 pm," said Grace. "We can't leave yet, it's only 4 pm and Father isn't back yet."

"Girls, I'm sorry but the bus won't wait for us. We have to leave now, or we'll miss it. We'll come back first thing in the morning."

Grace started welling up, her heart thudded in her chest and she felt sick.

Eleanor took her hand. "Come on Grace, your father would be awfully cross with us if we missed the bus." Grace nodded, but every step she took was torture.

Giles grabbed her other hand after a short time. "We 'ave to run, or they'll scoot without us."

Running was hard as they were so tired, and Grace so reluctant, but even Grace sighed in relief when they turned the last corner and saw the Charabanc still there.

Back at the vicarage, neither of them wanted to go to bed so they fetched their pillows and blankets and made a makeshift bed in the Morrison shelter. When they heard the planes flying overhead, Grace started crying uncontrollably. Eleanor wrapped her arms around her and held her tight.

"Please God," said Eleanor. "If you're real, please look after Richard. Bring him home to Grace, and I'll never doubt you again."

The next morning the two of them ran to Thomas's house, where the bus had been stowed away from sight under the branches of a huge willow tree nearby. It was still pitch black and they thought they would be the first ones there. They were surprised when they found nearly everyone gathered inside Thomas's house.

Mrs. Brown, Thomas's mum, was handing out cups of tea. Grace searched through the crowd looking for Jonathon, the local bobby who was organizing everything.

"When do we leave?" she asked when she found him.

"We can't go yet, Grace. We won't see where we're driving and we can't put the headlights on. We need to wait another half hour at least before we set off."

Grace wanted to argue but knew it would do no good, it wasn't safe to leave yet and that was all there was to it.

"They say there must have been over one hundred and fifty aircraft last night. They've dropped so many bombs that the whole of Manchester is lit up."

Grace turned around slowly and walked over to Joe, who had a group around him listening. "What do you know, Joe?"

Joe looked up at Grace, his face bleak. Now was not the time for lies or trying to soften things up. "'Tis not good, Grace. They didn't let up last night, it was worse than the night before."

Grace felt someone take her elbow and turned to see Eleanor looking at her with tear-filled eyes.

"Oh no. He's not dead. No, he's not. I would feel it if he was. He'll be fine, down an air raid shelter, somewhere safe."

They waited for a tiny bit of light and then set off, with the ride to Manchester seeming like an eternal torture to Grace. She had never been so frightened in her life. She tried to focus on her father's sermon but images of him being crushed under a building wouldn't leave her.

Eleanor held Grace's hand tightly the whole way there, wishing she could comfort her friend in some practical way.

The bus pulled into the outskirts of Stretford and came to a halt. Everyone stood up and peered out of the windows.

Yesterday, they had driven through Stretford on their way to Manchester without a problem. Today the road was blocked and there was no way through. Thomas opened the door and climbed off the bus, the others coming after him.

A young man rushing past suddenly stopped and turned to look at them. "If you've come to 'elp, Stanley Road was hit worse, they're still looking for survivors."

"So much damage in one night," said Eleanor.

"Aye, missus, right terrible. Over 'eard a copper sayin' 140 bombs hit us I t'night, its amazin' anyone's left alive to be honest with ya. Anyway, gotta rush, me Mrs went into labour during night and is over at th'ospital. Not sure how they copin' with no water and no electric, like." With that, he nodded and rushed off.

"It looks like we'll be helping out in Stretford today, folks. Everyone back here by 4 pm, no stragglers, we won't be waiting for anyone."

Grace rushed forward. "No, Thomas, we can't stay here. I've got to find my father, please let's just drive around and find another way into the centre."

Thomas put his hands on Grace's shoulders. "Grace, love, we canny. We're needed here, anyway."

"Please Thomas, I've got to get to the city."

A policeman came up to them. He had lost his hat. His uniform and face were filthy and he looked exhausted.

"You need to reverse that bus back a good few hundred yards, sir. The fire engines will be coming up this street shortly, heading into the city, and we're clearing the way."

"Oh, thank heavens. See, Thomas, we'll help clear the road and then we can go to the city." Grace was pleading, but Thomas looked over her head and saw quite a few of their group had dispersed in search of someone to help.

"We can't, Grace, I'm sorry. Officer, the five of us left here will help clear the way."

There was nothing more to be said and the small group from Newton Le Willows joined the police officer and a few men from Stretford and started clearing the road. It was almost clear when the first fire engine turned up.

"Don't you need the engines in Stretford?" asked Thomas.

"Another would be good, but the city is burning, there'll be nothing left of it if they don't get help right away."

Panic rippled through Grace and her whole body started shaking. Eleanor wrapped her arms around her and couldn't help the tears that fell.

"I've got to get to Manchester," whispered Grace.

"You'll not be able to get in, sweetheart, they've blocked the roads to all except the fire engines," said the policeman wiping his brow.

Grace pulled herself out of Eleanor's arms and ran to the firemen who had come over to help clear the last of the rubble. She grabbed one by the arm.

"Please. Please, I beg you. Please take me to the city with you."

The tall chunky fireman looked down at Grace with sad eyes. "'Tis not safe, lass."

Grace could feel herself getting hysterical. "Please, for the love of God, please will you take me with you?"

The other fireman came over to Grace. "We can't be responsible for you, you will have to take care of yourself."

Hope. "Oh, I will, I will. Thank you so much."

"I have to come too," said Eleanor, smiling sweetly at the two firemen.

The second fireman looked at the first, questioningly.

"Aye well, suppose we could squeeze two in behind us."

"God bless you," said Grace, turning around and instantly going back to helping with clearing the road.

It wasn't long before a space big enough for the engines to pass through had been made and they were on their way. They sat in silence, all of them observing the horrific sights of a bombarded Manchester. It wasn't long before the flames could be seen, leaping into the air and engulfing the city with their awesome red tongues.

Tears rolled unchecked down both Grace and Eleanor's cheeks. The devastation was breathtakingly awful.

"Ladies, we can't take you any further, you're going to have to get out here." As the engine pulled over, the firemen jumped out and helped Grace and Eleanor down the vertical steps. "You should turn around and go back, you're not going to be able to get anywhere near the centre."

Grace nodded. "Probably true, but I have to try."

"God speed, to you then," said one of the firemen getting back onto the engine.

"Be watchful, ladies," said the other fireman before climbing up.

They watched the fire engine move away and head towards the fire-filled streets.

"What are we going to do?" said Eleanor, staring at the fire.

"We're going to pray, and then we're going to trust." Grace took hold of Eleanor's hands and the two of them closed their eyes. A prayer fell from Grace's lips but she felt in her heart it offered no confidence and therefore lacked the faith necessary to move God to action. Still she prayed, crying out for the Holy Spirit to fill her with faith and trust. When she could think of no more to ask she whispered, "Amen."

"Amen," Eleanor repeated, "now what?"

"We walk."

The two set off and carried on walking down Stretford Road. The road didn't go directly into the city centre but swung to the left and skirted the city a little.

"We'll keep walking until we find a way in to the city that's not on fire."

Eleanor didn't answer Grace, for some strange reason she trusted that God would show her which way to go.

They'd only been walking for fifteen minutes when they arrived in Oxford Road. There was a tonne of activity with people walking into the city. A wedding party passed them and both women stopped and stared agog at the bride in her full gown and the guests all in their best togs.

Eleanor put a hand out and stopped one of them. "Where are you going?"

The woman grinned at her. "All Saints Church took a direct hit, nothing left but a mountain of bricks, so we're off to the Methodist church in Hulme. Despite the heavy bombing there, the church is still standing, apparently."

"Life goes on," said another woman in the group, "nothing will stop Susannah marryin' her fella before 'ee goes off t' war."

"Being in the family-way might have something to do with it," said one of the men, who promptly received a smack on the arm from one of the women.

"Don't you listen t'im. He's knows nought of love, the miserable old so and so."

Eleanor noticed that Grace was shaking from head to toe. "What's the matter?" she said grabbing Grace's arm.

"That's Henry's church," Grace whispered.

Eleanor's face took on a deathly pallor. "Which way is it to All Saints Church?"

One of the women pointed down the road. "You just have to go down Oxford Road for about ten minutes and you'll come to it, but you won't find anyone there. The firemen have been through the rubble, no bodies to find."

Grace started shaking uncontrollably.

"'Ere lass, you be all right?" asked one of the wedding party coming over to them.

"It's her father," answered Eleanor, "the last we knew he was going to that church."

"Not a vicar your dad, is he?" asked the woman.

Grace nodded.

The woman smiled. "Well then, you tain't got nothin' to worry about do you, lassie. Two vicars got caught up in the incendiary bombing, but they escaped with their lives intact. I overheard the groom sayin' that they spent the night helping others caught up in the bombing and giving absolution to the dying. He said he found them in Gartside Gardens. Vicar Henry couldn't do the marriage due to the state he was in, but he assured the groom there would be someone at Hulme who would be able to perform the ceremony. So there, you turn that frown upside down, and stop ya frettin'."

Grace threw herself at the woman and hugged her tightly. "Thank you," she said before turning and running down the road.

"Wait for me, Grace." Soon Eleanor was running next to her. They dodged people who were, unbelievably, making their way into the city to go to work.

"Can you believe people?" said Eleanor, nodding towards five men in their suits.

"Life goes on," laughed Grace, and Eleanor grinned at her.

Five minutes later they entered the park to find it full of people who were obviously exhausted and taking a rest. Despite the freezing weather, quite a few people had curled up under the trees and gone to sleep. They hurried through the park, searching everywhere until they found Richard. Grace stopped in her tracks, her chin quivering as she tried to hold back the flood of relief washing over her.

Richard glanced up, and instantly smiled as he caught sight of her. She ran and threw herself into his arms, sobbing.

"There, there, my little love. I told you I would be all right." After Grace had calmed down, Richard looked at her sternly. "What were you thinking, Grace? The city is burning. There is a complete wall of fire from Piccadilly to Portland Street, if they can't get it under control soon we will lose the entire city. You should have stayed at home."

"I would have gone insane at home. Anyway, we're here now, so let's see where we can help."

"Hello, Grace," said Henry, coming back from talking to a policeman.

"Hello, Henry. I'm very glad that you're okay, I hear the church has been flattened."

"Yes, your father and I were very lucky, we just made it out before it collapsed, but not before we were fighting off those blasted incendiary bombs. They scattered everywhere and before we knew it there were too many fires to put out. Inventions from hell they are. We were totally covered in dust at one time, had to wash off as much as we could with a bucket of water, but I still feel it's embedded in our clothes and we should change before we ignite."

"We should make that a priority then," said Eleanor putting her hand out towards Henry. "I'm Eleanor."

"It's nice to meet you, even in these dire times. I'm afraid changing clothes needs to wait a while. I've just found out that the Royal Infirmary has been badly hit and they need all the help they can get to bring out the patients and doctors."

"Is it far from here?" asked Eleanor.

"No, lass. It's just down the road a bit and over towards Brook Street, we'll be there in ten minutes."

The four set off, and as Richard and Henry had been working all night and were near exhaustion, the pace was relatively slow. The bitter, oppressive smell of burning filled their nostrils, whilst the ash flakes in the air stung their eyes.

As they turned the corner of Grafton Street, they could see the carnage of the bombs and fire and they froze. The street was full of patient beds and people were grouped together doing various tasks. Getting over their initial shock, they walked briskly up the road looking for someone who might be in charge. Just then, a fire engine pulled into the street. "Thank God," uttered just about everyone present.

Two doctors talked to the firemen briefly before they set to work. Richard decided they might know what help was needed.

"You can't go in," said the young doctor. "There's fires erupting all over the place and there are several people trapped inside. To be frank, I'm not sure what you'll be able to do."

"I could do with a cuppa," laughed the older doctor, "not had a drink in nearly ten hours."

It seemed frivolous, but Eleanor and Grace went off to find someone who would make them cups of tea, whilst Richard and Henry started praying with people. A short time later Eleanor and Grace returned with trays full of luke-warm cups of tea. A small thing, to offer a cup of tea, but the heartfelt thanks they received from everyone was touching.

The fire seemed to be under control which filled everyone with relief, as it hadn't spread to the nearby buildings. There was an unreal atmosphere in the smoky street, and Grace kept getting the impression that she was watching something on the big screen as opposed to being right in the middle of it.

A cheer rang out down the street and Grace looked to see what had caused it. Two nurses and a doctor stumbled out of a side door. Their news quickly spread through the street. The doctor had been trapped in a room, with fire in every corridor surrounding him, so the two nurses set about rescuing him. They found an incendiary bomb burning in a fireplace and braved the smoke and flames to smother it. Then they dug through a two-foot wall to push open a door and release the trapped doctor.

"My angels," the freed doctor was heard saying, as someone wrapped a blanket around him and hurried him down the street away from the burning building.

"They're so brave," said Grace, choking up.

Just then, a thunderous bomb blast filled the air and the ground shook. Immediately people started screaming and running for cover.

"It's all right," yelled one of the firemen. "The army have brought in experts and they're blowing up houses to stop the fire spreading." People began to calm down and returned to their tasks and when a second boom went off they cowered in fear, but didn't run.

Richard took out his pocket watch and had a quick look at it before putting it away.

"What time is it?" asked Grace.

"Nine-thirty."

Grace felt like she had lived a whole week in just a few hours. The emotions were exhausting but she felt alive. Everywhere she looked things seemed to be ultra-clear. She didn't know how to explain it, but things appeared more real, more vibrant, as if she had never truly looked at anything properly before.

The feeling stayed with her throughout the day, and even as the afternoon wore on and she felt weary to her bones, she still felt alive.

"We need to head back to the bus now," said Grace, looking at everyone as they had stopped for a break. To her surprise, no one argued but nodded their agreement.

"You'll come back with us tonight, Henry. We'll call the diocese tomorrow and see where you should go." Henry placed his hand on Richard's arm and tried to smile his thanks.

The walk back to Stretford felt long and all four of them had to force their legs to keep moving. There were many sighs of relief as they finally caught sight of the Newton Le Willows bus, still where they had left it.

"Glad to see you, Richard," said Joe, patting Richard on the shoulder and giving Grace a grin. "Been worried sick about the pair of you all day," he said shaking his head.

The bus ride home was completed without conversation. People were either lost in their thoughts and memories of the day, or else asleep.

Grace couldn't sleep. She held her father's hand tight as he slept, his head bouncing up and down, chin hitting chest and springing back up again.

"Thank you, God," she whispered, "for the only Christmas present I could ever want."

Chapter 8

Christmas Day
1940

Because of the blackout Midnight Mass had been cancelled, a short family service arranged for Christmas Morning at nine o'clock instead. Another year with no nativity and not much cheer, yet surprisingly the church was packed. Every pew was full and there were people standing at the back.

Grace looked around at the people she had grown up with and felt a love for them. They saw that love, as she smiled and welcomed them into the church.

"Merry Christmas, Grace," said Giles' wife, hugging her tight.

"Merry Christmas, Beth."

"Merry Christmas, Grace," said Giles, shaking her hand.

"Merry Christmas, Giles."

This greeting had been exchanged repeatedly, since the doors opened. With not much food to serve later that day, and with the exchange of homemade gifts and simple wares, one might have expected a cloud of misery to hang over the service. Instead, it was joyous, for it was another day, and they were all still alive.

"Yesterday was a day I will never forget," began Richard. Instead of standing in the pulpit, he was on the tiled floor, in front of the pews.

"Never has there been such a fire in Britain, since the Great Fire of London. People lost their lives. Homes were destroyed. Historical buildings are no more." Richard's eyes were smiling as he searched the faces of his congregation.

"How will you remember the last two days?" He let the question sink in before continuing.

"I shall remember, to my dying day, how wonderful the people of the great city of Manchester are." There was a lot of agreement from everyone present.

"I was speaking to a policeman just before we went to find the bus yesterday afternoon. He told me that not a single crime had been reported anywhere in Manchester for two days. Coppers had been drafted in from all over the place to help keep the peace and protect shops and people's homes. There was no crime. They spent their time instead helping the stoic Mancunians rescue people from burning and crumbling buildings. Despite the devastation of the city, people still came in to go to work, by any means they could. I saw bicycle after bicycle with people riding in to see if their place of work still stood.

"It was something that moved me deeply, here." Richard placed his hand over his heart. "Every single person I saw was pulling together to help in any way they could. Babies were born. People got married. Life went on. As I watched Manchester people fighting to save their city I wished that Mr Hitler could have been standing next to me." A few people started hissing.

"So that he could see that he will never break the British people. That we will always fight for justice, and that we will never, ever, roll over and surrender." The church erupted into cheers.

"War is a dreadful, evil thing. The loss of life is so tragic. The damage is horrific. Should we pray, then, that wars cease to be?" Richard looked around at the congregation; they were sitting straight in their seats with pride filling their lungs.

Grace wondered what her father was about to say, she always prayed that this war would come to an end and there would never be any more wars. She prayed it daily, giving the prayer earnest, heartfelt passion.

"I don't think so."

Grace looked at her father, puzzled.

"I believe that evil will exist in the world until the end of time. We can't wish it away; it is here for a purpose. Greed, for one, will always drive some men forward, bringing corruption to everything around them. This, then, is how I am going to pray from this day forward. That God would elevate people of honour into politics. Men and women who go out of their way to avoid temptation, and don't let themselves be blinded by greed and lust for power. If every country in the world was governed by such people, we would surely have peace and justice.

"I don't want to arrive in Heaven to have my Father tell me that things could have been different if only I had prayed differently. Therefore, I start my prayers by calling the Holy Spirit and asking Him to guide me towards the things the Father wants me to pray about.

"I encourage you to do the same. Today is Christmas Day, and in a moment we shall sing our carols with great gusto. As we sing the hymns we know so well, without reading the hymnal because we have sung them so many times before, let our souls cling onto the truth of God's sacrifice that was given to the world. His Son, who came as a baby and was born in a stable so that we might know Him."

As soon as they opened the door to the vicarage the smell of roasting turkey and vegetables greeted them. Taking off their coats, hats, scarves and gloves and throwing them onto the hallstand, they stood smiling at each other.

"So, let's get started. I'll get the fire going in the front room," said Richard, and took himself off.

Grace and Eleanor went to the kitchen to finish off the dinner. They usually ate at the kitchen table, but today Eleanor went to set up the table in the dining room, whilst Grace made the gravy. They hadn't been home long when the door opened, letting in a cold gust of wind.

"Hello," yelled Henry, "we're here."

"Welcome, everyone. Come on inside quickly and shut that door," said Richard.

A group of people piled in. No sooner had they taken off their coats than there was a knock at the door. Henry opened it and welcomed another group of people in.

Grace poked her head into the hallway. "Hi everyone. Dinner won't be long, make yourselves at home."

Mrs Tilbury followed Grace back into the kitchen. "Are you sure I won't be in the way?"

Grace looked up at her and smiled. "Of course not, it's lovely to have you here."

"I've made a figgy pudding," said Mrs Tilbury, putting a large bowl on the table, which was covered by a frilled checked cloth. "I would have liked to make a Christmas cake for you but I couldn't get icing sugar from anywhere. I even asked my relatives in London to help me out but they said there was none to be found."

"That's very generous of you, Mrs Tilbury, I'm sure everyone will appreciate it."

"Grace, as you are a grown woman now, I really do think it would be appropriate if you just called me Edith."

Eleanor came bouncing into the room. "Did I hear someone say figgy pudding?"

"Yes, Edith has very kindly made one for us," said Grace.

Eleanor took Edith by surprise when she threw her arms around her and gave her a tight squeeze. "Oh Edith, I do believe you have just become my favourite person."

Twenty-one people squashed themselves close together and sat around a table designed for sixteen. Richard sat at the head, and Grace sat opposite.

"That's it, Dad, everything is here," said Grace pulling up her chair.

"Ladies and gentlemen, we don't normally hold hands when we give thanks, but today I would ask for an exception. Would you mind very much if we held hands whilst I pray?" Everyone nodded and smiled at the person on either side of them as they all held hands.

"Dear Lord, I give you thanks. For the wonderful meal you have supplied, that will nourish our bodies and keep us fit. For the roofs over our heads that give us shelter and protect us. And for the clothes on our backs that keep us warm and cover our modesty. For these things Lord, we are truly grateful. But Lord, on this day when we remember your dear Son given for us, we say thank you, from the bottom of our hearts, for the life you have breathed into us, and for the gift of eternal life.

"We lift our loved ones, who are far from us today, Lord, and we ask that you bless them and keep them safe. For our men and women who are serving our country today, I ask that your angels protect them. Lastly, dear Lord, I thank you for everyone around this table. I thank you for their lives and for their friendship. God, please continue to bless us and protect us, in the name of your son, our Lord Jesus Christ, amen."

"Amen," said everyone around the table.

Despite the horrendous events of the last two days, dinner was a joyous occasion with non-stop talking as people passed the serving plates around and helped themselves to the best meal they'd had in ages. Richard carved the turkey at the top of the table, giving thanks to Giles and his wife who had given them the turkey as a Christmas present the day before.

Grace would have liked more people to have been there, and if she could have possibly squeezed anyone else around the table she would have done. The jovial nature of everyone was enhanced by the complete lack of war talk, or of going over the things they had witnessed recently. No one had said, let's not talk about it, it just happened. The past was grim and the future looked bleak, but for today they were full of life and delighted in every simple thing that happened. William constantly came to Grace's thoughts, but she gently put him aside. She would pray in earnest when the day was done, and then she would let herself ponder on what kind of day he might have had. It had been a month since his last letter and, as much as she tried not to, worry for him constantly filled her.

At the end of the day when the last guests had gone, and Henry had been shown to his room, Richard called Grace over to him.

"I have a present for you, my little love."

"Oh, Dad. We agreed no presents this year."

"I know, but it's not exactly my present, its William's, actually."

Grace gasped in surprise as Richard pulled out a small white envelope from his desk drawer.

"I hope you don't mind, but it came a few days ago, and this idea just came into my head that it would make a lovely Christmas present for you."

"It was a lovely idea, Dad. Thank you so much." Grace threw her arms around his neck and hugged him tight. However, after only a moment in the embrace Richard started coughing and Grace let him go.

"You okay, Dad? Shall I get you a drink?"

Richard shook his head and fought to keep the coughing under control. "I'm fine."

"You sure?"

"Yes, I'm sure. Now go and read your letter. You can tell me in the morning if there is anything you want to share."

Grace stood on tiptoes, and Richard leant down so that Grace could plant a kiss onto his cheek. "Night, Dad."

"Night, Grace."

Grace charged up the stairs two at a time and ran to her room. Just as she was about to shut the door, Eleanor popped her head into the corridor.

"Night, Grace, thank you for a lovely day."

"Night, Eleanor, sleep tight, don't let the bedbugs bite."

"You too, night."

Both of them closed their doors at the same time and Grace walked slowly to her bed and sat down on the edge, holding the letter in both hands, looking at William's squiggly handwriting. She opened the envelope carefully and took out a single sheet of paper, slight disappointment creeping into her spirit at the fact it was such a short letter.

10th November 1940

Dear Grace,

It gets harder to find time to write to you, for which I am sorry.

Good news, I have been promoted again. I am now a Captain and work very closely with my Major General. It means that my pay has been increased - that is if I should ever see any pay. My duties keep me running many errands, and being constantly on the move makes it hard for me to find time to sit down with paper and pen. I am currently in Greece, of all places, just fifteen miles from the Albanian border.

What Mussolini was thinking when he decided to invade Greece is anyone's guess. Hats off to the Greeks though, they are resourceful and dedicated. I watched as they went to battle with only a handful of Great War weapons and farmers' rakes, can you believe that? The discipline though was amazing, and they literally pushed the Italians and Albanians back within just a week. Oh Grace, if only all battles could be over so quickly. The British government will have no choice now but to send in the army to help protect them, and I believe we, that is the Major and I, will be here for some time to come.

I am sorry to fill the page with items of war but I am afraid it has become my life; there is very little time to think of anything else. What time I do get to reflect, wish and hope, that time is dedicated to you, my special friend.

Grace put the letter down on the bedside table and got ready for bed. Once she was tucked up under the blankets, she picked up the letter, gave it a kiss and placed it under her pillow. She was happy to receive news from William, and to know that he was still alive and well, but the letter had felt impersonal and she was left wanting more. She scolded herself for being needy and instantly prayed that God would forgive her and help her to be gracious and understanding.

If you would bring him home safely to me, Father, I would be eternally grateful.

Chapter 9

Pickles Galore
1943

"How did you manage that?" Grace challenged.

"Ask me no questions, and I'll tell 'ee no lies!"

"Seriously, Eleanor this is amazing. I'll be able to make tons of jam now. I don't know what to say."

"Thank you will do."

Grace threw her arms around Eleanor and kissed her on the cheek. "Thank you. Oh, and by the way, next time you see Teddy, be sure to thank him for me too!"

Eleanor burst out laughing. "He's so good to me. Besides the sugar, he gave me a pair of stockings and a bar of chocolate. You're welcome to the sugar, of course, but I'm afraid the rest is for me."

"Oh, I'd much rather have the sugar," Grace laughed back.

"You might, but I think William would prefer the stockings when he comes home?"

"Eleanor!" Grace started blushing.

"What's that?" asked Richard sticking his head around the door.

"Sugar, Father, I have three pounds of sugar."

"Very happy for you, I'm sure," said Richard before retreating into the parlour.

Grace and Eleanor got the giggles.

"I need to get this soup made," said Grace, going back to the chopping of vegetables. "Are you staying for supper or going to meet Teddy?"

"I'll be seeing him tomorrow as they have something going on at the airbase tonight."

"Good, then you'll be able to have supper with us tonight. I have to say, with all the extra work you're doing, then with you stepping out with Teddy, we hardly see you anymore, and I have to be honest and say I miss you. I have no idea what I'll do with myself when this war is finished and you leave us."

Eleanor came around the table and put her arms around Grace. "You daft thing. We will always stay friends, always. And, anyway, who says I am leaving when the war finishes?"

They both laughed.

"I am sure Teddy will be whisking you off to America as soon as he can."

"Oh, I hope so, Grace. I love him so much. He's everything I've ever dreamed of. Besides being *so* handsome, he's also kind and thoughtful. I have my fingers and toes crossed that he will ask me to marry him any moment now. You know Cathy, from Earlstown way? Well, her Texas pilot proposed to her last week and they're getting married tomorrow. I'm so jealous. I'm happy for her, of course, but still… I wish Teddy would ask me."

"I'm sure he will, why wouldn't he? You're beautiful and funny and lovely, everyone loves you."

"Not as much as they love you, Grace. Seriously, I think even the cats and dogs follow you around with love in the hope that you will smile at them."

"Don't exaggerate, I know I'm a plain-Jane, but I don't care because my William will be coming home soon."

"Wow, has he had his release papers?"

"No." Grace put the chopping knife down, with a huge sigh. "He's been wounded."

"Oh no! Not too badly I hope?"

"I don't think so, the letter I received didn't say too much, just that he was wounded and that he could finally come home for some leave. I know he's been hurt, Eleanor, but I'm so happy I could burst." Eleanor gave her another huge hug. "It's been two years since he last came home on leave, his Major always seemed to have some good reason to delay it, but now he's been wounded he can come home."

"That's good news. But back to what I was saying, I didn't mean people are *in* love with you, just that everyone loves you. Seriously, Grace, I've never met a nicer person in my entire life."

Grace could hear Eleanor choking up and felt her own eyes prick with the sting of oncoming tears. "I love you too, Eleanor."

A fit of coughing from the other room broke into their moment, and concern instantly came on Grace's face.

"It's not getting any better, is it?" said Eleanor.

Grace shook her head. "I persuaded the doctor to come again, just this morning. He's prescribed some cough mixture but I know he doesn't actually know what's causing it."

"Can't we take him to the hospital?"

"He won't go. He's adamant he's just got a cold in his chest, and nothing I say about coughing for nearly a year will make him listen. I wasn't too worried at first, but now I'm sure he's beginning to lose weight and I don't think that's a good sign."

After their supper of soup and bread and cheese, the three of them settled into the living room to listen to the BBC Home Service on the wireless. Richard, who now wore round spectacles, was reading the newspaper. Grace and Eleanor curled up on the sofa to listen to the music. After only a short while, Eleanor yawned.

"How's it going in the Vulcan Foundry these days, Eleanor?" inquired Richard, peering over the rim of his glasses.

"It's hard work. I've never felt so exhausted in all my life. I thought shifting hay was bad and that moving to the factory was a good idea, but I was wrong. It's long, hard days of physical labour and my body is developing the most unfeminine muscles a lady could possibly get. You know, we spotted the Luftwaffe flying over us yesterday taking photographs. Everyone's in a tis-was now, believing they will be back soon to bomb us. The gaffer has ordered that absolutely no one is to be on site after dark."

"Surely, this war must end soon?" said Grace.

"Four years," said Richard. "I never would have believed that we could fight for so long. I keep thinking that today will be the day when we can ring the church bells ring again." Suddenly, Richard spluttered and started coughing so harshly that his body rocked with the force of it.

Both Grace and Eleanor jumped up and rushed to his side.

"Dad, try to drink," said Grace holding a cup of water in front of him.

As the coughing fit eased off, Richard accepted the cup and took several sips of water. When the coughing had completely stopped, he sighed and sat back into his chair.

"Seriously, Grace, Eleanor, I'm fine. It's just a cough; I don't feel ill at all."

Grace opened her mouth.

"No, Grace, seriously, I won't listen to another argument for visiting the hospital. Those poor doctors and nurses have enough to do without me appearing for a stupid cough. I'm fine." He flicked his hands at them. "Go on, shoo. Let's talk about something more cheering, shall we? Eleanor, tell me something new about this young man of yours, we haven't seen much of him lately."

Eleanor sat back on the sofa and couldn't help the smile that lit up her face.

"Well… Teddy's been at the Burtonwood base since the beginning of February, so that's…" Eleanor counted on her fingers.

"That's five months, gosh, it's frightening how quickly time flies, isn't it? It only feels like yesterday when I met him."

"And is he going to make an honest woman of you?"

"Dad!"

Eleanor laughed. "I certainly hope so, Richard."

"Are you going to bring him home, sometime soon?" asked Grace.

"I was hoping as he is off this Sunday that he could come around for dinner after church, if that's all right with you two?"

"Of course, delightful young man, be a pleasure to see him again," smiled Richard.

"It would be rather nice to see him again, and cooking him a dinner would be a lovely way to say thank you for the sugar," said Grace.

"He'll be so pleased. He's missing home very much; I think a family dinner will cheer him up no end."

"Listen," said Grace getting up to turn the volume up, "Worker's Playtime is coming on."

"Oh good," said Richard folding up his paper. "I could do with a laugh."

"Rather," agreed Eleanor.

The three of them spent the next hour laughing and putting the horrors of war out of their thoughts.

The next day Grace was up before the birds, dressed, washed and out of the house before either Eleanor or Richard had even stirred. She pedalled to the farm in the dark, glad of her warm coat. Although it was June, the weather hadn't been great, and the swirling morning mist was damp and cold. Propping her bike against the cowshed she went straight to work. She had mucked out and fed the pigs before Giles came out to find her.

"Ee-gods Grace, what ya doin' 'ere at this time o't mornin'?"

She laughed. "I have pickling to do, Giles. Tons and tons of pickling. Need to be home as early as possible so I can get cracking."

"You're crackers, lass. Go on, get yerself off 'ome. We'll mange without 'ee today."

Grace needed no second telling. "Thank you, Giles. I'll stay a bit longer tomorrow. I have something to ask though, before I go."

"What's that then, lass?"

"Do you think I could take today's batch of ripened strawberries? It's just that I have been given some sugar, and I'd love to make a batch of jam."

"Goodness me, girl. Go 'elp yerself. For dear life, how many times do I have to tell 'ee? Food is for sharing and you earn your share, good 'n proper."

Grace's grin nearly split her cheeks. "Thank you. William is going to be coming home soon and I know he loves strawberry jam. I'm just so excited to be able to make him some."

"Get on with you, lass. I'll see 'ee tomorrow."

Grace waved as she raced off down the field to the strawberry patch. It was a very small patch this year, as nearly all the land had been turned to producing high volumes of vegetables. However, Giles' wife had insisted on having one small run to plant her favourite fruit. The sun was creeping into the sky, throwing a soft, warm glow over the land, and when the rays fell on Grace's face, happiness radiated through her. Birds tweeted merrily in the hedgerow, oblivious to the horrors of war, and she was flooded with feelings of well-being and a moment of contentment.

"Thank you, God. Thank you so much for sending my William home to me."

With her basket heavy with ripened, plump and juicy strawberries, Grace rode home slowly so as not to shake it and knock any out. The High Street was coming alive by the time she got back to town.

"Morning, Grace," called the butcher, propping open his shop door.

She waved back. "Morning George." The bike wobbled and she nearly lost her precious load.

"Steady on, lass," called Joe, laughing.

"Morning, Joe," she called as she turned the bike into the drive that ran down the side of the vicarage.

Eleanor came out of the back door just as she was propping her bike against the shed. "What's wrong? Why are you home?"

"Nothing's wrong. Giles said he could do without me today and I'm going to do some pickling and make some jam."

"Umm," said Eleanor putting a strawberry into her mouth.

"Hey, you," laughed Grace.

"Can I take your bike today? I think mine has a slow puncture and I don't have time to look at it."

"Sure, no problem. Have a good day, see you later."

Grace took the strawberries straight to the sink and gave them a quick rinse through. Not long after that, the smell of strawberries wafted through the house as they bubbled away in the sugar. It wasn't until she heard her father coughing upstairs that she realised he was late getting out of bed.

Not able to leave the jam she started her daily chat with God, lifting up her father again, and asking for a full and swift recovery.

She'd just screwed the cap onto the twelfth and last jar of jam when Richard came into the kitchen, still in his dressing gown.

"Don't look like that, I'm just feeling a little tired today and thought I would rest. I'm fine, and before you start, I don't want a lecture today." He sat down in the rocking chair by the fireplace and Grace washed her hands.

"Tea?"

"Yes please, dear."

She had recently filled the large teapot and placed the cosy over it to keep it warm, ready for when he came down. She knew how much he liked a strong cup of tea, and so she had used her last ration to get some yesterday.

"Here you go, Dad," she said placing the cup down on the small table near his chair.

Richard reached up and grabbed her hand. "You're a good girl, you know that?"

"I'm hardly a girl any more, Dad."

"You'll always be my little girl. You know your mother would be so proud of you."

Grace reached down and hugged her dad tight. He never mentioned her mum much and for some reason mentioning her today seemed to spark a bit of fear inside her.

Richard didn't want any breakfast, nor did he want to go and sit in his study, so Grace carried the heavy wireless into the kitchen and tuned into the BBC so that he could listen to 'Music while you Work'. She was glad she had lit a fire in the kitchen today, something not normally done in June, but she wanted to jacket some potatoes. She also put a pile of clothes up to dry on the pulley-maid, which hung from the ceiling, because although it was sunny now she knew it was going to rain later. Grace was only thirty-one years old but suffered terribly from arthritis, and by the amount of pain her knees were giving her just now, she was sure it would rain within the next couple of hours.

As she threw the peppercorns, mustard seed, bay leaves and onions into the pan and hummed along to Bing Crosby, she was aware that, without words, she was having a special moment with her father.

From an early age, her father had told her to watch out for special moments and to make a clear record of it in her memory. It would be these recorded memories that she could recall when needed, that would help her to get through tough days.

The first special memory that she had stored in her mind was a day with her dad on the beach in Blackpool. Since then, she had squirreled away moments aplenty.

As she put the now-cooled onions into jars and poured the malt vinegar over them, she knew her father was watching her, she could feel his love in his gaze. For the second time that day, well-being washed over her.

I'm so blessed. A wonderful father, a fiancée coming home, the best friend anyone could want, a lovely home and to top it all off the reassurance that God was real and cared about them.

To conclude a special day, Teddy came for dinner and had all of them howling with laughter. He really was a dream, and

Grace totally understood why Eleanor was head-over-heels in love with him.

Chapter 10

Falling
1943

"I'm not sure about this, Eleanor."

"Trust me, Grace, you look amazing."

Eleanor had been asking, can I do-you-up, since the day she arrived, and until today Grace had always replied with a resounding, no. Not sure what had happened, Grace had given in and put herself in Eleanor's hands. She had been primped and preened until she didn't recognize herself anymore. Seriously, looking in the mirror in that moment was like looking at a mannequin in a shop window. Her hair was sprayed stiff, and then wrapped into large curls on the top of her head; adding both a little height and an air of sophistication. Eleanor had carefully painted her face with a myriad of cosmetics, splashes of blue over the eyes, black kohl on the inside of the eyelids, powders to subdue her natural sun-kissed, freckle-filled cheeks and deep red lipstick.

To finish it off Eleanor had bought Grace a new dress, and that was where most of the arguing now stemmed from. Its heart-shaped neckline was slightly too revealing for Grace's mind, and although the material was most wondrously soft and lovely to touch, it hugged her figure in a rather revealing manner. But... the nail in the coffin, to coin a phrase, was that the dress was the deepest and richest colour of red Grace had ever seen.

"I'm sorry, Eleanor, you're just going to have to take it back, I can't wear it. It simply isn't me."

"Don't be silly, Grace. You look amazing. Go on, for once in your life let your hair down, just go along with it and have some fun."

"To be pedantic, my hair is actually up."

Eleanor came and stood behind Grace and put her hands on her shoulders, as the two of them looked in the mirror. "Seriously, Grace, you look amazing, please come out with me just as you are?"

"I don't know, Eleanor, I'll only be a gooseberry with you and Teddy anyway."

"Grace, the place is going to be packed, of course you won't be a gooseberry. Come on, say yes, we'll have so much fun."

Grace stared at Eleanor's pleading eyes in the mirror and after hours of debating, finally gave in. "Okay, then."

Eleanor threw her arms in the air. "Hallelujah!"

"Oy," said Grace, giving Eleanor a tender thump on the arm.

Laughing, Eleanor grabbed her clutch bag off the bed and opened the door. "Come on, let's go before you change your mind."

As Eleanor headed downstairs Grace picked up a hankie, placed it in-between her lips and pressed down hard. When she removed the hankie most of the lipstick was left on it in the impression of her lips. There was only a hint of red on her lips now, but absolutely enough as far as she was concerned. She was just about to go after Eleanor when she stopped and looked at her finger. Without hesitation she pulled off William's ring and left it on the dresser; there was no way she was going to risk losing it.

As she went rushing down the stairs, a car horn beeped three times.

"Come on, Grace, they're here." Eleanor flung open the door, and then went running down the path.

"Have a nice time," Richard called, popping his head around the door. Grace blew him a kiss before shutting the front door. Despite not wanting to go out in the first place, for at the age of thirty-two she felt she was well past going to dance halls, she was surprisingly giddy as she hastened down the path after Eleanor.

As she approached the black Hillman Minx she slowed down, in debate with herself once more on exactly how good an idea this was. Eleanor pushed her head out of the car window.

"Come on, slow-coach."

The passenger door was open and Grace caught sight of the driver as he leant over to smile at her. Bump! Her heart felt as if it had stopped for a moment as the sparkling blue eyes of the driver caught hers. A weird sensation rippled through her as she climbed into the car. Her mouth was dry and her face flushed as she pulled the door shut.

"This is Milton," said Eleanor leaning between the two front seats. "Milton, this is Grace." She looked at both their faces and the realisation that they liked each other was obvious, making her laugh. "I knew you two would get on," she said, leaning back and snuggling into Teddy.

"Nice to meet you," said Milton putting out his hand.

"And you," Grace replied, tentatively giving him her hand. She was surprised when he gave her hand a tight squeeze.

"Let's go dancing," Milton said, with the nicest smile Grace had ever seen.

A short time later Milton parked the car and the four got out into a packed street. Grace looked around, slightly shocked to see so many people. Milton offered Grace his arm, which she took automatically and the four of them joined the throngs of people heading towards the Parr dance hall.

The Saints jazz band weren't due to start playing for another hour and yet the queue to get in went right round the block. Grace was bemused at the joviality and good-natured banter that was all around.

"I take it you haven't been into town for a while?"

Milton's American drawl felt like honey to Grace's ears and for a moment, she forgot to answer. He raised an eyebrow at her, and she lost herself for a heartbeat in his deep, speckled-blue eyes.

"Oh, yes, it's been a very long time since I've been into Warrington during the evening. I didn't realise there was still such vibrancy around."

"People need to let off steam," chipped in Teddy.

"Too right they do. Dancing is a wonderful release from fear and misery. When I'm on the dance floor I can forget, for a while, about everything else and just have fun." Eleanor threw her arms up in the air and spun around. Teddy instantly took her in his arms and flipped her backwards over his arm. She landed smartly on her feet, dress demurely back in place around her knees where it should never have left. Grace was agog. Everyone laughed at her.

"You telling me that you won't be dancing the jitterbug with me? Darn, I was so looking forward to swinging your tiny body around."

Grace stared at Milton in horror, which only made him laugh louder.

"I'm jesting with you, Grace. I'm no dancer, you'll obviously be pleased to hear."

Relief flooded through Grace and she couldn't help the sigh that escaped her lips. Milton's laughing eyes locked onto hers and for a moment the bedlam of the mobs of people completely faded. Silence, and nothing but fell around her as she looked up into the most alluring eyes she had ever seen.

The moment was broken by a sudden commotion that didn't sound good natured.

"I've told you. Read the sign. No blacks allowed, now get out of here, I won't tell you again."

Grace's mouth dropped open as utter horror at the man's words washed through her. "He can't be serious," she whispered.

Eleanor came and locked her arm through Grace's. "I'm afraid he is."

Three black men stood in a clearing as people moved back from them.

"I signed up for this war," the tallest one announced with pride in his words and his stance. "We weren't conscripted, we volunteered to come and help you beat the Germans. You're happy enough to allow us to carry your weapons and fight side-by-side with you, but you won't let us drink and dance with you? You're hypocrites, the lot of you."

"Oh no." Grace was so upset she started trembling. "I don't understand, I thought our government rejected the US stipulations that we impose segregation. Why won't they let them in?"

"I'm afraid our lieutenants have visited the pubs and dance halls and told them if they let blacks in, the white GIs will be forbidden to come. Of course there are more whites here than blacks, so they're set to lose money if they pick blacks."

"It's simply outrageous," said Eleanor.

"Diabolical," agreed Grace. "Isn't there anything you can do?" she said, looking up at Milton.

He shook his head.

As the three men walked off Grace was struck by their air of dignity. "I wish I could do something for them."

The hushed atmosphere was heavy and permeated with shame. Eyes cast down and faces turned away, too guilt-ridden to look the three black soldiers in the eye.

"The line's moving now, we'll be inside soon," said Teddy. It was obvious that he was uncomfortable about the whole thing but wanted them to enjoy the evening.

Grace dropped it, but a sympathy demanding action was born in her heart. Just as her father had told her to store up precious moments in her memory, she became aware that she was now storing up moments that caused her anguish.

By the time they reached the entrance the crowd was once again jolly and loud. Like a mirage, the incident with the three men faded and was pushed to the farthest recess of logical thinking. Tomorrow there would be time to dwell on yet another injustice in the world, tonight was for abandon and gaiety, and the proof that they were still alive.

Teddy steered them towards an empty table near the edge of the dance floor. He spotted another couple heading towards it and let go of Eleanor's hand so he could quickly by-pass the couple and slide into one of the chairs.

"Sorry, they're taken," he said smiling his most charming smile at the couple. The man seemed none too pleased and was about to say something when the woman grabbed his arm, declaring that she wanted to be near the bandstand.

Milton raised his eyebrows at Teddy, who was now lounging back with his arms spread along the back of the seats. "What can I get you to drink, ladies?"

"An orange juice, please," answered Grace.

"Whiskey and coke for me," said Eleanor giving Teddy a wink.

"Eleanor!"

"Oh, come on, Grace. I've been drinking for years; you really ought to try drinking more than a sherry at Christmas. It's fun!"

Milton looked at Grace questioningly.

"Oh, no thanks. I'm quite happy with an orange, thank you."

They watched the two men walk off to the bar and when they were out of ear shot Eleanor turned to Grace. "Well?"

"Well what?"

"What do you think of Milton? He's a dreamboat, isn't he? Got to love those sparkling eyes."

"I thought you were in love with Teddy?"

"I am, silly. No, what I mean is, I think Milton is perfect for you. He's a six foot four inch dream boat."

Grace sat back in her chair and frowned at Eleanor. "You know I'm engaged."

"Yes, I do. But I've also seen some of the letters he's sent home to you, and Grace, I'm afraid to say it, but he doesn't sound like a man head over heels in love."

Grace started playing with her hands. What could she say?

"I knew it, you're not so in love with him either, are you? Grace, life is so short, you can't get married to a man you don't love."

"I love William, Eleanor."

"Umm, but are you *in* love with him?"

"Drop it, please. I am very happy to be marrying William, we go together extremely well."

"Grace, I wish you could hear yourself. And anyway, where's the ring?"

Grace rubbed her finger where the ring should have been. "It took a lot of William's savings to buy me that ring, I don't want to lose it."

"Poppycock and fiddlesticks."

"They're coming back, Eleanor, drop it."

Eleanor passed Grace a look that clearly said we'll talk about this later, and then turned to grin up at Teddy as he passed her a drink.

The evening was fun. Grace's face lit up when the Saints came on and she stood on the side and clapped along, as the floor flooded with dancers.

"Are you sure you don't want to dance?" Milton asked as he watched her tapping foot.

"I'm sure, thanks." Then it hit Grace that maybe Milton wanted to dance. "If you want to look for a partner and join in the dancing I'm very happy to just watch. The dancers here are amazing. Look at Eleanor go, I didn't even know she could dance like that and she's been living with us for years now."

"I'm good, thanks. Like I said, dancing isn't my thing."

The evening was over and Grace had no idea how it had reached midnight so quickly. They drove home slowly in the dark. No street lights and filtered headlights meant dim visibility. Luckily, the full moon helped light the way.

Milton got out of the car when Grace did and escorted her up the path, leaving Eleanor and Teddy to a heavy kissing session on the back seat.

"Thank you, I've had a lovely evening."

"Was my pleasure, Ma'am," he said giving her a snappy salute. She giggled.

"Grace, would it be okay for me to take you out to the pictures next weekend?"

"Oh, I'm sorry, I..." Grace didn't know what to say. For some reason she didn't want to tell him that she was engaged.

Disappointment showed on his face and the sparkle left his eyes. "Yes, of course, I understand."

Panic rose in her chest, she couldn't let him leave thinking she didn't like him. "Actually, when I think about it, I think I am free. Yes, that would be very nice, thank you."

His sparkling eyes were instantly lit up. "I probably won't be able to borrow the car again next weekend, so are you happy to ride to the movies with me?"

"So long as Eleanor hasn't gone off with my bike, yes of course I will ride."

"Night, then." Grace could see his desire to lean forward and kiss her so she took a step backwards.

"Night. See you next Saturday, about six?"

"That's a date."

Before Grace could go into the fact that it wasn't a date as in stepping out together, Milton had turned around and was off.

Grace unlocked the door and waited for Eleanor, who came slowly, with a very slight wobble and an ever-so dreamy expression on her face. Once inside, Grace helped Eleanor off with her coat and then took her by the elbow to help her up the stairs.

"Isn't he dreamy?" she hiccupped.

"He certainly is."

"He's got to ask to marry me soon, surely?"

"Surely," replied Grace as she ushered Eleanor into her room.

Chapter 11

Entanglement
1944

She never set out to lie, but then presumably no one ever did. Why Grace continued to remove her engagement ring when she knew she was meeting up with Milton she didn't analyse, just shoved the guilt to the back of her mind. She also paid particular attention to skip over any feelings that she had for him when she prayed for his safekeeping.

After several months of meeting up, and, being honest, acting like a couple and sharing a few tender kisses, Grace was happily caught off balance when she opened the front door and found Milton standing there.

"Surprise," he declared opening his arms.

She rushed into them and held him tight. "It's a lovely surprise, I thought you couldn't get any spare time today?"

"A few of us were given last minute leave due to an early start tomorrow, and I thought to myself, what can I do with a few spare hours? Then I thought, I know, I have this very cute, but irritatingly prudish friend, I'll go pay her a visit."

"Oh really? Why did you knock on *my* door then?" They both laughed. "Come on in, I'll pop the kettle on."

Milton hesitated. "Is your father in?"

"No, he went to Manchester after the service to visit an old friend. Why?"

Milton obviously relaxed. "I don't think he is taken with me."

Grace wanted to lie and say, of course her father liked him. But she couldn't, it was obvious to everyone that he didn't like him, and she could hardly explain to Milton that the reason was because he thought he was drawing her away from William.

She smiled at him instead. "Come on, let's go to the kitchen, I'm cooking and it's the warmest room in the house."

"I got six letters from home today."

Grace was filling the kettle, and she paused to look over her shoulder. "Really? That's lovely, fancy getting six all in one day."

"My sister just had her first child, I'm an uncle! It seems everyone wanted to be the first to tell me."

"Oh, how lovely. Congratulations. I bet that makes you miss home even more doesn't it?" After lighting the stove, Grace came and sat opposite Milton at the table.

"I never realised how much I was going to miss home. I mean, we've always been a close-knit family and I love my home town. But I wasn't prepared for this constant pain and longing to be back with them."

Grace reached out and took hold of his hands across the table. "I'm sorry."

"It's not your fault, Grace darlin'. It's just the way it is."

"Tell me about home, and your family."

Milton grinned and went off into a very lengthy description of his family and their wonderfully unique characters. The tenderness he felt towards them all was very touching, and Grace was jealous for the size of his family.

"I wish I'd had a sister or a brother," she said getting up to turn the gas off under the whistling kettle.

"Well, maybe one day you will."

She was puzzled by his answer, until it dawned on her that he was hinting at a proposal. Her cheeks flushed, and excitement tightened her stomach.

As she poured the boiling water into the teapot, her hands were shaking and Milton reached over to help her. Abruptly, he snatched his hands back. Puzzled, Grace looked at him and nearly spilt the last of the water from the kettle.

"You'd better put that down."

She took the kettle back to the stove, unwound the cloth from the handle and slowly returned to the table.

"What's wrong?" she asked, sitting back down opposite him.

"So, do you want to tell me who the lucky guy is?"

Grace watched Milton's gaze drop to her fingers. When she looked down the sparkling blue sapphire seemed to be laughing at her. She shoved her hands under the table.

"I think it's a bit too late for that, don't you?" He stood and headed out of the room.

"Milton, wait. You don't understand, let me explain."

"You're engaged," he barked as he flung open the front door. "I don't think there is much to explain."

"Wait please," called Grace running to catch him up. "Please," she said reaching for his arm.

He jerked away from her touch. His eyes filled with so much anger that Grace took a step back. "You know, the joke is I thought you were *such* a lady. What an idiot I am, or rather what a good actress *you* are."

Grace's chin was wobbling, her eyes stinging. She wanted to reach out and hold him and let him know that she loved him in a way she'd never loved William, but he had turned and was marching away. She sat down on the steps, dropped her head into her hands and cried like she'd never cried before.

The next morning at five o'clock Grace could stand it no longer and got out of bed and dressed. She hadn't been able to sleep. She loved Milton, loved him with a passion and a longing she never thought she'd experience. She had to see him. She had to make him understand.

It was still dark as she pulled her bike out of the shed but she didn't care, she had to get to the base to see him. She had no idea where the energy came from but she raced along the road, keeping her fingers crossed that she didn't hit any potholes. Half an hour later, she jumped off the bike and approached the gates to the base.

"What you doing here, Miss?" demanded one of the guards.

"I need to see Senior Airman Milton Simmons, it's urgent."

Unbeknown to Grace, quite a lot of women had been turning up at the gates demanding to see some GI or other. They'd all had the same tale to tell, they were in the motherly way and it was so-and-so's fault.

The guard sighed and embarked on his normal patter. "Sorry, Miss, but no unaccompanied civilians are allowed on site."

Grace saw movement on the airfield and strained to concentrate; it looked like Milton.

"Please," she said pointing, "I think that's Milton over there, please call him." The guard turned to look, and then turned back to Grace.

"Sorry, Miss. Airman Simmons is on duty. You won't be able to speak to him today."

Panic rose, she had to tell him. "Milton," she cried, waving her arms like mad. "Milton." He must have heard her because he stopped and looked in her direction. "Milton please, let me have five minutes."

It looked for a moment as if he'd come over, but then he changed his mind and carried on walking across the airfield.

Grace let out a moan of frustration.

"Look, Miss, it's the first daylight raids we've ever done, today. He truly doesn't have time to talk to you. Why don't you come back tomorrow? At a more appropriate time."

"They're doing daylight raids?"

"Yes, Miss. I hear they're heading to Berlin."

"Oh my Lord." Grace's hands flew to her mouth. Her body started shaking. "That's too dangerous," she sobbed into her hands.

"Our boys will be fine. Why don't you take yourself home now?"

Grace moved along the fence and watched the shadows of men as they checked and re-checked their planes. "Oh Father-God, please forgive me for being deceitful, please, please keep him safe."

She didn't have the strength to ride home, instead she decided to push the bike through the fields, a more direct route but not suitable for riding. All the way she cried out to God, over and over again, for forgiveness and for protection over Milton, and the other pilots.

8th March 1944

Grace leant her forehead against the window as she watched the landscape rush past. She was glad she'd managed to get a window seat, the train was full and the carriages packed tight with people from all walks of life. Mostly soldiers though, their pea-green uniforms dominating the spectrum of colours. She found the chuff-chuff of the steam train soothing and leant back in her cushioned seat. Not wanting to talk to anyone, she closed her eyes.

What was she going to say to William? Her dear, dear, friend. How could she tell him that she no longer wanted to marry him? She assured herself with the fact that he was home safe and sound, and that the reason for marrying her was probably not so pressing. Still, no amount of camouflaging or looking on the bright-side could fully convince her that if he still loved her and wanted to get married then she would have no alternative but to comply. She had entered into the arrangement willingly and quite happily when it suited her. She now felt honour-bound to marry him, if he still wished it.

Yet her hands were trembling in her lap. God had heard her prayers and bought Milton home safely from the air raid over Berlin, but she still hadn't been able to speak to him and she didn't know which thing caused her to feel sick the most – the thought of talking to William or Milton. If she could break off her engagement to William she would, then she would go and make Milton listen to her story. If William was too upset at the prospect of breaking off the engagement, then she would stick to it and firmly put Milton out of her mind forever.

She felt glad as the train pulled into Blackpool Station for she was closer to her confession to William. The sea breeze was cold and she quickly did up the buttons of her dark grey woollen trench coat, and then pulled the belt in tight. She fished her hat out of her bag and put it on, but it was obvious straightaway that without pins it wasn't going to stay on, and as she had forgotten them, she shoved the hat back in her bag.

She asked the porter for directions to the sea front and he pointed her the right way. She only been to the beach a few times whilst growing up and couldn't help but stop and stare when she reached the promenade. It was blustery, the waves high and loud as they crashed on the sandy beach. She loved the sea and always had a longing to swim in it, even though she wouldn't go near it on a day like today. Not only could the current quickly carry her off, but it was also so cold that she'd probably freeze to death.

Blackpool front was a hive of activity and she watched the never-ending line of ambulances as they queued for the hospitals. She wondered if the patients felt any safer being here by the sea than they would in hospitals in Liverpool or Manchester. Probably they would, because despite the threat of invasion by sea, air raids over Blackpool rarely happened.

The further along she went, the slower her steps became. She didn't want to hurt William; maybe she shouldn't mention anything and just forget about Milton. She spotted the Miners hospital straight away. The huge, redbrick building was breathtakingly impressive. She hastened her steps as she walked up the front path to the hospital, reluctantly leaving the promenade and the salty sea spray.

The receptionist informed her that Mr Shelby was on the third floor and pointed her towards the stairs. She arrived surprisingly breathless; it seemed that despite being fit the never-ending stairs were just a bit too much for her. A nurse showed her to William's room and she stood in the doorway for a moment until she found him. Luckily for him he was in a bed next to the window, and he was sitting on the edge of it looking out to sea. She walked slowly past the other beds and came to a halt behind him, then paused, not wanting to startle him.

"Hello, Grace," he said without turning around.

"How did you know it was me?" she asked, surprised, as she came around the bed to stand beside him.

"Your lavender rushed to greet me way before you did." He looked up at her and she had to stop herself from gasping. He was gaunt, his eyes black, lifeless hollows.

"William," she whispered wrapping her arms tightly around him. "Oh, William."

For a moment he didn't react, and then slowly he raised one arm and placed it around her. "I'm all right, Grace."

She commanded the tears to desist their threat of spilling, clenched her teeth and sat on the bed beside him. "Are you really all right, William?"

He gave her a weary smile and placed his hand over hers, which she had put on his thigh. "We're all grown up, Grace."

She didn't know what to say. They sat in silence, both staring out of the window.

"It's beautiful, isn't it? I understand why the miners' commissioners decided to build a convalescent home here. The sea and the fresh air practically force you to recover."

Grace looked at the sparkling tips of the waves and had to agree. "It's beautiful."

After a few moments of silence, Grace fished inside her bag and pulled out a jar of jam. "For you," she said handing him the jar with a smile.

"Thank you," he said. Without directly looking at it, he placed it on the cupboard next to his bed.

Grace felt disappointed but smiled to hide it when he turned back to face her.

"Grace, sometimes a promise is made for all the right reasons." He cupped her fingers in his hands. "And sometimes, for all the right reasons we must break a promise."

Grace tensed, did he know about Milton? Was he giving her permission to call off the engagement? He looked at her properly for the first time since she'd arrived.

"Grace, will you try to understand when I tell you that I can't marry you anymore?"

Her eyebrows shot up in surprise. "Of course I will, we're best friends, remember?"

Before she could rush on and tell him about Milton, he carried on. "I didn't have anything to worry about you know, when I joined up, about you know what. How foolish I was to think they would be bothered as to where my affections lay when we were face-to-face with death and the horror of war. When I asked you to marry me, Grace, I truly believed that we could make each other happy. And now I must ask your forgiveness because I can't go through with it, I can't live a lie. For as much as I love you Grace, and I do love you, marriage would be a lie."

"What made you change your mind?"

"Death, and the clarity of life that death brings."

A single tear fell from the corner of William's eye and Grace found herself speechless and lost in his sorrow.

"I fell in love, Grace."

She smiled up at him. "You did?"

"Yes, with my Major." He went quiet, but Grace didn't say anything and waited for him to tell his story. "He doesn't know, of course. He has a wife and three children, I'm sure he would be horrified if he knew how I felt about him."

"I suppose being with him every day makes that hard for you?"

"Yes and no. I love working for him, he's such an intelligent man, Grace. And he cares about his men strongly; he's what you call a real decent, solid type of bloke."

"If he is never going to know about your feelings towards him, do you really want to break off our engagement?"

William wrapped his arm around her shoulders. "Grace, how sweet you are. Yes, I'm sure. One day you will meet someone who you fall head-over-heels for and then you'll be free to marry them. I can't tie you into something that's not real. Life is too short, way, way too short."

"Well, as it happens, I have something to tell you too."

William turned his head to look down at her. "Do tell."

"I have met someone, and I am in love!"

"That's great, gosh I'm so happy for you… wait, does he feel the same towards you?"

"Yes. Well, yes, I think so. I think he hinted that he wanted to take me home to Ohio, and that his family would become my family."

"Wait, wait, wait. And you were still going to marry me?"

"Yes, if you wanted to. I made a promise to you and I wasn't going to break it without your blessing."

"Goodness, Grace, you have my blessing, heaps of blessings."

For the first time since she came into the room the atmosphere relaxed and the two of them chuckled together, as they had done in the days of their youth.

"You'd better invite me to the wedding."

"Of course I will. Although, I mustn't jump the gun, he hasn't asked me yet."

"He will, Grace, he will."

"When do you get out of here?"

"Soon, I hope. I'm walking with just one stick now and getting stronger every day."

"Will you come home after that?"

William shook his head. "There's nothing in Newton Le Willows for me any more, Grace, only you, and I've seen you now and I'm happy that you're happy. No, I'm going back to my regiment as soon as they release me."

"I thought they would discharge you now you've been wounded?"

"Not serious enough, they want me back as soon as I am able. It's all right Grace, I am quite happy to go back. We're a team now, and if we lose a team member we all suffer. Will you still write to me?"

"Yes, of course. I love receiving your letters, William, and so does my father. He's always bragging about how brave his son-in-law-to-be is."

"Will he still be bragging when he finds out the wedding is off?"

"He will, he has a very soft spot for you."

"I know you've come a long way, but I'm feeling rather exhausted. I think since your letter arrived saying you were coming to visit, I have been on tenterhooks and now all the tension has left, all I want to do is go to sleep. Is that terrible of me?"

Grace reached up and stroked his face. "Of course not. You have a good sleep and get well and strong soon. Write to me often, promise."

"I promise."

Grace stood up and kissed his forehead. "Take care of yourself, William."

"You too, Grace, and thank you for the jam."

She took a good long hard look at him, firmly planting the image of his face into her memory. She smiled softly then turned to leave, but had taken only a few steps when she remembered the ring.

"Oh, sorry, William. I almost forgot to give you back your ring." She pulled it off and offered it to him. He took it, and looked at it for a moment and then reached over to grab her right hand. He slipped the ring onto a finger.

"It might not be an engagement ring any more, but it is still a ring of love. Your friendship means the world to me, and I will always love you. Keep it, and when you look at it, remember I love you."

She threw her arms around his dreadfully thin body and hugged him fiercely. "I love you too," she said before hastening out of the room.

She couldn't wait to get out of the hospital. She had to get home; she needed to tell Milton she was free to marry him. As she walked along the promenade once more, she thought of William and his friendship. "I love you God," she cried out to the heavens under the thunderous roar of crashing waves. "Please look after William, send your angels to guard and protect him, and offer him comfort whenever you can." She lowered her head and caught sight of a few people looking at her as if she was crazy. She laughed and started running. She was free of her obligation and she was free to love Milton.

It was another two weeks before Teddy could persuade Milton to listen to what Grace had to say. By the time she'd finished telling him everything, she was crying.

"Tell me you understand," she pleaded.

For an answer he took her in his arms and held her tight, covering the top of her head in kisses.

27th July 1944

The air was electric. Milton held her hand tightly and worked his way through the crowd to get near the makeshift stage. Grace kept sneaking a look at him as they made their way through a sea of olive-green uniforms. He stood out from the rest of them and it wasn't just his height, he carried a notable air of confidence.

Once he was happy he couldn't get her any closer, he stopped and pulled her in front of him, wrapping his strong arms around her waist and protecting her body from the excited audience. The band finished warming up and then beckoned the sergeant who was waiting on the side. He took a few brisk steps forward and then climbed the couple of steps onto the stage and went to the microphone.

"Ladies and gentlemen, welcome to Burtonwood." This was followed by a loud cheer. "From the United States of America, Uncle Sam presents…" he turned to the right and lifted his hand, "Glenn Miller!" The crowd went nuts – clapping, cheering and whooping.

From the second the band started, goose bumps went up Grace's arms. When the trumpet blasted she was caught up in an ecstasy of music she'd never felt before. The band played all the latest tunes and the crowd was ecstatic, clapping and dancing on the spot, whilst trying not to knock each other over. When the Crew Chiefs came on, toe tapping turned into full-blown jumping when they started singing Jukebox Saturday Night.

"You enjoying it?" Milton shouted in her ear when the Crew Chiefs went off.

"Yes, oh goodness, yes." Grace laughed up at him.

Towards the end of the show, Johnny Desmond came on. When he started singing Speak Low, Milton pulled Grace tightly against his cheek and started singing along softly in her ear.

"Wherever I go that tomorrow is near. That tomorrow is here. Is here and always too soon."

Grace melted in his arms. *Thank you, God,* she thought. *Thank you for one of the most precious moments I've ever had in my life. I love you so much, Father. Thank you, thank you.*

The show ended with Johnny Desmond and Gloria Brent singing 'At Last.' Grace thought if she could be any happier, she would burst.

When everyone started dispersing, Eleanor came over and whispered in Grace's ear.

Grace tried to hide her shock. "Are you sure?"

"Absolutely," Eleanor answered, then took hold of Teddy's hand and disappeared into the crowd.

Milton walked Grace home. It had been a perfect evening and there was no need for words.

As they got close to home, they both slowed their steps, wanting the evening to last a little longer. On their way past Willow Park, Milton darted across the damp grass, pulling Grace with him. They were laughing when he pulled them under the branches of an enormous willow.

Grace tilted her head back to look at him and Milton took the opportunity to cup her face in his hands.

With slow intent, he leant down until his lips were touching hers. She moaned and sank into his arms. He kissed her like never before, passionately, and by the time he stopped, she was breathless.

He leaned back a little and smiled at her. "At last, my love has come along," he sang.

"My lonely days are over," Grace sang back.

All at once, Milton dropped to one knee in front of her. At first, she thought he had tripped but then she saw him reach into his pocket and pull out a ring.

"Now this is only a plastic ring that I stole off a little girl last week," he said lifting the blue plastic ring up. "But when I told her why I needed it, she said I didn't have to steal it, I could have it. When we go home to Ohio, I'll be giving you my grandmother's diamond ring which is being kept for the lady of my dreams. You are that lady, Grace. Will you marry me?"

Grace let him slip the ring on her finger. "Yes, Sergeant Milton Simmons, I will marry you."

He jumped up, pulled Grace back into the open and then picked her up in his arms and swung her round and around.

She was laughing when he put her down. "I didn't think this day could be any more perfect."

This picture was taken at Burtonwood camp in December 1944. Joe Loss, Vera Lynn and Major Glenn Miller ©historicaviationmilitary.com

Shortly after this photo was taken Glen Miller flew to Twinwood Farm in Bedfordshire and then onto Paris. However, his aircraft never arrived in Paris, presumably having crashed in the English Channel.

Chapter 12

Everything Changes
1944

Telling her father about William had been difficult, made worse by the disappointment on his face.

"So, he just decided he didn't want to marry you anymore? And it had absolutely nothing to do with Milton?"

Sarcasm was rare from her father and Grace couldn't help cringing. "I think he's found someone else, he just didn't want to talk to me about her. I would never have been disloyal to him, Dad, but now he doesn't want to get married I am free to court whoever I want, and I happen to want Milton."

"Oh, do you now. How long, exactly, have you wanted Milton?"

"Dad! Don't you know me at all? I've done nothing to dishonour myself. Milton and I have been going out as friends only." She felt the heat rise in her face, she didn't want to lie but at the same time she couldn't reveal William's secret. Richard started coughing, his shoulders shook and his hands grasped his chest.

"Oh Dad, please let me take you to the hospital."

When the coughing fit had eased off, Richard leant back in the chair and regarded Grace who was now kneeling in front of him.

"I liked William."

"He's not dead, you can still like him. We're still best friends and when the war's finished he's going to come and stay with us for a while until he gets his life sorted. He gave up his rented room last year, believing he'd never come back, so I wrote to him telling him to stay with us."

"What will Milton have to say about that?"

"Nothing. He knows William is my best friend in the whole world, well, besides Eleanor."

"Umm."

"Dad, can I call the doctor? Please?"

"Make me a cocoa will you, love?"

Grace was frowning but Richard gave her a soft smile. "Please, love, I think I'd like an early night tonight." Grace stood up and picked up Richard's hand to give it a quick squeeze.

"Of course. Won't be long."

Monday 4th September 1944

Looking at her ration book Grace wondered what she would be able to buy so that she could out-do herself with tonight's meal. Giles had given her an extra portion of vegetables that morning. She had also been in the garden and picked a huge number of apples to make an apple pudding, so she had a good bulk of it already. She wondered if the butcher would let her use two weeks' rations so that she could buy a leg of lamb.

Milton had been to the house several times in the last two months and she did feel like her father was coming around to him. Today she wanted to cook for the five of them, and if it went well then at the end of the evening Milton was going to ask him if he could marry his daughter. She was nervous. She had grown up by her father's side and they were extremely close. To her knowledge, not marrying William was the first time she had ever disappointed him. She didn't want to do it again.

133

She was in luck. The butcher's was empty when she went in and she was able to ask George about using a double portion ration in exchange for a leg of lamb. Not only did he give her a large leg of lamb, but he threw in four rashers of streaky bacon.

"I don't have a coupon for bacon," she said, as she watched him wrap the slices in brown paper.

"I know your father's not feeling so good these days, Grace. This is from us, from our own ration book, you give him a good breakfast on Sunday morning, get him fattened up and healthy."

"I don't know what to say. Thank you so much." She was touched by his kindness.

"We'd miss your father if he wasn't behind that pulpit on Sunday mornings; we've grown up with his sermons."

The butcher went quiet for a moment as he finished wrapping the meat. "You take good care of him, lass."

"I will do." The brass bell over the door tinkled as Grace left. She felt flat and sick at the thought that the townsfolk should think her father was that ill. She got on her bike and rode straight to the doctors.

She had to wait over half an hour before he could see her.

"Grace, my dear, what can I do for you?"

"What's wrong with my dad?" she blurted out.

Concern settled on his face and he sighed. "Is he all right? Does he need me to come out?"

"He seems all right this morning but he coughed all night. What is it? What's wrong with him and why won't you make him go to the hospital?"

"Your father should be the one you are talking to, Grace."

"You know how stubborn he is. Please, tell me what's wrong?"

He seemed to consider for a while and she thought he was going to tell her, but instead he slowly shook his head. "It's not up to me to tell you, Grace. You need to ask him."

Grace started crying. "I knew it was more than just a cough," she said getting up.

"You've had a lovely life with him, Grace. Try to remember that when you talk to him. Think of all the good things. There are many folk in this world who don't have a father who is such a good man, and many who don't have a father at all. You've had a blessed life, Grace."

She got a handkerchief out of her bag and wiped her eyes then blew her nose. "Thank you."

She rode home with the shopping in her handlebar basket jumping up and down as the wheels hit bumps in the road. Panic was setting in. Fear clawed at her skin and she felt like bringing up her breakfast. She dumped the bike against the wall of the house, went in through the back door, dropped the shopping on the kitchen table and strode into the hallway. She was a bit out of breath, having ridden so hard, so she paused for a moment before pulling open the study door.

Richard looked up and smiled. "You've been a while, love, all okay?"

She walked slowly up to his table looking at his face, her pain and love radiating from her face.

"Tell me," she said.

He put down his pen then stood up and came around the table so he could hold her hands. There was no mistaking what she was talking about.

"It's cancer," he said. He watched her as the colour faded from her face and felt her trembling hands. "It's not so bad," he continued, "it doesn't hurt, in fact if it wasn't for the coughing I don't think I would even know I was ill." He looked at her, waiting for her to say something. He saw her chin trembling and the water filling her eyes. "Oh Grace." He pulled her into his chest and wrapped his arms tightly around her.

"Dad, why haven't you been to hospital? Maybe the doctors could have done something."

"I didn't want to go."

Grace pushed herself out from under his arms. "Why not?"

"Let's have a cup of tea, love," he said his face awash with sorrow.

Grace looked at his stooped shoulders and wondered when he'd started doing that. She seemed to see him clearly for the first time in ages. He'd aged. How had she not seen the excessive lines around his eyes and his hollow cheeks?

"I could do with a brew," she answered and headed into the kitchen.

When the kettle started whistling, Richard came in and sat at the kitchen table.

"I love this table, you know." Richard ran his hands over the rough surface of the wooden table.

Grace covered the teapot with the cosy. "How come?"

"You read your first line of the Bible to me while sitting at this table, Grace."

She looked up and smiled at him. "That was a long time ago."

"I remember Millie teaching you to make pastry," Richard chuckled. "You were covered from head to foot in flour but when you presented those hard-as-nails jam tarts to me, you were so proud."

"Good old Millie, I miss her so much. I wish they hadn't had to move so far away when she got married."

"She was an angel when we needed one, and I will admit I also missed her cheery singing. You did your first school homework at this table, Grace, and when I listened to you trying to spell out your words, I was crushed that your mother wasn't there to help you."

"Oh, Dad. We did okay didn't we?"

"Yes, we muddled by, didn't we? But you never had a mother, Grace, and I think that must leave a hole in you."

"I might not have had a mother, but I have two Fathers, so I am very blessed."

"And your Father in heaven will be with you always, Grace."

Floods of emotions washed through her.

"This table represents our life together, Grace, years of love and happiness. Yet now I am tired, my little love, and I want to go home and be with my Annie once more."

Grace sobbed. The pain in her chest was severe and tears splashed down onto the table that had watched her grow up.

"I know it will be hard for you when I go. But you will heal, for that is the way we are designed. Dying is, unfortunately, a part of life. Moreover, we will meet again! Your mother and I will come to greet you when your time comes, never forget that. Your American beau will take care of you, for which I am eternally grateful. It means so much to me, to know you will be happy after I go."

"I don't want you to go, Dad." Grace dropped her head onto her arms, which lay folded on the table, unable to stop crying.

Richard got up and came around the table. "Come here, my sweet thing."

Grace leaned against his chest and he held her tight until the crying began to ease.

"Tea's getting cold." Grace sniffled, tenderly shooing Richard back to his seat.

When her father took himself off for a nap in his favourite chair, Grace nipped to the Post Office on her bike and telephoned the base to leave a message to ask Milton and Teddy not to come that night.

Later that night, when Richard was in bed, Grace sat in the dark in the front room and waited for Eleanor to come home. She had been glad that no one arrived at dinnertime, but now she was worried, because she thought Eleanor would have come straight home to find out what was wrong.

"Eleanor," she called softly, as she heard someone close the front door.

"Grace, what are you still doing up?"

"I needed someone to talk to."

Eleanor put her coat on the stand and came into the front room, sitting herself down as close as possible to Grace.

"What's happened?" she asked reaching for Grace's hand.

Grace filled her in on the events of the day.

"Oh Grace." Eleanor flung her arms around her and squeezed her tight whilst the two of them tried to keep their crying as quiet as possible.

"I'm so sorry I wasn't home earlier, I've just had a bit of a ghastly day myself."

"That's all right, you weren't to know, and I'm glad you're here now."

"I'm family now, aren't I? And you have Milton too, and when he takes you back to America you will have a whole new family, and they sound so lovely. Maybe when Teddy and I are married we will be able to travel from Illinois to Ohio. I've been to the library and looked it up on a map, the states are only about six hours apart by car. Wouldn't that be grand?"

"Why Illinois?"

"That's where Teddy's from, of course."

"Are you sure?"

"Of course I'm sure, he's talked to me about Springfield many a time. Why do you ask?"

"It's just I thought Milton said he was from North Carolina."

"You must have misheard, Teddy's definitely from Illinois."

"Oh, okay."

Just then, Richard started with a coughing bout.

"I'll go and check on him, then I need to turn in, I'm shattered."

"I'm coming now too, I'll just get a glass of water. See you upstairs."

Richard was asleep by the time Grace leant over his bed. She stroked his head very tenderly and then tiptoed out. Eleanor was standing outside her bedroom door when she came onto the landing.

"Grace, I know this is terrible timing, but I actually have some news of my own."

Grace followed Eleanor into her room and sat on the bed beside her.

"Please don't think harshly of me, Grace."

"I'd never do that."

"You might when you hear my news."

"You're not leaving us, are you?" Grace asked in sudden panic.

Eleanor grabbed her hands. "No, I'm not leaving, well, unless you ask me to."

"Why on earth would I ever ask you to leave?"

"Because I'm pregnant."

"Oh, Eleanor, that's wonderful news. I'm so happy for you, Teddy must be delighted." The smile slowly slid off Grace's face as she looked into Eleanor's sad eyes. "Oh no."

"He flew off the handle, Grace, called me a hussy and all sorts of names."

"It will just be the shock, you wait and see. Once he has had time to digest the news he'll be happy. Of course he will, he's bringing a new life into the world. He probably just thinks the timing is wrong. Maybe he is afraid that he won't come back one day and he's left you all alone with a baby. Yes, that's what it will be. You'll see, it'll be fine."

"I do love you, Grace."

"I love you too."

Sunday 10th September 1944

This was the sixth day that Richard had been unable to get out of bed, his health's deterioration shocking. He had stopped eating solids three days before and the nurse warned Grace that it wouldn't be long now.

She spread the Sunday Times out on his bed and read to him. To talk about something different besides the war she tried to find all the articles that stood alone.

"The Cornwall–Massena earthquake occurred on September 5 at 12:38 am in Massena, New York. The earthquake is the largest known in New York's recorded history and was felt over great distances. The earthquake was felt as far away as New York City, Quebec City, Toronto and Boston and caused a terrific amount of property damage. Several large aftershocks were felt in the general area, described as a low rumble followed by a loud bang." Grace stopped reading and looked at her dad.

"Can you believe that, Dad? As if there wasn't enough going on with a world war, God has to throw in an earthquake as

140

well?" Silence. She flicked through a few pages and came to a stop on another American article.

"Really? This is too much. Dad, why on earth did you ever read the papers? So right next to the submarine U-865 being lost after leaving Trondheim in Norway, we have Venus Ramey, Miss District of Columbia is crowned Miss America! Seriously, Dad, the world's gone crazy, no wonder you want to leave it." Grace screwed up the paper and threw it across the room. She pushed her chair back and got up. Pacing the room she felt anger burning in her chest.

"I don't want you to go, Dad. Can't you stay with me a while longer?"

Silence.

"Aghh." After a time of pacing the floor, the anger began to ebb and sadness seeped in. She pulled the chair back up to the bed and sat back down.

The Bible on the bedside table caught her attention.

"So let's see what you were reading last." She opened the book to where the bookmark lay. She was drawn to a paragraph that her father had underlined, and read it aloud.

"Matthew 25:35. For I was an hungred, and ye gave me meat: I was thirsty, and ye gave me drink: I was a stranger, and ye took me in: Naked, and ye clothed me: I was sick, and ye visited me: I was in prison, and ye came unto me. Then shall the righteous answer him, saying, Lord, when saw we thee an hungred, and fed thee? Or thirsty, and gave thee drink? When saw we thee a stranger, and took thee in? or naked, and clothed thee? Or when saw we thee sick, or in prison, and came unto thee? And the King shall answer and say unto them,

Grace stopped reading and stared at the words. She felt numb and empty. These words were empty. Faith was empty. What good was having faith if you lost everyone you loved? She closed the Bible and put it back down.

"I just need to stretch my legs, Dad," she said before kissing his forehead. She flew through the house, longing to be outside, and ran down the garden to the back, where her childhood swing still stood. She sat on the swing and then the internal heavens opened as pain washed through with the passing of tears.

Sometime later, she looked up to see Eleanor walking down the garden towards her. She knew from Eleanor's expression that her father had at last found his peace, and left her all alone. Calm descended and she got up and started to walk back to the house.

"You're not alone, Grace."

She looked up at Milton and wondered why, when she loved him so much, did she still feel alone and isolated. She didn't have words so she attempted a smile and when that didn't work, she squeezed his hand.

She hadn't cried another tear since she had sat on the swing. She was all dried up inside. Friends, neighbours, churchgoers, all gathered round offering their sympathies and respect; there was no doubt about it, her father had been a truly loved vicar.

Henry had taken the service and he'd done a lovely job. Her father's resting place was next to Annie's, a lovely spot near the brook where the sun shone most of the day. He had loved it here, Grace knew. Michael, her father's best friend from days gone by had been too ill himself to travel. Joy had come in the surprise arrival of a much older, plumper Millie. Millie sobbed on Grace's shoulder and Grace hugged her for ages, but did not join her in crying.

Eleanor was always close, as was Milton, the two of them watching over her like parent bears, and she, the helpless cub. She was glad when the day was over and she didn't have to accept condolences any more, she just wanted her bed.

Thursday 14th September 1944

The next morning she found Milton asleep on the sofa. She loved him so much but something was wrong inside her. A heavy iron wall had started to grow around her heart. Didn't everyone die and leave her? Wouldn't Milton do the same? Grace felt herself putting her love for him in a closed box.

The smell of toast woke Eleanor and Milton and they both came rushing in to check she was okay. Not reassured when she said she had 'never been better,' they sat in silence and watched her fetch the breakfast things to the table.

"I have to report back in today, Grace," Milton said.

"That's fine, I'm fine. Everything is okay. I am going to spend the day sorting through Dad's stuff, see what I can donate and what needs to be thrown away. I'll be busy and that'll be good."

"I also have to go to the Foundry today, but I will be home as soon as I can."

"If you don't stop fussing about me I will go insane. I'm glad you're both going to work. I need time on my own. I have to think of what I'm going to do next."

"What do you mean?" asked Milton.

"The Bishop of Liverpool is coming for refreshments at eleven this morning, no doubt, to tell me that I am now homeless. I need to think of somewhere to live."

"Noo," said Eleanor.

"That can't be," said Milton, "you've lived here all your life, they surely won't ask you to leave just like that?"

"I'm afraid they can. Now please hurry up and eat your toast because if I don't get some time to myself soon, I think I will fall apart."

"I'm going, Grace," said Milton standing up, "but I will be back this evening." He came over to her to give her a kiss but Grace dropped her face, which meant he could only kiss her forehead. He looked hurt and Eleanor shook her head in sadness.

"I'll go too, Grace. To be honest I don't feel hungry. My shift finishes at six, so I'll be home about half past." Not caring if Grace hugged her back or not, Eleanor wrapped her in a huge bear hug. Grace remained stiff and eventually Eleanor let go, feeling rejected.

As soon as the front door shut, Grace poured herself a cup of tea and went to sit in her father's chair by the unlit fire in the front room. She was numb. She was still sitting there three hours later when someone banged the knocker on the front door. She jumped up, slightly disoriented and realised that she must have dozed off. She hastened to the door, trying to pat her hair straight after she caught sight of herself in the mirror and realised she hadn't brushed it yet.

"Hello, Grace."

"Good morning, Your Excellency. Please come in."

She led him into the front room and they sat on chairs opposite each other.

"How are you doing?"

For a moment, she ground her teeth against the pique that rose inside her against this week's most asked question. She made an effort to be civil. "I'm fine, thank you, Your Excellency."

"Ah, I see. Well that is understandable."

Grace's face screwed up in puzzlement.

"Your father was a most respected man, and he will be greatly missed by everyone, especially you, of course. I am truly sorry for your loss, Grace. And please, for today call me Albert."

"Sorry enough to let me stay in my life-long home, Bishop Albert?"

"Actually, I did advocate that you should be able to remain here until you found somewhere else to live, however long that takes. But I am afraid I was outnumbered. You have three months Grace, and then unfortunately you will have to move. I am dreadfully sorry. I know losing both your father and your home at the same time must seem quite overwhelming."

He looked at Grace, waiting for her to respond, but she didn't.

"I will help you find somewhere else to live. I have many contacts and know lots of superb people who now have to rent out rooms to be able to pay the bills."

"I'm sure I will be able to find somewhere on my own, thank you. I am quite capable."

"I never thought anything less. I am just trying my hardest to help you."

Remorse washed over her in waves. Her father would be ashamed of her. "I'm sorry, I haven't offered you a drink, would you like some tea?"

He smiled. "That would be very nice, thank you."

It wasn't long before Grace returned with a tray topped with two cups and saucers, the cosy covered teapot and a small jug of milk.

"I'm afraid I don't have any sugar left," she said putting the tray on the table.

"That is fine. I haven't had sugar in tea for years now."

When the tea had been poured, they settled back in their chairs and the Bishop looked at Grace and started again. "Liverpool has been dreadfully bombed, you know. You have been very blessed here in Newton Le Willows."

"Yes, very blessed indeed," she retorted sarcastically. Did he not know she'd just buried her father and that two of her school friends were lost in action? But yes, living here was a blessing, wasn't it?

Undeterred by her cutting tone he carried on. "We lost many churches you know, amongst all the other things as well. We also lost most of our congregations, either from death or from a sudden dislike of everything religious. Your father did a marvellous job of helping the people here to hold onto their faith, you must be very proud of him."

Shame. Guilt. Loss. Pain. Pride? No, not pride.

"I was wondering if you might consider a job in Liverpool diocese and help me in restoring people's faith in both God and the Church?"

She looked up at him in shock. She was a female; there was no role for her in the Church other than washing the toilet floors.

As if reading her mind he continued, "Things are changing, Grace, and a good deal for the better. The role of women in churches will also change over time. I am not asking you to stand up and preach on Sunday mornings. I am asking you to assist me. Help in counselling people, leading them in prayer meetings, and practical stuff like re-housing. What do you say? Will you at least consider it?"

If Milton hadn't been in her life she would have jumped at the chance to serve both God and man. Now there was a new reason to carry on, though. As the thought of moving to Liverpool entered her head she had known instantly by the cramping in her stomach that she couldn't leave Milton, no matter how horrid she had been to him that morning.

"That is very kind and generous of you, and I do appreciate it. However, I think my path lies elsewhere. Thank you, though."

"You are welcome, and if you change your mind just let me know."

The Bishop stayed for an hour and half, talking of the new kind of England that had to emerge now that so many women were working. They discussed their hopes for fairer working conditions and their prayers for the war to end. By the time he left, Grace was feeling incredibly calm. She tuned in the wireless and set about cleaning the house and cooking tea for when the two people she loved most in the world came home.

Grace had slow-cooked the beef brisket, placing the vegetables around it. She had thickened the gravy around the joint with a little corn flour and added plenty of chopped lovage and parsley fresh from the green house. The aniseed smell wafted through the house.

Milton had the loan of a car and so picked Eleanor up from work, tying her bike to the back of the car. As they walked down the side path of the house, they could smell the cooking dinner. Eleanor gave Milton a worried look as they entered the kitchen through the back door.

Grace was sitting in a chair gazing into the fire.

"How did it go?" Eleanor asked.

"Good, actually, it was really good. The Bishop is a lovely man. We have three months to find somewhere else to live though. I'm sorry, Eleanor."

Eleanor flew across the kitchen and pulled Grace into her arms. "Why on earth are you sorry? It's not your fault. We'll be fine, all of us, you'll see. I am believing in Him upstairs," she pointed to the ceiling, "to sort everything out for us."

"Dinner's ready if you want to freshen up?"

Both of them wanted to wash so they left Grace to lay the table and raced each other up the stairs, laughing all the way, to see who could reach the bathroom first. A few minutes later, they were sitting around the table.

"I'd like to pray, if you don't mind?" said Milton.

Grace smiled, although Milton had told her he was Catholic they had never prayed together before and it warmed her heart. Milton held out his hands and all three of them took a firm grip of each other, transmitting their love in their reassuring touch.

When he had finished praying, Milton took the lid off the pot roast and served everyone, something her father would normally have done. Grace watched him with a mixture of sad and happy feelings chasing each other around inside her and fighting for dominance. Happy won and she smiled.

"Grace, I spoke to the Colonel at the base today. I told him we're going to marry as soon as we can and I asked him for family quarters for us."

"You did?"

"That's wonderful," said Eleanor, "of course that would solve all your problems."

Grace reached for Eleanor's hand. "I'll not leave you on your own, we'll move in together or not at all." Grace turned to look at Milton questioningly.

"It seems that all the houses are occupied at the moment so we can't move in now anyway. He said once we're married, he'll put us on the list and we'll get something as soon as possible. I am going to hope that something comes up before the next three months have gone by."

"See? Everything will work out," said Grace looking at Eleanor.

"Grace?" She looked up at Milton. "Grace, after the war I wanted to take you home to Ohio. My parents have a large farm there and I have a house a short distance from them. You'd want that wouldn't you?"

Grace's heart swelled with love. "Of course I would." She turned her glance back to Eleanor. "And when Teddy comes around to being a father and asking you to marry him, we'll all live happily ever after in the U, S of A!"

Eleanor smiled back at her with hopeful eyes, and neither of them noticed that Milton looked down at his food and started eating, avoiding their smiles.

Chapter 13

Goodbyes are not forever
1944

For two months, Eleanor had besieged Burtonwood camp with a countless number of letters pleading with Teddy to see her. Today, all the letters had been given back to her un-opened, and she received an embarrassing dressing down from a Lieutenant who told her she was acting in a manner unbecoming to a lady, and not to return, harshly attesting that Teddy had sworn he wasn't the father of her forthcoming child.

"What will I do, Grace?" Well past heartbreak and tears, Eleanor was full of fear for the future. Her bump was obvious to anyone who cared to look, and the women around town were beginning to look down their noses at her. "I can't stay here, the shame is killing me."

"Where will you go?"

They were once more in the vicarage kitchen, sitting at the table, drinking tea. The smell of washing powder filled the room from the clothes covering the clotheshorse stationed around the fire.

"I'm not sure, I just know I can't stay here anymore." She reached out and grabbed hold of Grace's hand. "We'll write though and stay in touch, and you'll come to see me whenever you can, before you go to America?"

"Of course I will."

"I was talking to a girl from the Foundry last week. She is in the same position as me. Her parents are sending her to live with an aunty in Brighton. When the baby is born, they are going to give it away and she is going to come home as if nothing had happened. I feel so sorry for her, Grace, she is beside herself with grief, but her parents have said they will disown her if she doesn't do it."

"Honestly, as if there isn't enough sadness in the world already. Have you thought about doing that and giving the baby away?"

"I did think about it, but it's not for me. I'm thirty-seven and this is probably my last, maybe my only, chance to have a child. I'm keeping it and to hell with what the world will think of me."

"What if you were married?"

"Don't be silly, Grace, who would marry me now? I'm soiled goods."

"You are not, and you should never say that."

"I'm sure it's what God thinks."

"He does *not!* No one is perfect, we all make mistakes. It is why Jesus had to come to save us; if we could remain sinless then He would never have needed to come. He loves you dearly, and don't you ever forget it."

Eleanor wrapped her arms around her stomach, feeling maternally protective over her little one.

"What I mean is, what if people *think* you are married?"

"Hey?"

"Wait a minute." Grace went running out of the room and upstairs. Eleanor could hear her pulling open drawers in one of the bedrooms, and then she was running back down again. "Try this on." She held out a small gold ring.

Eleanor took it off her and looked at it, puzzled. "Why?"

"Just try it on. No, not on that finger, on your wedding finger."

Eleanor slipped the ring on.

"Keep it, and if someone who doesn't know you sees the ring, what are they going to think?"

"That I'm married."

"Precisely. If anyone asks, tell them your husband went missing in action. No one will question you. This way you can bring up your child respectably."

"Oh Grace." Tears of gratitude fell, leaving streaks down Eleanor's pale complexion.

Friday 27th October 1944

Dearest Grace,

I am weary to my bones and can hardly find the words or the strength to write to you. This war, this total horrific, man-created hell on earth is taking its toll and I am afraid I have abandoned hope that it will ever cease. It will, of course, it has to, but I know I will not be here to see it. For me, and for those lying in the makeshift hospital tent with me, it is the end of the road.

Having dodged bullets and bombs, I am, alas, undone by the bane of the earth, the devil himself incarnate in the form of disease carrying fleas.

We waste away under the terrible curse of dysentery. I am sure if we could only get home we might survive. My anger has gone, Grace, I am left with disappointment. We die for our country, but it seems our country does not see us and cannot be motivated enough to come to our rescue. We are too far inland and apparently if we were nearer the coast we might have a ship to whisk us home. We're too ill to sit in a truck for two days, they say it would kill us, ha, are we not dying anyway?

What was it all about, Grace? To push boundaries? To annihilate unjustifiable racism? Why? Why did so many have to die because of a mad man. I don't understand how God could let it happen. I don't understand why we didn't kill Hitler and stop it before it began. Surely, the death of one evil man would justify the saving of millions. Don't rebuke me, Grace, I can hear you now arguing against taking a single life. But this is too much for me to bear.

I am glad my time has come. I long for peace and quiet.

I have written to the solicitors on the High Street and told them the bank has my will, they will be expecting you. I made sure that you would have all of my savings. Use them to build your life, my dear friend. Don't let the seeping wickedness of this war pull you down. Smile and be happy, live your life for both of us.

I have the strangest request to ask of you, Grace. Should an opportunity ever arise to go to Kenya, will you take it? I have this recurring dream that you are under a blazing sun watching animals move across a red earth. You look so young, Grace, like you did that day we went to the fair. Your hazel eyes sparkle with love and your tiny nose is sprinkled with freckles. You are at peace and happy, and I am flooded with joy when I see you turn your head slightly and smile at me. You'll think me mad, I know. And well, maybe I am, I fall in and out of consciousness as the fever takes me. But there is a voice in the dream. Such a rich, deep voice and I am drawn to it like a moth to a flame. Each time the dream ends in the same way, with the voice saying, 'When I was hungry you fed me, and when I was thirsty you gave me a drink.' Just that one line, every time, I have pondered on it long and hard as I've lain here, in my misery.

And now my strength is failing me and it is time to say goodbye.

Remember our moments, Grace, our special moments when we shared a laugh or a secret. Where we walked across the lands of our fair England and enjoyed the beauty of it, so rich and so deep. Remember the good times, Grace.

Remember too, that goodbyes are not forever. Goodbyes are not the end, they simply mean 'I miss you' until we meet again.

With all my love my dearest friend,
William

Ps My only regret is not watching you get married.

Friday 10th November 1944

"I want you to have it."

Eleanor backed away from the envelope. "I can't possibly take William's money, he meant it for you."

Grace grabbed hold of Eleanor's hand, which she had pushed behind her back. "He did give it to me, so it's mine, and I'm giving it to you. For you and the baby, so you can start a new life."

Eleanor couldn't talk, her throat was gripped so tightly it was hard to breathe, she gulped as her eyes became large pools of water.

"Go to Dorset, Eleanor. Find a nice cottage and bring up your little one, but most importantly, be happy."

"I don't know if I will find my cousin, she might not even live in Dorset anymore."

"Then make friends and start a new life."

"I can't leave you."

"Now you're just making excuses. I am fine, more than fine, I'm great. The wedding has been delayed whilst we wait for the paperwork and permissions, but Milton and I will get married despite the government's opposition, and then we'll go and live in America."

Eleanor looked down at the envelope, now in her hands. "It's so much money," she whispered.

"William always wanted a son you know, he'd be happy to be helping you and your child out, I know he would."

"Then if I have a son, I will call him William."

"Eleanor, that's perfect."

"It might be a girl."

"No, I mean, why don't you say that William was the father and take up his name? The Register Office in Liverpool has been bombed you know, so anyone who got married there has completely lost their records, no one could prove you weren't telling the truth. You won't be able to claim a war pension because you don't have the marriage certificate, but at least you'll have respectability."

"Grace, that's so devious of you, clever too, very, very clever. What a marvellous idea. Oh, you will have to pray I have a son so I can call him William… after his father."

"Well if it's a girl you could call her Wilhelmina or Willow?"

Eleanor smiled and threw her arms around Grace.

"I love you, Grace. I'm going to miss you so much."

"I love you, too," said Grace, hugging her back tightly. When they let go of each other, Grace asked. "When will you go?"

"I was thinking of catching the train to Euston on Wednesday, then getting a connection as soon as a train is available to Dorset."

"This Wednesday?"

Eleanor nodded.

"Oh, that's so soon. I wasn't expecting you to leave straight away."

"I told them at the Foundry that I wouldn't be returning this week, and I thought the quicker I find somewhere to live before the baby is born the better. But if you want me to stay a little longer I will."

"No of course not, it's fine. It took me by surprise, that's all. Of course, you need to go now, get settled and everything, before the birth."

Eleanor reached up and gently nudged a curl away from Grace's eye. "Are you sure?"

Grace took hold of Eleanor's hand, and kissed it. "Yes, I am perfectly sure. You've helped me so much with the cleaning of the house and getting rid of everything that doesn't belong to the diocese; I don't know what I would have done without you. But we're finished now and I'm ready to hand back the keys."

"When are they coming?"

"I got a letter yesterday saying the new vicar and his family have been delayed so I still have three weeks left, but I don't know if I will stay here on my own. Joe and Betty have offered me temporary lodgings in their house and I think I will take them up on it. It will cost money, but not much, and I'd rather be out of here sooner than later."

"Oh Grace, your home."

"It's fine, don't get me going again, I've had enough of crying. Anyway, goodbyes are not forever, they simply mean I'll miss you, until we meet again."

Wednesday 15th November 1944

Eleanor had found a seat next to the window and lowered it as far as it would go. Pushing nearly half of her body out of it, she started waving like mad. Grace waved back until the train had chuffed its way out of sight. She stood on the now empty Earlstown platform staring down the track. Where had the last four years gone? It only seemed a moment ago when the land army lady from London had arrived.

As Grace ambled home, she thought of everything that had happened since Eleanor arrived in Newton Le Willows. She concluded it was a good job that back then, they hadn't known how long the war was going to drag on for. The thought of years of blackouts, rationing, bombing and poverty, not to mention the death of family and friends; she might have felt like giving it all up there and then. As it was each day had passed with its own problems, but they had worked through them. She missed her father, missed his reading the Sunday papers aloud, missed their chats on life, and missed his quotes. Mostly, though, she felt lost without his cuddles, how she longed for one more embrace.

Cherish the moments she could hear him say.

Saturday 18th November 1944

The sound of the knocker wasn't loud, meaning someone had tapped it opposed to banging. As she opened the front door she

157

wondered who it could be at this time in the evening, surprised when she saw Teddy.

"What do you want?" she snapped.

"Will you invite me in, Grace?"

"No, I won't. Now what do you want?" Grace glared at him, showing her full contempt of him, but as he looked back at her she became aware of the sadness in his eyes.

"If you want to speak to Eleanor you're too late, she left on Wednesday. She's gone to Dorset if you feel like chasing after her!" *Sarcasm, Grace, is the lowest form of wit, and totally unbecoming to a young lady. Yes, yes, Dad, I know, but seriously, how can he stand there?*

Teddy didn't answer, nor did he leave. Fear crept up Grace's shoulder, its icy fingers sending shivers down her back.

"What do you want, Teddy?"

"Please, Grace, can I come in?"

All the fight evaporated with the realisation that Teddy was the bearer of bad news. She opened the door wide and then turned and went into the front room.

Teddy shut the door and followed her. She sat in her father's chair by the empty fireplace.

Teddy pulled over a chair and sat in front of her. "I'm afraid I have some bad news."

She didn't answer, just folded her hands sedately on her lap.

"Milton was on a mission, he was on his way to Germany." He stopped and looked at her, waiting for her reaction, but when she didn't move or speak he carried on. "His plane went down over Dortmund." He stopped again, waiting, and when there was no response he carried on. "His plane was hit and instantly burst into flames, there was no time for him to jump out, and he went down with the plane."

Grace was staring at him.

"Do you understand?"

"Milton is dead."

"Yes, I'm sorry, Grace, he is."

Grace stood up. "Thank you for telling me." She walked out of the room and opened the front door.

He followed her out, worry and concern on his face and in his movements. He reached up to touch her but she jerked her arm out of his reach.

"I'm so sorry, Grace."

"And what about Eleanor? Are you sorry that you've left her to bring up a child on her own, to live with the stigma of being a wanton woman, and bearing a bastard child? You're despicable."

Teddy stepped through the door but turned back to look at her. "I never lied to her, Grace. I never told her I loved her or that I would marry her."

"That doesn't make it any better, you idiot."

"I would have married her if I could, but I'm already married. Now before you fly off the handle and start screaming at me, try to put yourself in my shoes. Every time I take off, I wonder if I will return. Most of the guys I came over with are dead. Now even Milton has gone, and I will probably be next. I needed something light in my life, I needed to have fun and just for a short time have special moments and pretend the war wasn't really going on. I needed to escape."

"Well your escapism caused incredible damage to Eleanor's heart. She wept for weeks. Why couldn't you have at least responded to her letters?"

"That was my Lieutenant, he told me it would be best not to, and she would get over me quicker. I thought he was right. And if I'm honest, I don't think I could have faced telling her that I'm married."

"Coward."

"I am. I know it, but I'm also a coward who climbs into a plane and goes to fight an enemy to help save others. I could have stayed in America but I didn't, in fact I was one of the first to arrive in Newton Le Willows."

"Please leave, Teddy."

She could see him fighting internally, but eventually he turned and started walking down the path. "Tell her I'm sorry, Grace," he called as he disappeared past the hedgerow.

She stood like a statue on the front door steps for a long time, staring blankly at the huge willow tree at the bottom of the garden.

"Goodbyes are not forever, they simply mean I'll miss you, until we meet again."

Grace closed the door, went into the kitchen and lit the gas lamp. Empty boxes were scattered around the room. She picked one up and put it on the table, then she began filling it with the crockery from the dresser. She wrapped the plates in newspaper and laid them one on top of the other. Her movements were mechanical, and she'd packed one box and then started another on autopilot. Then something snapped.

A spark of pain stabbed at her and she bent double, a moan escaping her lips. She stayed bent for a while then slowly straightened up.

"It is what it is. There is nothing I can do but accept." She went back to packing, but it was hard to concentrate, hard to even open the paper to take another sheet. Everything was moving in slow motion.

"Aghhhh." Grace screamed as pain ripped at her insides and she crumpled onto the floor, dropping and smashing the teapot. She lifted her head back and howled at the ceiling. Her arms clenched tightly around her body trying to stay the pain.

Her chest heaved with the effort of breathing through the pain. She fell forward again onto all fours, panic choking her as she fought for air. Her vision blurred and a high-pitched note drowned her hearing. She flopped onto her side, breathless, believing she was dying. She shook on the cold tiled floor and then thankfully tipped over the edge in the blackness of a faint.

As she came to, Grace realised the excruciating spasms had ceased and in their place a cold, dark presence had settled. Gingerly, she turned on her side and pushed herself up. She swooned slightly and gripped the edge of the table until she steadied.

"I need a good cup of tea," she said walking over to the stove. With shaking hands, it took three attempts at striking the match before it would light. She went to the dresser to fetch the bowls for wrapping. She placed the bowls on the table then lifted one and began wrapping it in newspaper. She put it in the box and picked up the next one. She froze, staring at the bowl. The blue patterns on the bowl began to swirl together and became all she could see.

"Aargh!" she screamed and threw the bowl against the wall. The cracking sound it made and the tinkle of broken crockery spilling on the floor was somewhat satisfying. She picked up another bowl and threw it at the wall. Yes, for some reason there was something very satisfying about breaking crockery!

She picked up a third bowl but this time as she threw it, she screamed, "I hate you, God." Bang. Crash.

Before she knew it, another bowl was in her hand. "You're a liar." The bowl flew through the air. "You're *not* just." Bang. Crash. No bowls left, she ran to the dresser and picked up the tea-plates. Bang. Crash. "I hate you. I wish I had never known you." Bang, bang. Crash. "I am no longer your daughter." Bang. Bang. Bang. Crash.

She was just looking at the dresser for something else to throw when the kettle started whistling. She felt the anger evaporate. The adrenalin slowed and she felt her heartbeat drop.

She made a small amount of tea in the milk jug and took it into the front room, where she perched on the edge of the sofa and waited for the leaves to brew. While she waited, she searched around inside her, seeking out the anger that had just enveloped her. It was gone. *Maybe I should cry?* Nothing happened. No more anger. No tears. Nothing. She sat staring at the tea and became aware that she was empty. Devoid of emotion and feeling. Cold.

Chapter 14

A governess in Guildford
Sunday 10th December 1944

Grace stood in the shadows of the upstairs landing and listened to the Reynolds as they prepared to leave for church.

"I think we ought to look for another governess, a God-fearing one to be sure. I can't believe I overlooked asking her whether she was a Christian, which really was rather remiss of me."

Mr Reynolds muttered under his breath.

"What was that, dear? I didn't quite catch you."

"She's a perfectly capable governess, Gillian, stop your moaning and leave her be."

"Here, Katy, let me tie your hat on. Stay still, stop shuffling your feet."

The front door opened and Grace heard Harry skip down the steps. She could see Mr Reynolds's reflection in the tinted glass of the door as he held it open for his wife and daughter to leave.

"You only want her to come to Church so that she can look after the children whilst you chitter-chatter to your cronies. Now I'll hear no more of sacking her, do you hear me?"

"Yes dear, of course, whatever you think best."

Grace let out the breath she had been holding as the door shut. She hadn't lied to Mrs Reynolds, but she also hadn't been particularly forthcoming. Her past was her own, and she had no desire to spill her life history out to her new employers. In fact, she had no wish to divulge her loss of faith to anyone. She knew how the jargon went, and what platitudes would spill forth from their built-in automatic ecclesiastical replies. She'd had enough of it. She would never let religious mumble-jumble pass by her ears ever again.

Grace went to the end of the landing and climbed the narrow staircase to her attic bedroom. Today was her day off and she was longing for freedom. It was freezing outside, the wind whistling through the avenue and across the Merrow Downs, but despite this she had a longing to be outside. She grabbed her coat, picked up her boots, and went running down the stairs. She'd only been given a key to the side door and she let herself out there, locking the door behind her.

The Reynolds's home was the last one on the left, at the bottom of Downside Road. She literally only had to walk twenty yards and she was in the great expanse of the Downs. The Surrey Downs were renowned for their outstanding natural beauty and Grace was eager to explore. She set off along a well-worn footpath, eager to see where it would lead.

The wintery greens and browns broke up the undulating hills like patchwork. Naked trees shivered under the power of the wind and yet the starkness of winter did nothing to hide their splendour. Exhilarated for the first time since the loss had deprived her of feelings she started to run, her arms thrown open, embracing nature.

Grace was cold, hungry and tired by the time she got back. Yet she felt good, somehow cleansed. She'd spent the time deliberating her past faith and wondering how she could have believed without question. It seemed a puzzle to her that she could have spent her entire life, until a few weeks ago, believing in something that now felt so alien and unfathomable. She accepted the fact that she was alone now, and probably would be until her dying day. The pain of the situation was that no matter how she longed to end her life, something prevented her. If she tried to analyse why she couldn't commit suicide, her head would start to hurt and she would go blank. She decided not to think on it again and to concentrate on getting through each day, knowing that each night when she went to sleep she was a day closer to her last day.

She entered the house quietly, with every intention of sneaking upstairs and avoiding everyone. She shut the door as softly as she could and turned the key, and was just pulling off her boots when Mr Reynolds appeared.

"Did you enjoy your walk?"

Grace felt herself blush as she awkwardly stood up straight. "Yes, thank you. It was very refreshing."

"Cook has left you some dinner on a tray in the kitchen."

"Oh, that's awfully kind of you. I don't want to put anyone out."

"As she's cooking for us, doing an extra plate for you was no trouble for her, and those were her words by the way."

"Thank you." Grace felt like a child, caught doing something wrong and waiting for the telling off. It came, albeit in a very gentle form.

"We were worried about you. We assumed you had gone off onto the Downs. I must admit I love to walk there myself whenever I can. But in this weather, you might have caught pneumonia."

"I felt a good walk would help me clear my head. I'm very sorry if I've caused you any worry."

Kenneth observed Grace thoughtfully. "I don't know what you have been through, Grace, the letter of recommendation that I received from the Bishop of Liverpool didn't go into any specifics about you. He simply stated that you would make a marvellous governess to our children." He paused, scrutinising her with worried eyes. "I just want you to know that we respect your privacy and your wish to remain detached."

"Thank you."

"However, I do request, most sincerely, that you do not let your sorrow transpose to Harry and Katy. I ask you, therefore, to do your utmost to mask the pain you are carrying."

Grace was shocked. She hadn't realised that she was wearing her grief for all to see. "I promise to be nothing but professional, educational and positive whilst I am around your family, Mr Reynolds."

"Thank you, Grace, now enjoy your supper. I shall tell Nanny to have the children ready for you by nine am sharp. Good evening."

"Good evening," Grace returned. When he left, Grace went into the kitchen, picked up the tray of food that had been left for her, and took it up to her room.

Later, washed and in her nightgown, Grace sat on the stool in front of her little dressing table. Mrs Reynolds had given her a small round mirror encased in an intricately carved, gilded stand. Although expertly designed, it was over the top for Grace, the golden birds and flowers harsh against the poverty she had seen in her life. She peered into the glass and scrutinised her reflection. *Who am I?* She reached up and traced her finger along her freckled cheekbone and down to her lips. She felt irritated under her skin and realised that being told what to do was going to be hard for her. She longed for her old life and for the touch of someone dear.

The memory of Milton's lips on hers flashed before her and she closed her eyes, trying to hold onto it. *Milton.* Tears of sadness, loss and loneliness trickled down her cheeks. After a moment, her runny nose made her open her eyes to look for a handkerchief. Once her sniffles had stopped, she placed her hand on her mother's Bible. She would never read it again; however, it was one of only two things that she possessed of her mothers, and although she loved the earrings they didn't comfort her the same way the book did. She reached over to the suitcase that still lay open on the floor and pulled out her father's Aran cardigan, gathering it into her arms and lifting it to her face. Eyes closed, she breathed in deeply to draw in his scent, then lay her face on it, imagining she was leaning on his chest and that his arms were around her. Pulling on the cardigan she climbed onto the bed, staring at the open suitcase.

When she arrived a week ago she had been unsure whether she would stay or not, and so had decided not to unpack. Tomorrow, she would put everything away. Not that she had brought much with her, just a few changes of clothing and some books. She decided that the morning would bring a new day, a new life, and a new Grace. She might not consider herself a Christian any more, but she was still a good person who was kind and thoughtful, and these traits weren't lost with her faith.

*****

Life as a governess in Guildford, despite the war and being thrust into a family of strangers, was surprisingly good. Grace soon settled in and developed an instant fondness for both Harry and Katy – although Katy pulled on her heartstrings the most. She'd also become good friends with Mary, the cook. As the months slipped by, miraculously quickly, Grace found a new kind of peace within her spirit. There were moments when stark loneliness would rise up like the coldest of fogs and swamp her, and other times when she would pine for Milton until she felt the pain would surely kill her. It didn't, however, and she grew used to it, accepted it, and as much as possible kept herself completely busy so as not to have time to ponder the loss she wore like a halo.

Wartime Guildford

Her eagerness to keep busy and be helpful meant that both the cook and Mrs Reynolds grew reliant on her and very fond of her. Between the children, Cook and Mrs Reynolds, her name was being called all the time, and she was happy for it, for there lay a certain amount of comfort in feeling needed.

August 1945

Waterloo Station was a hive of activity. Grace had never been in such a crowd in her entire life. She clutched her heavy suitcase handle tightly, fearing it would be swept away with the rushing throng of people should she loosen her grip. Her shoulders hunched and taut, she gazed around her with wide eyes. People ran this way and that, all with their eyes straight ahead, not acknowledging anyone they knocked into in their haste. A sudden thought came to mind and she turned to Mary, with fright.

"Is there is a fire, should we run too?"

Mary laughed. "No, there's no fire. It's always like this in London, everyone always seems to be on a life or death mission to arrive somewhere or other on time. Totally amazes me that they just don't leave a bit earlier to save themselves the burden of clock watching. But there you are, that's Londoners for you."

"Oh." Grace went back to watching the people and soaking up the atmosphere that yelled 'we're alive.'

"Come on, dearie. Let's get going."

Grace nodded and followed Mary as she wove her way through the crowds towards the exit.

"Let's get the bus, I can't be doing with that hot and dirty Underground, always gives me the chills going down and down. I know they saved thousands of lives whilst the bombing was going on, but I don't know, I still feel they are morbid, for me anyway."

"I'm more than happy to go by bus. I can't wait to see London."

"Your first time here then, dearie?"

"It is indeed," Grace replied with a sparkle in her eyes.

"Well it will take at least an hour to get there, so let's get cracking."

A young soldier rushing up the steps stopped half way and came back down again. "Let me take that for you, love," he said with a grin.

Mary nodded at him. "Eee, but that's grand of you, thank you kindly, young man." When they reached the top of the steps, the man handed back the case.

"Thank you," Mary repeated. He tipped his hat with his finger, and then went rushing on his way. "This way," said Mary leading them across the road.

The noise was overwhelming, and Grace found herself trying to shrink in her skin to get away from the stares of people rushing past. For the first time in her life she felt like a complete country bumpkin. Looking at the fashion statements walking past she realised she must look like something out of an old magazine.

"You look just lovely, don't you go a frettin'. My sister's a seamstress, if you fancy something new after pay day I'll take you over to her place. Spruce you up something pretty, she will."

"Thank you."

"Fifty-five, this is our bus." It looked like the red double-decker was full when it pulled in towards the curb, but despite this, there was a surge from the people waiting to get on board before it set off again.

"Just put your case between your legs and hold onto one of those handles," said Mary pointing at a rubber loop. "Once we get past Walworth the bus will pretty much empty and we'll be able to sit down."

When the bus lurched forward Grace nearly toppled, but two men on either side of her swiftly put out their hands to steady her.

"Thank you," she said, embarrassed. As she got used to the bus's jostling and jerking stops, she looked out of the window, trying to soak in as much of the city as she could. She quickly concluded it was simply amazing. Two wars had tried their hardest to destroy both the architecture and the people and yet, despite the rubble of buildings that had been hit by bombs, here was a metropolis obviously thriving. The streets were packed with cars and buses and the pavements overflowed with crowds on the move.

When Mary finally told her they had reached their stop, Grace was grateful. The Reynolds, along with Nanny, had driven to London the previous day, Mr Reynolds being keen to return to their normal life now that London was considered to be safe again.

Grace and Mary had been left behind to do a final clean up, before shutting down Mrs Reynolds's old family home. They had been up since the crack of dawn doing final checks before heading for Guildford station. That seemed like a very long time ago, and although she was excited to see the city, Grace was grateful for the thought that a good cuppa-tea was just around the corner.

"This way," said Mary, "unfortunately, the bus doesn't go straight to our street so we've about fifteen minutes to walk now." Grace moaned, causing Mary to laugh. "Here now, which one of us is the old maid, may I ask?"

"I honestly don't know where you get your energy from," answered Grace, picking up her case and stepping in line with Mary.

"That bus stop is called Maze Hill, should you ever take yourself off into the city. There's a couple of buses you can get but if you stick with the number fifty-five you'll not get lost as there are no changes on that route. Back there," Mary pointed backwards, "is the Greenwich Royal Observatory, right interesting that place – you ought to check it out. The astronomers don't come any more like, they say the city smog stops them seeing the sky. Still, it survived two world wars, that's saying something, right? Anyway, the park we're walking through now is called Blackheath and the children love it here, so I suspect you'll be seeing a lot of it."

As they walked out of the park, Grace was instantly in awe of the houses. Those in Guildford had been grand compared to what she was used to, but these were something else altogether.

"This road here is Morden Road, we live about half way down. Nearly home now."

Grace's jaw had dropped as she goggled at the houses they passed, they were surely houses fit for royalty.

"Here we are, home sweet home. Oh, how I missed this place. Come on, I'll show you to the back door where we go in and out."

Grace was beyond words as they skirted around the building to the door down the side.

"Mam," came a yell, which was followed by the appearance of a young man who came running up to Mary, and before she could object, had picked her up and was swinging her around. "Ye gods, Mam, I ain't half missed ya."

"Put me down, you silly boy!" Once down on the ground again Mary looked at her son for a full minute before throwing her arms around him. "Oh Billy lad, I've missed you grand I have." Mopping her happy tears away, Mary introduced Grace to her son. "He's Mr Reynolds's chauffeur," she said with pride.

Introductions made, they went inside the biggest kitchen Grace had ever seen. Mary visibly swelled with pride as she watched Grace looking around in awe. "Best kitchen south of the river, this is."

"Yep, and Ma is the best cook this side of the river too," chipped in Billy.

"I've tasted her cooking, and I think it might be fair to say she's the best cook in London."

"Now that," said Mary pointing at Grace with a pleased smile, "is why I like you so much."

*****

Of course the servants' quarters are in the attic, thought Grace as she forced her legs to take the next steps to the third floor.

"This is your room," said Billy opening a door. He ducked as he went through the doorway into the room and Grace smiled, as she was just able to walk through without stooping. "I'll see you tomorrow at breakfast. Goodnight now."

"Goodnight, and thank you for fetching my suitcase for me."

He grinned at her before leaning forward and going through the door, which he closed behind him.

The room was small but looked comfortable with a single bed, a washstand, a dresser and a small wardrobe. It was hot and stuffy, and Grace walked across the room and opened the window. Instantly, a fresh breeze filtered through and she sighed with relief at its cool touch. She leant against the windowsill and looked out at her new surroundings, wondering how long this would be her home. *Home?* She had actually thought of this place as home and she had only been there five minutes. She kicked her stout black shoes off and with great care peeled off the stockings, which were sticking to her legs with sweat. These were the last pair Milton had given her and she wanted to keep them for as long as possible. Along with Milton's memory, she also wasn't very keen to go back to rubbing gravy browning on her leg, and then drawing a line down the back with her kohl pencil. She found it extremely difficult to draw a straight line! Sighing with relief at being cool at last, she sat herself on the floor and opened the suitcase.

Neatly folded on the top was her father's Aran cardigan and lying next to it her mother's Bible. She traced her fingers over the Bible and then picked up the cardigan and took a deep breath. It was very faint now, but she could still just about smell her father on it. Despite the heat, she put the cardigan on and wrapped her arms around herself, imagining the bear hug that she missed so much.

Sunday 2nd September 1945

'Euphoria'; never in the history of man had a word been more aptly created to describe a scene, such as today. The no-alcohol drunkenness that drenched the crowds was intoxicating. *I wonder if Pentecost had been like this.*

"Grace." She turned her head and grinned at Billy. "If we lose each other, make your way back up to Trafalgar Square and sit on the fountain until I come and find you."

"Don't worry, I'll find my own way home if I lose you, it'll be fine."

Just then, a cheer rose and rippled through the streets of Whitehall, and they turned their attention to the government buildings. A deafening roar erupted, and Grace and Billy squeezed their way through the thick throngs of people until they could see the balcony of the Ministry of Health.

Winston Churchill was waving at them and Grace found herself screaming and waving as madly as everyone else. This man of inspiring speeches had, at last, brought this country to peace, and he well deserved their admiration and thanks.

"God bless you all," his voice boomed through the loud speaker.

The crowd erupted into song, *For he's a jolly good fellow,* and Grace found tears streaming down her face. William and Milton hadn't made it, but today for the soldiers still standing this was the most tremendous day.

When it was clear Mr Churchill wasn't coming back onto the balcony, the crowds began to disperse slowly, showing their reluctance to leave behind the memory of today. Grace drank in the atmosphere of merriment as they strolled through the streets. What a colourful lot they were, with most people wearing red, white or blue. Union Jacks flew from nearly every window and most hands waved miniature flags on sticks.

In this moment, Grace was so proud to be British she could burst. Not because Great Britain was great, but because the people were amazing. *We're a nation of steadfast people, with faults, warts and all, yet still we believe in the greater good and strive for something better. I wish you were here Dad – you would have loved this. We have done our best as never before, we neither sought nor glorified in this war, and we have gained nothing. Indeed, it seems we are losing our Empire and acquiring an unfathomable amount of debt. Our governments may do things we don't agree with, but as a people we are peaceful and self-reliant, and the sacrifices of war have fallen hard upon us. If I were a Christian, I would be on my knees now praying in earnest that this would be the last world war in the history of mankind.*

Sunday 14th June 1953

Sitting at a small wooden table in the courtyard, just outside the kitchen door, Grace flicked through the pages of the Sunday Times, glad that Mr Reynolds was an early riser and happy for Grace to read the paper once he'd finished with it.

Mr and Mrs Reynolds and Katy had gone to church and the house was peaceful. As they were going out for lunch after church, Cook had been given the day off and went to visit her sister, taking Billy with her. With no one around to see her, Grace was wearing her father's large cardigan and enjoying the comfort it still brought her. She watched two robins hopping on the grass pecking for worms and felt tranquil. *I wonder what's next for me.* Harry had left for boarding school years ago and only came home for holidays, and in all honesty Mr and Mrs Reynolds didn't seem to be too fussed about the education that Katy received. Grace felt the only reason she was still here was that they were loath to kick her out. Katy was fifteen now and in the nine years Grace had been with the family she had watched her blossom into a lovely young lady. Unfortunately, she had no wish to be clever, as she constantly reminded Grace, and eventually the 'lessons' with just the two of them turned into something more like adventures, with the pair of them visiting every place of interest London had to offer. Grace always repeated the history of a place and was sure Katy was broadening her mind as much as she could, but marriage (sigh) seemed to be all Katy was interested in.

Grace was nearing the end of the paper and turned the page to the employment section; it was about time she found herself another position. Her eyes scanned over the huge paper, looking for positions for governesses. Just as she found a section that showed a possible three jobs, the wind picked up and a sudden gust flipped the pages over.

"Woo," said Grace, spreading her arms on the newspaper to hold it still. With an arm on each end of the paper, she found herself looking down at a large square box advertising a job in Kenya. A bolt of something hit her and her heart started beating fast. The wind died down and Grace sat back a bit so she could contemplate the advertisement.

> *Administrator wanted for Mombasa office. Good rate of remunerations.*
> *No prior experience necessary.*
> *Must speak and write excellent English and be free to travel immediately.*
> *Contact the Imperial British East Africa Company.*

She closed her eyes and William's dream-letter flashed before her eyes…

> *I have the strangest request to ask of you, Grace. Should an opportunity ever arise to go to Kenya, will you take it? I have this recurring dream that you are under a blazing sun watching animals move across a red earth. You look so young, Grace, like you did that day we went to the fair. Your hazel eyes sparkle with love and your tiny nose is sprinkled with freckles. You are at peace and happy, and I am flooded with joy when I see you turn your head slightly and smile at me.*

Her eyes sprang open and a joy washed through her; she didn't hesitate or stop to consider all that was involved. She gathered up the paper and rushed inside to Mr Reynolds's study. She took a piece of paper and wrote a very short letter applying for the position.

Saturday 25th July 1953

Grace stood in her bedroom doorway taking a last look around, it was practically impossible to imagine that this had been her home for nine years. *Where does time go?*

As she stepped off the last stair into the hallway she was surprised to see everyone gathered there. Mary was openly sobbing, as was Katy, even Mrs Reynolds looked sad.

"Let me take that for you," said Billy taking the suitcase out of her hands.

"I'll miss you," wailed Katy, who ran into the front room, threw herself on the sofa and buried her face in a cushion.

177

"It has been a pleasure having you as part of our family, Grace. I wish you well and God speed for your journey and your new life in Kenya."

"Thank you, Mrs Reynolds, that means a lot to me. And thank you too, for employing me without prior experience. I know that was hard for you and it means so much to me that you took that chance."

They hugged briefly and then Mrs Reynolds went to console her daughter.

"It has been a pleasure to see the pain vanish from your face." Mr Reynolds came up to stand before her. "I know you experienced a lot of sorrow, but I pray for you often, and will continue to do so even though you will no longer be with us, that you will find your way back to God. He misses you, Grace, and you should remember that He will always welcome you back with open arms."

"Thank you, that is very kind of you."

"I want you to have this." He offered her an envelope. "It isn't very much, but I'd feel much better letting you travel around the world knowing you have a small amount of money on you. It is for emergencies and such like. Also, it is enough that if you find Mombasa is not for you, then you can purchase your return ticket and come straight back to England."

"I don't know what to say."

"No need for words, just take care of yourself, promise me?"

"I promise." Grace had a lump in her throat and was beginning to think she had made the worst decision of her life.

"Billy will drive you to the docks. Goodbye, and may God bless you always."

Grace followed Billy through the kitchen and out into the courtyard.

"Bye, dearie," said Mary with bright red eyes.

They hugged long and hard.

"We don't want to miss boarding time," said Billy, opening the car door.

"Thank you for treating me like your family." Grace rubbed her eyes with a big handkerchief.

"God speed, luv."

Grace had just climbed inside the car when Katy came charging into the yard.

"I made this for you," she said, pushing a small piece of cloth at her.

Grace took the cloth and looked at it. In not so expertly sewn embroidery, she read… *I was hungry and you gave me food to eat. I was thirsty and you gave me a drink. I was a stranger and you welcomed me.*

"It's beautiful, I will cherish it always."

Katy ducked her head into the car and gave Grace a big kiss on her cheek. "Don't you forget me."

Grace smiled. "I'll never forget you, you mean far too much to me."

Katy's chin trembled and she turned around into the arms of Mary who hugged her.

Part Two
Mombasa, Kenya

She grimaced behind her delicate china cup, and sipped her insipid tea, wondering if she would ever stop missing a proper-good cup of English tea. Putting her cup down, she smiled.

"I can say, without a shadow of a doubt that the lesson that has most impacted me since coming here is… you can't out give God."

Chapter 15

SS Uganda
July-August 1953

As they left the Thames on the SS Uganda and emerged into the North Sea the crowd on deck cheered. The excitement that only an adventure like exploring the unknown can bring flooded through all those present, except the crew who had done the trip several times in the last year and were busy going about their duties.

Grace felt the thrill of embarking on a new life, and her skin tingled with the anticipation of discovery. She clung onto the rail as she stood on the deck near the bow of the ship and closed her eyes. The salt water kissed her face as the wind scattered the spray across the deck.

She felt a yearning in her spirit to talk to God but squashed it; that was her past. Now she was moving forward, carried to an unknown destiny by this powerful ship built for the British-India Steam Navigation Company only a year ago.

It wasn't too long before the excitement left most people as they found it impossible to keep any food down. For days, the smell of sick was pretty much everywhere Grace went, so she began holding her lavender scent-covered handkerchief to her nose at all times. She felt very grateful to Mrs Reynolds, who having been on a ship herself some years before, had insisted that Grace take the small bottle with her. Thankfully, by the time they started skirting the North Atlantic seas past Portugal, leaving the Bay of Biscay far behind, most people had grown accustomed to the ship's movements and were at last keeping their food down.

Most nights, a band would play music and the passengers would drink and dance. Their chatter and laughter would make Grace smile, as she sat alone on deck reading. She had been over the moon when she discovered the Captain had a library and that the passengers were free to read the books it contained. Never in her life had she been bored, she had always been busy and active, and she was finding the idleness of a passenger's life unbearably tedious, until she discovered the library. Now her hours and days sped by and blurred together as she lost herself in War and Peace, Uncle Tom's Cabin, Huckleberry Finn and all of the Brontë books. The characters captivated her imagination and she laughed with them and sobbed at their sorrows.

The heat was sometimes unbearable, and on especially hot days she became more and more grateful to Mary's sister, who had made her the simplest dresses from light cotton. Short sleeves prevented her shoulders from burning as she did her daily walks around the ship. The front buttons made dressing easy and she had abandoned the belts at the beginning of the trip so that the dresses hung loosely around her now very thin body.

Being used to Mary's excellent cooking she found the ship's meals mostly unappetising. She was glad when they called into Gibraltar and the Purser and the Chief Cook went ashore to stock up on fresh fruit and vegetables.

Sailing through the Mediterranean brought calm waters and the passengers became more active, playing games on deck and going swimming. Grace had never learnt to swim, but sat happily in her deck chair watching children jumping in and out of the pool on deck. To her amusement, some people with blonde hair who went swimming in the small square pool found themselves with green hair. The Captain had assured those who complained that the colour would come out eventually and the strong chlorine was necessary to kill the germs in this heat.

One man was most put out by the new colour of his hair.

"I look ridiculous," he moaned to no one in particular after the Captain had finished explaining.

"I think it quite suits you," said Grace who was sitting nearby on a deckchair.

He came over and sat down next to her. "It isn't amusing. I've been told I practically have to wait for my hair to grow out before it will be gone."

Grace couldn't help the sparkling laugh that bounced around her eyes. "Never mind. What about wearing a hat?"

He looked at her in dismay, and then saw the funny side and started laughing. "Christopher," he said, offering Grace his hand.

"Grace Clifton, a pleasure to meet you."

After that, whenever their paths crossed, Grace and Christopher would stop and exchange small talk for a while. These moments soon became the highlight of Grace's day, until the day he told her he was engaged. After that, she was careful to avoid him whenever she could.

When they docked in Naples Grace was one of the first people off the ship. She experienced the city like a sponge, soaking in the atmosphere, people and different aromas. For the first time in her life she tucked into a plate of pasta al pomodoro and thought it was one the tastiest things she'd ever had, with the rich tomato and garlic flavours enhanced by the sprinkling of fresh basil. If her stomach hadn't shrunk so much in the last weeks she might have ordered a second plate.

The next stop was Port Said at the entrance to the Suez Canal. Here, a lot of trepidation washed through both the crew and passengers. That night at dinner, the captain assured them that they would be traversing the canal in the safety of a convoy of at least twenty ships and they had nothing to fear.

It felt closed-in moving down the canal. Not only could they see the banks on either side, but they formed part of a convoy heading south, whilst convoys of ships heading north passed them nearly every hour. Grace had no idea the Suez Canal would be so busy and could appreciate now why it had been vital to fight over free passage for so long. It was a relief when they came into the Red Sea and Grace didn't feel so hemmed in any more. It was even better when they came out of the Gulf of Aden and into the Ocean.

For six weeks the SS Uganda had ploughed its way at a steady 16 knots and now at last was gliding through the Indian Ocean on its last leg before reaching the port of Mombasa.

The lull of passage began to wear off and Grace found it more and more difficult to concentrate on her books. She wanted to be in Kenya. She wanted to see what her new home looked like, and ultimately to find out if she had made the right decision in going there.

In the last few days a number of passengers succumbed to a gastrointestinal illness, and the decks and hallways had been quiet. Grace was grateful that she kept herself to herself and rarely ate anything that didn't look washed or thoroughly cooked.

The Chief Steward had informed her that today they would reach Mombasa, and for the last couple of hours she had been

switching from sitting and trying to read, to standing and
looking ahead.

Finally, the ship veered slowly to the right and headed
towards land.

Chapter 16

Mombasa
Friday 4th September 1953

Wearing her lightest sundress and a big straw hat, Grace took her first step onto Kenyan soil and felt a thrill of excitement grip her like nothing she had ever experienced. Her eyes darted back and forth across the docks, drinking in as much as possible.

"Excuse me, dear," said a woman behind her and she jumped, quickly sidestepping to let the other passengers off the ship.

"Sorry," she offered, but the woman was already walking off at a brisk pace. Grace clutched her suitcase tight and chewed her bottom lip as she debated which way to go. Undecided at the last minute about how to reach the address she'd been given, she dived into her bag and brought out her well-read map of Mombasa island.

"I'm getting a taxi to the hospital, if you'd like a lift to Old Town I could drop you off?"

Grace smiled as she looked up at Christopher. "That's very kind of you, but I want to explore… I think I'm going to go on a bus!"

"Well, you're braver than me." Christopher smiled down at her. "I will be at the Aga Khan if you should need me for anything in the next few days. But, if I don't see you again, I wish you a very pleasant stay in Kenya."

"Thank you, same to you." Grace slowly followed and watched as he climbed into a taxi. Part of her longed for the comfort of a man's arms and gentle conversation, however, he was engaged and extremely handsome, so that meant sharing a taxi with him was probably not the best thing to do.

She shook her head to chase away the yearnings of belonging to someone and set a brisk pace, for she had decided she was going to walk the long Kilindini Avenue for a while, then jump on a matatu (local bus) to take her to Old Town. At first, the cool sea breeze followed her along the road, but as the morning began to fade and noon approached, Grace began to regret her decision to walk. The fresh warm air of the morning was steadily rising and beginning to creep towards 28 degrees and she needed to rest. Her case was heavy, and no matter how much she waved at the matatus, none stopped to pick her up. Sweat poured down her back and off her forehead, which she tried to keep dry with constant wiping, but her handkerchief had long since become soaking wet.

She looked at the local tradesmen selling their fares from push-along wooden stalls and longed to be adventurous enough to try their food. Not quite ready to risk an upset stomach, she finally made her way into an old colonial hotel and asked if non-residents could eat in the restaurant. She was given assurance with many smiles and bows, that she was most certainly welcome to eat there, and was ushered through the lobby and out into the gardens. As she sank into a comfortable wicker chair under the shade of huge palm tree she sighed with relief.

She enjoyed a light salad and lemonade and left the young waiter a generous tip before heading back to her road of discovery. She walked slowly, having given up completely on stopping a matatu, her eyes searching everywhere whilst she drank in the atmosphere of Africa. She marvelled as three women in brightly coloured dresses, which seemed to be no more than a length of cloth wrapped expertly around them, walked past with huge baskets on their heads, one also carrying a child on her back. They didn't even use their hands to steady their heavy loads and Grace was in awe of their strength.

As she finally began nearing the Old Town section of Mombasa, her arms felt like lead from carrying the case. She had stopped a few times under the shade of palm trees and sat on the case until the feeling in her hands returned; how she wished she had accepted Christopher's offer of a lift. She promised herself she would never turn down a lift again.

The Old Town was cool in comparison to the more modern streets, where the sun blazed down, scorching everything it touched. Here, the buildings loomed narrow and tall keeping the sun off the narrow walkways. But the relief brought by the drop in temperature was replaced by overwhelming smells. The defective sewage works reeked up from the ground to be hit mid-air by the strong smells of Arabic perfume and tantalizing herbs and spices. However, the smell that had Grace literally holding her nose when she could stand it no more, was the knockout stench of bodily odours, it was simply too dreadful to ignore.

She stopped to catch her breath on a street corner that had opened up revealing the sea a short distance away, which allowed the fresh salt air to momentarily sweep all other smells away.

She rummaged in her handbag, fished out the now crumpled map and tried smoothing it flat against the wall.

"Habari."

Grace looked up to see a young boy looking at her.

Thinking she hadn't understood him the boy tried again. "Jambo."

"Jambo," Grace replied offering him a smile.

In response, he grinned from ear to ear, showing off his few teeth. "You lost, Mrs?"

"Well, yes and no. I mean I won't be once I can find what street we're standing on so I can find it on the map."

"Where you go?"

Saying it slowly, Grace answered. "Mzizima Road."

The boy dived forward, grabbed her suitcase, and started heading down the road.

"Hey," yelled Grace going after him.

"This way, Mrs."

Taking a chance, that he was actually leading her to the street she wanted and not down some alley to rob her, Grace followed him. They walked for about ten minutes and then the boy stopped and pointed upwards.

"Mzizima Road." He grinned and put out his hand, palm upwards.

She might not have travelled before, but she had taken the precaution on reading up as much about Kenya as she could, so she fished in her bag and brought out a coin. He snatched it from her hand and ran off.

"Well, how rude."

"Miss Clifton?"

Grace looked across the road to see an elderly white woman walking towards her.

"Yes?"

When the woman reached her, she put out her hand. "I'm Mrs Brinley, I run the guest house on behalf of the company, and I am very pleased to meet you."

"Pleased to meet you, too. I would have been here sooner only the buses wouldn't stop for me."

"Goodness me, we don't travel on the matatus. Why on earth didn't you take a taxi?"

"I was trying to save money; unfortunately I don't have a surplus of it."

Mrs Brinley raised an eyebrow at her. "Come along, it's much cooler indoors." The woman took off down the narrow street and Grace followed.

Indoors was indeed a good deal cooler. Net-covered glass doors were pulled back in the front room, which gave out onto a small courtyard. A gentle sea breeze rushed through and worked with the huge bladed ceiling-fan to keep the temperature at a comfortable level. Grace found herself instantly relaxing in the cool air and in doing so she realised how uncomfortable the heat had made her.

"Drop your bag down, I'll show you to your room later."

Grace put her bag down and followed Mrs Brinley into a cool kitchen. The shutters were down and it was dark, but Mrs

Brinley didn't bother putting a light on. Instead, she filled a kettle and lit the stove.

"There isn't much space for storing food and it goes off quickly in the heat anyway, so I suggest that you buy what you need for three days at most. I would keep everything in boxes too, otherwise, you will find it full of ants. There are seven of us here now you have come to join us, so we need to be respectful and considerate of each other. Now, the stove is temperamental so if it doesn't light the first time, just give it a moment and then try again."

Mrs Brinley chatted away whilst making the tea and setting up the tray, explaining the house rules and filling Grace in a little bit about the company. When the tea was ready they went back into the front room.

"Milk doesn't stay fresh for long I'm afraid, so we take tea with sugar and lemon, I hope that is okay?"

Grace nodded with a smile. She had never had tea with lemon but it sounded refreshing. As they got to know each other Grace couldn't help but wonder what had brought Mrs Brinley to Africa and why she had stayed. In her own words she was a true colonial, and Mombasa was her home. As her eyes drifted around the room, Grace felt it was like looking at a home in the England of about twenty years before. The old furniture looked worse for wear, and yet it was obvious that at its creation it had been the height of fashion and very expensive. This 'old' theme ran throughout the house, as did a horrendous amount of dust, and Grace couldn't help feeling slightly embarrassed for the landlady's obvious lack of cleanliness.

When Mrs Brinley finally grew tired of asking questions, for which she received only short non-informative responses, she told Grace her bedroom was on the top floor. Grace moaned internally, of course her bedroom was on the top floor.

Mrs Brinley pointed up the narrow staircase. "Just keep following the stairs up to the very top, your room is the only one in the attic so you can't mistake that you've reached it. I'd take you up myself but it's time to prepare supper and the others will be home soon. As it's your first day, supper will be on the house, after that if you wish to dine with us there will be a small fee on top of your rent. Mawanda has cleaned your room today and put fresh linen on the bed, in the future you will be expected to clean it yourself. Mawanda will wash your clothes for you if you wish and I will add the charge onto your rent. If you want to do it yourself there is a sink in the courtyard, but please buy your own soap."

"Thank you, that all seems extremely gracious of you. When should I come down for supper?"

"In about an hour, but I ring the bell when meals are ready so you'll know."

Four floors up, Grace finally pushed open her bedroom door and walked into her new home. The room was small and the ceiling low and she was only able to stand without stooping in the centre parts. She put the bag on the bed and went to the window, which had been propped open with a metal bar. A moment of joy filled her when she looked out and realised she could see the ocean. Sun-sparkles reflected off white horses and looked like jewels and she stared for ages soaking it all in.

She gazed down on the red rooftops and wondered about the people who lived under them. Someone close by was cooking curry, the overpoweringly strong smell wafted up to her window and she sniffed in deeply. It smelt exotic and she wished she could taste it. She could hear children laughing somewhere close by, and in the distance, cars and matatus driving around the island. There was a constant honk of motor horns and she wondered if today was a special day of some sort and they were beeping to celebrate – she would ask Mrs Brinley when she went back downstairs.

She opened her case and lifted out her Bible and her father's Aran cardigan. It was too hot to put the cardigan on so she held it to her chest as she closed her eyes and longed to hold onto the memory of the people she had lost.

Friday 25th September 1953

After three weeks of working for the company as an administrator, she knew she wouldn't be able to stay. The women had no backbone and the men thought themselves gods-over-all. She'd had enough, and after collecting her weekly pay envelope she informed them that she wouldn't be coming back. An argument had then ensued with the manager who demanded instant repayment for the passage over.

She assured him that she would pay them back as soon as she could and practically ran out of the building. Insufferable people, who did they think they were? She had never seen such injustice in her life and the way they treated the African employees was diabolical. She would have to find another job or return to England because she couldn't stand to watch such unfairness.

Her pride in being British had diminished. Was it something in the heat that made them insufferable, or was it just that self-righteous prigs found their way here? Their elitism made her cringe. Maybe she should go home? She knew the Reynolds would help her find another job. She was fed up with the heat, anyway. Sick and tired with the dust that immediately covered everything, laughing at your attempts to keep clean. She hated constantly sweating and the mosquitoes were simply going to kill her, either that or she would scratch the skin off her body and die from flesh wounds.

She could honestly say that except for moments when something of beauty caught her eye, that she disliked Africa and considered herself most assuredly 'homesick'. She found herself walking down to the docks and scouring the area for an England bound ship. She saw one that displayed the Union Jack from its top mast. Homesickness washed over her and helped to make up her mind. She hurried through the docks to the offices and enquired about passage home.

She was shocked at the price, it would take her every penny and Mr Reynolds's generous gift to buy the ticket and even then, she wouldn't have enough left to repay the company. She would have to persuade them that she would send them money from England. She gave her name to the clerk and told him she would be back tomorrow to board ship and pay her fare.

As she walked back to the boarding house the thought of going home didn't fill her with joy, in fact she began to feel low. *Maybe I am a coward with no backbone, wanting to run away after only five minutes.*

She had reached the Old Town and was walking mechanically back without taking in any of her surroundings, caught up in herself and the woes that life had bestowed upon her.

The sound of screaming and shouting shocked her out of her musings. She paused for only a moment and then started running through the streets to the place where the sound like a murder being committed was coming from.

Pausing as she came around the corner, she took in the scene before her. A young lad was the cause of the screaming. He lay on the ground fighting as numerous men grappled with him.

"Hey." She didn't stop to think that maybe a white woman shouldn't interfere with a group of African men, she just ran at them waving her arms. They paused only for a moment and then continued their struggle with the young man.

"What's going on?" Grace asked a young boy standing near by. He responded in Swahili, whilst waving his arms and shaking his head.

"I don't understand you."

"They try take him hospital," the boy said in broken English.

"Why?"

"He fell." The boy pointed to a nearby coconut tree. "His leg no-good, Mrs."

"Why won't he let them take him to the hospital?"

"Because everyone know, you only go there to die." With that the boy ran off.

Grace watched as the men finally got the lad to calm down so they could put him on a blanket. He seemed to give up and his screaming turned to crying. Tears left streaks on his dirty face and his large brown eyes, full of sheer terror, focused on her for a brief moment.

Help him.

Grace didn't know where the voice came from and didn't stop to question it, but hastened after the men as they jogged through the street with the lad on the blanket between them.

They weren't a great distance away from her lodgings, but they were in a part of the town she hadn't explored yet. The men carried the lad through the gardens of a largish building. Grace stopped and read the sign at the gate, it said, *Welcome to the Native Civic Hospital.* She looked up to see the men had stopped at the entrance. There was a lot of shouting going on and they put the lad on the floor. At last, someone in a white coat appeared at the door. They seemed to shout at him and then turned and jogged back out of the hospital grounds. The man in the white coat yelled after them, waving his arms. When it was obvious they weren't coming back, the man turned and walked back inside, leaving the young lad on the ground.

Her feet took control and she walked up to him.

His eyes, crazed with fear, locked onto hers, as he lifted his hand up to her. "Please, Mrs, don't let them take me inside."

Grace knelt down beside him. "What's your name?"

"Oborneo. Please, Mrs, please don't let them kill me."

"Doctors don't kill, Oborneo. They heal and make you better."

"Not in there." He started sobbing again.

Three people appeared in the doorway, one of them the man in the white coat. The other two men were shabbily dressed and basically looked like beggars from the street. The man in the white coat started shouting at her and shooing her with his arms. Although she couldn't understand him, she did get the gist of words.

"Okay, I'm leaving," she said raising her arms as if in surrender.

Help him.

Now what would you have me do? They won't even let me in the building.

Help him.

"I'm going to stay with him, until his family get here. He should have someone with him, he's only a minor."

The three men looked at her as if she was mad.

"You want to come inside?" asked the man in the white coat.

"Yes."

He regarded her for a moment then shook his head. "Crazy woman. Take hold of a corner then, and help us take him to a ward."

For the briefest of moments, she thought about telling him off for calling her crazy but shrugged it off. She probably was crazy; she hadn't seen one other white person in this area of town.

They carried him down a long corridor, passed through a door and then walked down another corridor. Grace felt the muscles in her arm protesting and was glad when they finally walked into a large room which was obviously the ward. The room had eight beds but only a few of them had mattresses on. Two beds had occupants, but the rest were empty. They laid the lad on the first empty bed that possessed a mattress.

The man in charge barked something at the other two and they went running off, then he turned to look at the boy who had been silent throughout the hospital walk. He asked him questions and the lad answered. It was only when the man began touching the boy's leg with gentle probing fingers that Grace realised he must be the doctor. When he'd finished he looked up at Grace and she studied him for the first time.

He was of Asian descent, not African as she had first thought, and he was much older than she had first reckoned as well. Lines filled his face and his black hair was full of white flecks.

"You should go, he has no family, and no one is coming for him." With that the doctor turned and walked out of the room.

"Excuse me," blurted Grace, thoroughly put out by the man's rudeness.

"What?" he muttered as he walked down the corridor.

Grace raced after him. "What about the boy? Are you able to fix his leg? Will he be all right?"

"Yes and no."

"What does that mean?"

"Who are you?" the doctor asked, abruptly stopping and turning to glower at her.

"My name is Grace Clifton, I work at the com… well actually I don't work anymore. That's beside the point. What do you mean by yes and no?"

"Yes, I will strap his leg together, and no, he probably won't be all right."

"Why ever not? It's only a broken leg, isn't it?"

The doctor rolled his eyes. "You do-gooders drive me crazy. You come here for five minutes all outraged at the state of the place and then you leave and don't do anything to help. Just go away, woman, and leave me be." He turned and started walking off again.

"Wait." Grace reached out and grabbed his arm, causing him to stop and give her a most threatening look. She dropped his arm instantly.

"What's your name?"

"Why? Want to report me to the authorities?" He laughed like he'd cracked a joke and started down the corridor again.

Not wanting to touch him again and make him even angrier, Grace decided to walk with him. "Actually, that hadn't crossed my mind, but maybe I should?"

"Do what you must; it makes no difference to me."

Grace was churning up inside, *why wouldn't the authorities be bothered?*

"Your name?" she tried again.

"Doctor Singh, not that it's any business of yours, of course." He turned into a room and Grace followed into what must have been the hospital office.

Grace waited for him to sit down behind his large desk, littered with documents. "Why won't he be all right?" she asked, genuinely concerned.

Dr Singh sighed, and resigned to the fact that she wasn't going to leave until she got her answers, leant back in his chair and regarded her. "Are you a Christian?"

She didn't hesitate. "No. Why, what has that got to do with anything?"

"The only white people who come in here are missionaries and the occasional bored Christian housewife who feels God has called her to help." He looked her up and down and tutted. "What do you want, Mrs Clifton?"

"It's Miss Clifton, and I want to know why he won't be all right if he only has a broken leg."

"You haven't been here long then, I take it?"

"Three weeks."

Dr Singh scoffed. "Well, *Miss* Clifton, the boy has no relatives, and that means he has no way of paying for medication. *That means*, if he gets an infection in his leg he will probably die. Now you have had your answer, please leave, you are giving me quite a headache."

Grace didn't know whether he was joking or not. She stood looking at him, waiting for him to smile and say 'just kidding.' When no such remark came, she made her way to a chair opposite his and sat down.

He groaned.

"If it makes you feel so bad why don't you buy his penicillin and pay for his nursing?"

She sat staring at the mountain of papers. That thought had already entered her head, but she only just had enough money to go home. If she spent some of it, she would have to find a job and stay a bit longer, save up a bit more money.

"I thought this was the 'free' hospital?"

"Oh really." He was irritated, but she waited for him to answer.

"I think the Company's intention, originally, was that it would be a free hospital. But over time the money dried up and that was that."

"The Company built the hospital?"

"Technically, the funds for the building came from Britain, their demonstration to the world that they care for the locals, or should I call them natives?"

"I did wonder about the sign at the gate, welcome to the Native Civic Hospital? Very condescending. So they built it and abandoned it?"

"Not at first. In the beginning the place was full of Asian and European doctors, all coming to help educate the poor natives and heal some if they could. There was a full house back in the beginning I'm told, all modern equipment was installed and it seemed to be a bit of a miracle."

"What happened?"

"With the decline of colonialism and then the war, we simply became a hindrance and the Governor no longer sanctioned funds for us."

"How long has it been this bad?"

"I'm not sure really, it was a slow decline."

"But you stayed. Do you have staff?"

"Yes, I have a young trainee doctor, very enthusiastic and quite hopeless. I also have twelve nurses who sometimes come in to work."

"They don't always come in? That's terrible, why don't you replace them?"

"They rarely get paid so I can hardly tell them they're sacked."

They went quiet for a while. Grace stared at the papers for a long time then looked up, her mind made up.

"Where do you suggest I buy his penicillin?"

Dr Singh said something she couldn't understand. "Pardon?"

"He is a lucky boy. Go to the pharmacy on the main street, Mr Lakviar is an honest man. Tell him I sent you, and he will not charge you wazungu (white man) prices."

"I thought you said he was an honest man, why would he charge a white person more for medicine."

"Because he is also a business man and white people can afford it."

Chapter 17

Broken Bones & the Prodigal Daughter
Wednesday 30th September 1953

Grace fled from the hospital ward, blindly running down the corridors until she found a door that let her out into the world. She pushed through the door and sucked in the moist warm air. It was no more refreshing than the room in the hospital. She stumbled and caught her toe on a loose tile as she entered the shabby, un-kept gardens. There was nowhere to sit and the heat was immense, so she took off across the dry earth towards the offer of shelter given by a solitary palm tree.

She crumpled to the ground and started crying. *Why won't you heal him, Father-God? If it is because of my sin then please, forgive me. Have mercy, not on me but on that poor boy. Please Lord, don't let him die. Let him live and reflect your glory.* No answer was forthcoming and slowly her tears subsided and came to a halt on a stuttering sigh. *What can I do, Father? Show me, help me make a difference. I promise never to forsake you again, only let me return to the shelter of your love and the comfort of your guidance. Help me, help him.*

Grace felt the blaze of the sun pouring down on her, wrapping its rays around her in a warm hug. She turned her head slightly and gazed up through the branches of the palm tree. The sun glistened and danced on the leaves, its lightness bouncing upon them. Then, as with all the mysteries of the workings of God, she knew this was where she belonged. The love of the Father flowed through her, causing waves of joy and peace to course through her veins.

She took a white cotton handkerchief from her bag and mopped around her eyes, giving a tiny laugh when she saw the dirt on her hanky. *Lord, but this dust is going to take some getting used to.* She picked herself up and straightened her skirt. She had no idea what she would do in the long term, but for now she still had a little money in her purse, so she would buy another course of antibiotics, then she'd stand over that poor excuse of a nurse and ensure Oborneo was given it this time.

Strength, Father-God, please. I am going to need loads of strength.

She crossed the desolate garden and took the pavement heading back towards town. How was it possible that a place could be both wondrous and dismal? There was a stark contrast between the beauty of the Campanula trees, the palms and the sun glistening on the sea compared to the grubby town itself. Neglected, that was how it felt. As if it had been built with pride and then left to take care of itself, which it had failed miserably to do.

The roads were littered with potholes, some of them big enough to fill with water and turn into swimming pools for infants. The paint on the buildings was cracked and peeling. And it was busy, oh so busy. People walked the street, and the road, carrying their wares on their heads and their children on their backs. Women wore colourful material wrapped around their bodies and heads, demanding you understand that you were no longer in the civilised, pretentious world of England. Instead, you were somewhere exotic and exciting, and to be clear, somewhere very, very different.

Then there were the beggars. Lord, but she had never seen such illness and poverty in her life before. She thought they'd had it bad in England during the bombing, and the soldiers in the war were faced with such horrors. Yet, in the strangest way people coped with them because they knew they weren't forever, eventually the war would end, and normal life would resume. It was this absence of hope in the future which infiltrated every spectrum of life that struck home for Grace.

The Africans in Mombasa had accepted their continual occupancy from different races. They bowed to the poverty and were grateful for scraps. They lived with death hanging over their heads, acknowledging it could come for them at any moment and that if you lived to the ripe old age of forty, you were very old indeed. The begging children brought Grace's spirits down, but not as much as seeing the beggars with Elephantiasis. She reeled in horror when she encountered the first diseased man sitting on the pavement. His humongous, stone like legs were totally incomprehensible to her, as it was when she learned that there was nothing that could be done for them.

In the last few weeks she had become used to the mixture of cultures. The Africans in their colourful clothes, huge smiles and very often, bare feet. The Asians in their gentle 'don't heed us' ways, which allowed them to slip into nearly every business Mombasa had to offer without objection or complaint. The Arabs with their men in white dresses and small bowl shaped hats dominating the streets, whilst their women stayed at home out of the way. Usually friendly, yet belligerent in a moment of bargaining in business, whether selling a house or a mango it made no difference, a sale was a sale. Yet they were warm and likeable, just hard to get a good bargain from.

Then, of course, there were the British, well let's say Europeans because in fact the British weren't the only white outsiders here in this British Protectorate. Ah, the European, so easy to spot carrying his airs about him, what a different breed of human he was, in his white shorts, long stockings and inevitable straw sunhat. To Grace they stuck out like sore thumbs and sometimes she had the urge to usher them all home and to leave the laid-back multi-nationals of Mombasa to get on with their lives, like they had done since the Portuguese swept in during the 1500s.

As she walked towards Mr Lakviar's small chemist shop, she looked at everything with new, fresh eyes. This was her new home.

She had lost God, he had drowned under her sorrow and she hadn't tried to find Him. She'd felt her Father in Heaven to be as dead as her earthly father. Yet today, that had all changed and as easily as turning on the light, He had returned. *No, I must be honest with myself, He had never left me, it is I who have returned.* For in this moment, Grace had need of a power far greater than any she could muster, she needed the miraculous help of God, for Oborneo was dying.

As quickly as it had disappeared, her faith returned. A real, live, prodigal daughter. The wall she built around her emotions came tumbling down. Her doubts about God's authenticity fell away. Her need and desire to help someone completely dissolved the darkness that had settled over her heart.

After buying the penicillin the first time, five days ago, she simply handed it over to the nurse on duty and left. She'd felt her part in his healing was over and tried to put Oborneo out of her mind. Yet for the next five days, he plagued her thoughts in every waking moment.

She had been lucky, she thought she might have had to return to the Company and eat humble pie and ask for her job back, but Mrs Brinley happened to mention that Woolworths just lost a few members of staff due to malaria. She hastened to the store in her best frock, applied her most English lady-like voice and enquired after a position. Fifteen minutes later, she was employed and shown immediately to an office at the back of the building, where she was to work as a purchase ledger clerk. It was a new job for her but she picked it up immediately and quite enjoyed it. The pay was also much better than the company, and she realised she would be able to pay them back within six months. Then when she was debt free she would be able to go home – well that had been the plan of yesterday. Today she felt different, more hopeful.

Woolworths Mombasa in the 1950's

Happy with her new job and new financial status, Grace found herself irritated that she couldn't get the young boy with the big brown eyes out of her mind. They were before her always, pleading and begging for help.

Eventually she could stand it no longer and returned to the hospital to check up on him, half expecting him to be gone. She walked briskly through the hospital until she reached the ward where she had left Oborneo. He was still there, lying so still that if it hadn't been for the sweat rolling off his forehead she would have assumed he was dead.

She'd raced through the corridors to Dr Singh's office, only to find it empty. She went running through the small hospital calling out his name. A young man in a white coat had finally stopped her, and asked her what was wrong. She told him and he sighed, many heavy sighs in fact, before explaining you never give the nurses the medicine because they might sell it to other patients. You needed to administer the medicine yourself and take it home with you to ensure your loved one received it all. Yes, he had confirmed, Oborneo had caught an infection in his wound, and there wasn't anything they could do for him.

She opened the door that made a brass bell tinkle, and welcomed the temporary relief from the heat provided by the shop's fans and dark interior.

"Ah, Miss Clifton, very nice to see you again."

Grace was puzzled, she didn't remember giving Mr Lakviar her name.

"You'll be wanting another course of antibiotics. Dr Singh mentioned you might be back. He told me to tell you, if he didn't see you, to give the medicine to the boy yourself. He forgot to warn you when he saw you last. The nurses haven't been paid in four months and some of them are in terrible need themselves, so unfortunately," Mr Lakviar shook his head from side to side with a frown, "they will do what they must to feed their own families. You mustn't be too harsh on them Miss Clifton, it is just the way of life around here, it is just what it is."

Grace handed the money over without saying a word, what could she say? She had wanted to strangle the nurse when she realised Oborneo hadn't received the medication, but she saw how the Africans lived and how dire the poverty was here. She wondered why the Africans didn't murder the Asians, Arabs and Europeans in their sleep, for they had all the wealth and the locals had nothing. It was injustice at its worst, and yet the Africans always seemed to have a smile.

She half ran, half walked back to the poor excuse of a hospital. She planned on having a hearty discussion with Dr Singh when she next saw him. Back at the ward, Grace looked around for some water. On a small table in the middle of the room was a glass jug half-full of water, and some glasses. Patrolling up the table leg, up the jug, across the lid and down the other side was an army of ants. Grace shuddered in disgust but forced herself to pick up the jug and a glass. Looking into the jug, she saw a few ants had fallen in and were now floating on the top of the water. She felt her stomach heave and wanted to vomit. She gritted her teeth and took herself, and the offensive jug, off to find somewhere to wash them and get clean water.

She found a door that opened to a small room that had a toilet and a sink, and heaved again as the most offensive smell hit her nose and she quickly shut the door. The young doctor appeared in the corridor behind her.

"The water has been off for two days now, it will probably come back on soon – it is rarely off for longer than two days."

"You don't have any water?"

"There is a water butt on the outside of the building, we fill buckets and flush the toilet with that, but it's empty now, so we wait."

"Oh my giddy aunt, this is dreadful. You're a hospital, you can't operate like this."

"No, we very rarely operate. Most die from illness, so no need to operate."

"Do you have any drinking water?" Grace rolled her eyes and ignored his misinterpretation.

"In the kitchen. The Company sends down some gallon containers at times like this. We keep it for strictly necessary requirements."

"Well this is strictly necessary requirements," Grace mimicked his accent and wobbly head. "Don't you know people die if they don't drink enough in this heat?"

The young man started barking at her in Hindi, waving his hands like crazy to emphasize his outrage at the utter insult she had given him. She didn't understand a word and when it looked like he would never stop she simply stormed off in search of the kitchens on her own.

The building was small and it didn't take long to find them. She tried not to take in the pile of mouldy plates in the sink, or the swarm of flies that circled the pans on the stove. Three large containers sat on one of the tables and she picked up a pan and poured a little water into it. She took the jug and glass outside and attempted to wash them in a tiny amount of water with no soap. Satisfied she had done the best she could and it was at least better than before, she filled the jug from the container and went back to the ward.

"Oborneo," she said softly, wiping his forehead with a small towel that lay on the bottom of the bed. He moaned and tossed his head from side to side.

"Oborneo, you must take this medicine." She slipped one hand under his head and tried lifting it a little, then as carefully as she could she tipped a little of the liquid out of the bottle and into his mouth. He coughed and spluttered, instantly covering her with the penicillin.

"Try to swallow it if you can," she said tipping a little more in his mouth. This time he seemed to swallow before he coughed and she felt sure he had kept it down. She brought the glass to his mouth and poured in a tiny drop of water. His eyes flickered and he looked at her. His lovely brown eyes were bloodshot and sunken to the back of his head. She put the medicine bottle down and sank onto her knees beside the bed.

"Oh, please Lord; in the name of your Son please hear my prayer. Do not forsake this child, please bring him back to full health. I will do whatever you ask of me, if only you would do this one thing."

A young woman, who lay on the bed next to a sick young boy, got up and pointed to the water.

"Of course, help yourself," Grace said. The woman filled a glass and took it back to the boy, who Grace assumed was her son. The other patient was a very old woman, who lay on her back staring blankly at the ceiling. Grace filled another glass and took it to her.

"Water?" she asked the old woman, who didn't respond.

"Maji," the young woman with the son said.

"Maji?" repeated Grace puzzled.

The woman lifted up her glass and pointing to it, repeated, "Maji."

Grace looked down at the old woman and lifted the glass up so she could see it. "Maji?" she said softly.

The old woman blinked and mumbled something. Grace looked at the young woman to see if she'd heard. She nodded at Grace.

Grace lifted the glass to the old woman's lips and gently poured a little in. She did this several times until the old woman raised her hand to indicate she'd had enough. Grace went back to Oborneo's side and started praying again.

She stayed all night, giving him sips of water when she could, and forcing him to take the medicine every few hours. She sat on a hard wooden chair and now and again slept a little by putting her head on the bed.

The sun poured into the windows announcing that it was a little after six am. She was dog-tired and aching, and worse, she had been bitten to bits by mosquitoes, but she had to go to work, she couldn't miss a day when she had been there for such a short time.

It was the longest day of her life and she nearly fell asleep at her desk several times. A co-worker brought her a cup of tea in an effort to revive her spirits a little, but the tea was weak and the milk off with little blobs floating on the top. She tried to drink, knowing that she should to avoid becoming dehydrated, but couldn't manage more than a few sips.

She took herself back to the boarding house, changed her clothes, ate a little cold meat and bread and then returned to the hospital.

The young doctor was checking Oborneo's pulse when she walked in.

"How is he?"

It seemed at first that the doctor was going to ignore her and he filled in some boxes on the boy's chart at the end of his bed.

"I'm very sorry about yesterday. I had no right to say that to you in the way I did. My only excuse is that I was very worried."

He considered her for a moment, and then offered her his hand. "Doctor Chopra, pleased to meet you."

Grace shook his hand. "Grace Clifton."

"Well, Mrs Grace, he is still in danger, did you bring back the medicine."

"It's Miss Clifton, and yes, I brought it back with me."

"Good, you can leave it with me. I will ensure that he receives it, you have my word."

"I think I'll stay if you don't mind? I would like to keep him company anyway."

"As you wish. I will be about the hospital until midnight, after that Nurse Mary will be here, call either of us if you need to."

"Thank you… Dr Chopra."

He smiled, revealing a row of immaculate teeth that seemed remarkably white against his dark skin.

"You're very welcome."

The two other patients were still in the room, the old woman didn't seem to have moved a muscle, but the young mother was sitting by her son and watching Grace intently. Grace smiled at her and she smiled back.

The evening dragged by slowly. Grace gave the medicine to Oborneo at regular intervals and made him sip water as often as she could. She prayed over and over and kept checking on him to see if God had worked His miracle yet. When the nurse arrived and saw Grace she quickly back stepped and left the room.

"Wait," said Grace, who had caught sight of her just before she disappeared. Nurse Mary went into a barrage of angry words and hand waving that involved hitting herself under her chin. Grace wasn't too sure what that was meant to emphasize, but she did understand the woman was defending herself.

"Do you speak English?"

"Yes."

"Then please know that I am not angry at you, in fact I am angry at myself for putting temptation in your way. I obviously won't entrust any more valuables, especially medicine, with you, but I want you to know, it is okay and I don't blame you."

The nurse reverted to Swahili, yelled a few things and walked off.

Grace sighed and went back to Oborneo's bedside.

The mother across the room came over and in halting English began talking. "You have God?"

Grace nodded.

"Your God save my son?"

Grace drew in her breath, what was she to do? She couldn't promise the woman that God would save her son, for in truth she didn't exactly believe that He was working a miracle on Oborneo; it was much more likely the antibiotics keeping him alive. Grace had noticed the woman had no such medicine to give to her son who was unnaturally inert and pale, and although she had tried to avoid looking at him, she did believe he must be close to death.

"You ask God."

Well, I can certainly do that. Grace nodded, although she was filled with irrational fear. What if the boy died and the woman blamed her? Or worse, blamed God? Grace had never seen a miracle in her life, and as much as she believed the Bible was the word of God she also thought it might be rather embellished somewhat in the passing down of the tales, after all, in the beginning these things were simply stories told around camp fires.

She went over to the bed with the mother and picked up the small boy's hand. It was freezing, and she looked up at the mother in alarm for he was already dead.

"You ask," the woman said.

Grace felt pains in her stomach as she looked at the mother and tears rolled down her cheeks. "It is too late," she whispered.

"You ask," the woman repeated.

With a lump in her throat and tears soaking her dress, Grace prayed. She poured out her love of God over the child and half-expected to see a miracle. None came and when her words dried up, she whispered amen.

The woman had been watching her son's face intently, and when nothing changed she began to wail, her body rocking violently as she threw her torso up and down, sobbing for all to hear.

Nurse Mary came running into the room and went straight to the boy; she checked his pulse and then pulled the sheet up over his head. The mother continued her wailing, and Grace was overcome with sorrow and went back to Oborneo's bed where she dropped to the floor and tried to pray. The nurse managed to put her arms around the mother and rocked with her until the sobbing quietened down. When the woman was calmer, the nurse spoke with her and tried to get her to come out of the room. The mother was having none of it, lay on the bed next to her son and cradled him in her arms as the crying resumed.

Grace watched as the nurse Mary stroked the mother's hair and whispered comforting words to her. It struck Grace that the nurse had nothing, no medicine or assistance but she gave of herself, pouring her compassion into the distraught mother.

"Mrs?"

Grace looked down at Oborneo who had opened his eyes.

"Mrs, don't let *me* die."

Grace took his hand and gripped it tightly. "I won't let you die, I promise."

The following day was Sunday, and as Woolworths was closed Grace didn't have to go to work so she stayed in the hospital. She felt beyond sick that God hadn't answered her prayers and given life back to the young boy, and she hung her head in shame as two porters carried his body out. The mother left only after they had taken her son away, not looking at Grace as she went.

Later that day the old woman also died and Grace was beside herself with grief. There was such lack of care here, they didn't have the right to call this place a hospital. Oborneo had been right not wanting to come here, the building was nothing more than a huge coffin.

Anger began to fill her spirit and replace her grief. Mombasa was rich. People were covered in money from tip-to-toe in their designer clothes, driving their American cars. The coffee and mango farms created an incredible amount of wealth into Kenya, why couldn't they share it a little and help take care of the locals? This was, after all, their home that everyone was pillaging.

"Where is Dr Singh?" she snapped at the young doctor when he came in to check Oborneo's leg. "He should be here taking care of his patients."

Dr Chopra unwrapped the dressings and inspected Oborneo's leg without answering her question. "This is good, the infection has almost gone. I can put a cast on his leg now to help keep the bones straight."

When he finished he looked up at Grace, his face full of disdain. "Dr Singh's mother died last week, he has gone to Nairobi to attend her funeral, he will be back in a few days."

The wind left Grace's sails and she collapsed into self-condemnation. "I'm so sorry, I didn't know."

"There seems to be a lot of things you don't know, Miss Clifton," he said as he left the room.

"Mrs Grace?"

Grace turned around and smiled at Oborneo, he looked so much better and she silently thanked God. "Yes?"

"Tell me about your God."

The request took her by surprise. She couldn't understand why he asked her about God, when God had obviously not saved the other two patients and also refrained from healing Oborneo's leg. "Why?"

"Because I want to be like you."

Grace stared at Oborneo, not knowing what to say. He reached up and took hold of her hand.

"Why would you want to be like me?" she said softly.

"Most wazungu are blind and do not see us. But you see us, Mrs Grace, and I see you. I think your God make you see, so I want to see your God."

Chapter 18

Mrs God
December 1953

These had become her favourite moments. Oborneo sat on the ground as she read the Bible whilst sitting on a bench in the park, as the sun began to dip and its intolerable heat subside. It was slow going as he constantly interrupted her and demanded to know what everything meant.

Today was no exception.

"No, no, no," he said shaking his head and wagging his finger at her. "That cannot be right, I think you made that up."

"I would never do that, why do you think I made it up?"

Oborneo was angry. "You tell me God is loving and just, He would never be cruel for no reason so why would He not look with favour on Cain? Cain brought to him a gift from his work so why didn't He be happy about it? I'd be happy if my son gave me a gift, it wouldn't matter if it were meat or grain, it would still be a gift."

Grace wondered at the simplistic belief that resonated from Oborneo. "It tells us in another book of the Bible that as a man thinks in his heart, then so he is. You see, God, who sees all things and knows all things, knew that Cain held wicked thoughts in his heart towards his brother, so God knew what he planned, and therefore rejected his offering."

"Maybe if He hadn't rejected the offering, Cain wouldn't have killed his brother?"

"He intended to kill Abel, whether God accepted it or not, God could see that."

"God has very big eyes."

Grace giggled. "He does indeed."

"So God hears all my thoughts in here?" he tapped his head.

"He does."

"If He knows all things and see all things then He must be really bored."

Grace laughed and closed her Bible. "I think we've had enough for today."

"Do you think God minds that I steal?"

"Yes, I think He minds very much."

"But if I don't steal, I go hungry, then I go thin, then I go ill, then I go die on you Mrs Grace, what you going to do then?" He flung his arms wide to emphasize the question.

"I would pray that God would forgive your sins and allow you to go to Heaven."

Oborneo appeared shocked. "You no be sad, I go?"

"Yes, actually, I would be very sad if you were gone, although I might be a little relieved that I didn't have to put up with your constant questioning."

"What shall I do if not steal?"

"Why don't you have a chat with God about it and see what He suggests."

Oborneo grinned. "This is excellent idea, you very clever woman."

Grace's shoulders shook a little as she tried hard not to laugh. In the past few months this dirty, cheeky street urchin had wormed his way into her affections and she had to admit she loved him, in a way she could only imagine a mother would love her child.

"Be good," she called over her shoulder as she set off for home.

"I'm always good, Mrs Grace," he called as he sauntered off.

"Dear Lord, please bless him and keep him safe this evening. Please don't let him get up to mischief."

Chatty Grace was back and God's ears were very aware of it as she talked to him all day long, and sometimes long into the night, kneeling by her bed and beseeching Him for help for the people of Mombasa.

"Jambo," she said to Mrs Kumah, who was washing down the steps outside her house.

"Habari," the woman returned, smiling up at Grace.

"Hellooo," Grace called out as she entered the lodgings.

"Hi, Grace," answered Mrs Brinley from the kitchen.

Grace went running up the stairs, once hated she now acknowledged that they helped to keep her fit as she climbed them up to her room in the attic. When one of the other tenants left, the landlady offered Grace his room on the first floor. Although it was considerably cooler than her room, Grace had declined for she loved the view from her attic window.

She leaned on the windowsill now, looking out at the ocean with peace in her heart. She couldn't believe she had been here for six months, nor could she believe that she had actually got accustomed to the heat. It only struck her a few days ago when she spotted tourists mopping their perspiring foreheads that she wasn't bothered by it so much anymore. The other thing that had dawned on her was that she was no longer gripped by arthritic pain, something to thank the heat for, she was sure.

As the evening breeze blowing from the ocean floated into her room, she relaxed under its gentle touch and instantly started thanking God for bringing her here. She had this week paid the company back for her ticket to Kenya and was now free to start saving for her return journey. She wasn't in a hurry to leave but she wanted to make sure she could always go home if she wanted to. Oborneo had become her priority, and she was trying her hardest to find him a job. She would never be able to leave knowing he still slept rough and had no one to look out for him. She gave him food every day, but she wouldn't be happy until she could get him off the streets and find a place for him to sleep.

Oborneo, unfortunately, was only one of a countless number of street urchins who constantly shoved their hands in front of her demanding money. She gave whenever she could, but her purse was nearly always empty, as her wages really didn't do more than repay her loan, pay her rent and buy a bit of food. She would have a little more now that the loan was repaid but she needed to be prudent and ensure she saved up for her passage home.

*****

As she came out of Woolworths after a long shift, she came face to face with a distressed Oborneo.

"What's the matter?" she asked, and her heart flew straight to her mouth with instant worry as Oborneo looked dreadful.

"Come. You come." Oborneo grabbed Grace's hand and started dragging her across the road.

She pulled against him, refusing to go anywhere until she knew what was going on. "Oborneo, tell me what's happened."

Oborneo looked at her, his big brown eyes swimming in water and Grace felt sick. "You come, Mrs Grace. You tell God to fix Wokabi."

"What is a wokabi?"

"Wokabi, is my friend. You come quick, they take her to the death building."

They raced through the streets of Mombasa until they came to Kisauri Road. Here Oborneo slowed, and Grace felt his hand

220

trembling in hers. As they reached the sign for the Native Civic Hospital, Oborneo let go of her hand, and giving her a frightened look he said, "You go, you bring her back out, like you did me."

"You want me to go on my own?"

Oborneo nodded.

"I can't do that, I still only speak a little Swahili, you must come with me so that I know who I am looking for."

He gulped, but nodded and started walking towards the door.

As during her previous visits, the hospital was fairly empty and they had walked down the hall to the main wards before nurse Mary appeared.

She barked at them in Swahili, clearly unhappy to see the English woman again.

Oborneo spoke to her and whatever he said made her demeanour soften and she stroked his head, speaking quietly to him.

When the nurse went rushing off down the hall, Oborneo gave Grace a look full of fear, and then he entered the ward. He cast his eyes around the room, all eight beds now occupied. When he spotted his friend he ran to her bed crying.

"You tell God, make her well," he demanded, with his teeth clenched.

Grace looked at the young girl lying in the bed and gasped, she had obviously taken a vigorous beating. Her face was swollen like a balloon and full of cuts and bruises.

"Who has done this?" Grace asked reaching for the young girl's hand.

Oborneo started rambling in Swahili and Grace put her hand up to stop him.

"In English, please."

"Tribe lords."

"Tribe lords, really? Why would they beat up a young girl to the point of death?"

Oborneo looked at Grace with sadness. "She is Maasai." Grace looked puzzled. "She came to Mombasa with mother two years ago. Mother dead now. Wokabi like me. No family, no home. She steal from wrong stall, the tribes men give her bad punishment because she not Taifa."

Grace wasn't sure what Taifa was, but she could guess that it was one of the tribes that still ferociously fought to keep their heritage alive. She came out of her thoughts to see tears streaming down Oborneo's face.

"We'll look after her, she'll be all right." Grace sank to her knees and started praying. After a moment or two she became aware that Oborneo had knelt down beside her and clasped his hands together in imitation of her. The truth of his tender faith produced tears falling down her cheeks.

Oh Father God, please answer his prayers.

March 1954

"What do you want me to do?" Grace yelled at the heavens. She had gone to every pharmacy on the island, and no one would give her the penicillin she needed. She had visited Mr Lakviar last, having already stretched his good will to the limit, but when no one else would help her she returned to him to plead. He remained polite but unmoving, and now she had to return to the hospital empty handed. She was out of money and she was out of options.

In a way, she felt like she was becoming a leper as more and more people pretended they didn't see her or rudely ignored her when she approached them. She knew she'd become obsessed with helping everyone who came to the Native Civic, but it had
222

taken over her life and she could no more stop it than she could stop a tidal wave. She had lost all her pride as she begged everyone, even total strangers, to give her money.

The wazungus turned their noses up at her uncommon mannerisms and the Africans thought her crazy. As for the Arabs, well dear me, they weren't known for handing out coin to mad English women. Even Mrs Brinley started avoiding her, and Grace felt as if she was falling apart. Going to work was getting harder and harder and her manager had given her two warnings for not coming in. One more and she would be out of a job, a home too, for although Mrs Brinley was a compassionate woman she also needed to pay her bills.

Grace pushed her hand in her pocket and brought out a couple of coins, not enough for medicine but enough to buy her a loaf of bread. Her stomach growled loudly, acknowledging the fact that she hadn't eaten in twenty-four hours. She made her way along Nkrumah Road and headed for the only bakery on the island that produced bread similar to home, quickening her pace as she weaved her way through narrow alleys since it was late in the afternoon and the baker would be closing soon.

As she opened the door the bell tinkled announcing her arrival, and she looked in dismay at all the empty shelves.

"Have you nothing left?" Grace asked a young Asian man who came to see who had come in.

He reached under the counter. "Last loaf just for you, Grace."

Grace couldn't help sighing in relief and handed over two of her three last coins until pay day. She was so hungry she almost sat down on the pavement to eat some bread but changed her mind. She had a little jam left in her room; she would wait until she got home.

As she made her way back to Nkrumah Road, she wondered if she was going crazy. She'd never heard God tell her to give every penny she had to the patients at the hospital, but that's what she'd been doing. If she needed to go home now, she wouldn't be able to with no money saved for her passage.

She stopped outside Keswick Book-shop and stared longingly at the Bible covers in the window. The only Bible she had was her mum's, now very old and worn, and also her prized possession. She longed for one of the Bible covers to keep it in, to hold off the insidious damp air that rotted everything. However, the price range was well over her pay packet. She sighed and started for home once more.

As she was approaching the Holy Ghost Cathedral she could hear someone crying.

He's hungry.

"Oh no," Grace spluttered, answering the voice in her head. "I've only got one loaf." She carried on walking, deliberately keeping her eyes straight ahead of her, but looking ahead didn't block out the sound of his pitiful sobs.

He's hungry.

"No, no, no. I can't God, I can't give up the bread. Please, they only had one left."

She carried on walking, although she had slowed down. The crying seemed to get louder and pierced her ears with its feeble, forlorn wail. She turned, waited for a space to open up in the traffic, and crossed the road.

I'll just give him the coin I have left, he'll be able to buy himself some ugali.

He's hungry.

Filled with irrational anger that God should make her give away her loaf of bread when she was hungry herself, Grace approached the boy in an irritated stomp. It wasn't that she was uncaring of his situation, or that she had become accustomed to the constant begging that besieged the island every day. It was just that she was tired, and deflated God hadn't come to her rescue and miraculously persuaded one of the chemists to give her the medicine needed for a young mother who was dying. The faith, that had been lost and found, was waning and she was running out of strength.

She looked at the tiny boy, maybe about two years old – it was hard to tell because he was so undernourished, and her heart went out to him. Sitting next to him was an old woman whose head was bowed and whose hands lay limply in her lap. She looked like she had no hope, and to Grace reflected the state of all paupers on Mombasa island.

Don't forget to tell her who's giving her the bread.

"God loves you," Grace said as she placed the bread in the boy's lap.

The woman's head shot upwards and she smiled at Grace.

Like a blast from heaven, Grace was pierced with joy. It exploded inside her like a feeling she had never experienced before. It rushed through her and filled her from her toes to her head. The woman's face was weather worn, lined and patchy. Most of her teeth were missing and the few she had were black. But it was her eyes that held onto Grace's soul. Crystal clear and blue! They sparkled with joy and Grace reeled up and turned around, giddy and drunk in happiness.

She didn't remember getting home, the next thing she knew was she was lying on her bed and pouring her heart out to God.

The next day she was dying to share her experience with someone and the only person she believed who would understand what had happened was Bernice, an American missionary who lived in Nyali.

She jumped on a matatu to Nyali, and then walked quite a bit out into the bush, an area very much only for the locals. Bernice lived in a small two roomed brick building that boasted running water and not much else. Grace knocked on the door, excitement filling her and she couldn't wait to share her experience with the godliest women she knew.

As she heard footsteps approaching the door, that voice returned in her head. *Don't say anything.* She was instantly disappointed, bursting to share this joy with someone.

A tall, black beauty opened the door and smiled warmly when she saw Grace. "Come in, it's so lovely to see you again."

Bernice fetched two glasses of homemade lemonade and they sat in the room together, both uncomfortably aware that a weird atmosphere hung between them.

After a short time, Bernice jumped up. "All right then, all right." Then she went stomping off into her bedroom. She came back and most ungraciously dropped a bag onto Grace's lap. "God wants you to have this," she declared sitting back down.

Bemused and interested at the same time, Grace slowly opened the bag. When she pulled out the contents she started squealing. "I don't believe it, I don't believe it."

Grace poured out how she had been longing for a Bible cover for the last year to help protect her mother's Bible which was beginning to fall apart, and then she went on to tell her about the loaf of bread. By the time she had finished the two of them were crying.

"I have a leather Bible cover, but I am in need of a new one and it has taken my church six months to finally answer my request and send this to me, it only arrived yesterday. But, the moment you walked in the room God told me to give it to you. I thought He must have made a mistake and had been arguing with Him the whole time we were sitting here. He just kept repeating, give Grace the cover, and in the end, I gave up. Oh, but I'm so glad I listened to Him now."

"God is so good," said Grace.

"He certainly is, and what's more, you can't out-give Him."

*****

The Bible lesson was over, and Oborneo and Wokabi were walking Grace home.

"Where's your husband?" Wokabi asked.

"I've never been married." Grace subconsciously started rubbing her engagement ring.

"Why not?" demanded Oborneo.

"The man I loved died during the war."

"That's sad," said Wokabi taking hold of Oborneo's hand.

"I'll find you another man," declared Oborneo smiling.

"Oh no, it's fine. I don't need a husband, I am perfectly happy."

"Really?" said Wokabi, with a look that said 'you're mad'.

"Mr Ysanki, his wife died. He be very happy marry you," said Oborneo.

Grace nearly fell over. "He's about eighty and can hardly walk."

"This make good marriage, you can look after him and he give you house," said Oborneo in complete seriousness.

"No thank you, I definitely don't need to be married."

"But you lonely," said Wokabi.

"How can I be lonely when God is always with me?"

"You like Him always be with you?" Wokabi asked sceptically.

"Yes, I do."

227

"It's like you're married to Him," laughed Oborneo.

"I guess in a way, I am."

"So you Mrs-God," said Oborneo.

"Well, no, not exactly."

"But you love God, you're always saying that," said Wokabi.

"Yes, I do."

"Then you be Mrs-God. Night Mrs-God," said Oborneo as he and Wokabi took off down the street.

Grace watched them until they turned the corner. *Please bless them and take care of them, Father.*

September 1954

Rarely did Grace feel afraid, but tonight as she walked the narrow streets home she was overcome with apprehension. Talk that the Mau Mau gangs were getting more desperate, and therefore more threatening, had been on the risc for days now. Today the people whispered their fears and rushed from place to place. The usual laid-back approach was missing, even from the old men who normally did nothing more than spit on the floor whilst playing stones. She shouldn't have left it so late to leave the hospital, or she should have stayed there as the night nurse had begged her.

She remembered her father's lectures on her independent stubborn streak and regretted not listening to him more.

Gunshot cracked the air and Grace automatically ducked her head and ran to press herself against the wall of the nearest house. She'd been ignoring a commotion for a while, pretending it wasn't getting closer as she raced for home, but now there was no denying it.

Sweat trickled down her back and her chest rose and fell at an alarming speed. She took a deep breath, trying to calm

228

herself down. Another gunshot filled the air, much closer than the last and although she knew she should be running, Grace was frozen against the wall.

Suddenly, a young girl appeared in the street in front of Grace. She was skinny and dirty, in ripped shorts and a hole-splattered t-shirt. Her arm whipped out and she pointed down a small alley off the street.

"Run!" the girl said in perfect English.

Like a bolt of lightning, Grace went sprinting down the alley. She didn't stop to see where the girl had gone, imagining she had returned to her hiding place where she had been before she stepped out to urge Grace on.

A loud crash echoed through the streets, immediately followed by screaming, and then she could hear people smashing windows. There was yelling and then another gunshot followed by laughter. Grace stopped; she was lost and didn't know where to go. She swung around on the spot trying to decide what to do.

"Grace." It was a hushed whisper, but she heard it and spun around. Hanging out of a door was a young Asian man who had a stall on the market. He beckoned to her, his face revealing his distress. She ran to him and he yanked her inside, shutting the door just as Mau Mau members came flooding down the alley. He put his finger to his lips and then took hold of her hand and led her to a back room.

His young family were huddled on the floor together. His wife held out her hand and both Grace and the man flopped on the floor beside them. Grace started praying, as did the young Muslim family. The Mau Mau weren't known for entering houses, only causing havoc in the streets as they swarmed through looking for food and ammunition, but it didn't stop Grace and the family being terrified, nor did it stop them praying long after the noise had faded away. Grace sunk her head into her hands as relief washed over her. She never purchased the newspaper, nor listened to the radio, but people seemed to delight in telling her when another white person met their end at the hands of the Mau Mau warriors. If they had found her, she would be dead now. She was sure.

When they were convinced it was all over the family showed Grace to the front door. She had said thank you a hundred times and still didn't feel it was enough. When she hugged them, they hugged her back with just as much warmth that they would give to their dearest loved ones.

10th February 1955

"Grace have you heard the news?"

Grace looked up at Dr Chopra and shook her head. "No, what's happened?"

"The Mau Mau have been offered surrender terms, praise to Brahma, we will all be able to sleep well again now."

Grace put down her pen. "Have they been given their land back in the terms?"

"Nothing like that has been mentioned yet, but I am sure something must have been agreed upon because they would never give up otherwise."

"Let's hope so, otherwise the last few years of bloodshed will have been for nothing."

"Have you heard the news?" asked Dr Singh coming into the room at speed.

"Yes, I've just heard. Do you think they will get their land back?"

"The Kisii Tribe won't settle for less, something must have been agreed I think," answered Dr Singh.

"Do you suppose they will release Kenyatta now?" asked Dr Chopra.

"Not until it is definitely over," responded Dr Singh.

"Then let's pray that this is the beginning of the end," said Grace.

Chapter 19

Fort Hall & a Holiday
1955

Grace sold her mother's pearl earrings to buy a return ticket to Nairobi. She had enough for one night in a cheap hotel and nothing more – she knew she had been swindled, but she had no choice. It was vital that she got to meet the Archbishop of Canterbury whilst he was in Nairobi. If she could persuade him to get the church to back the Civic Hospital, they would surely have funds to start treating the patients properly.

She decided to leave her bags in the holding room at the station and go in search of the Archbishop before finding lodgings for the night. After asking numerous people if they knew where the Archbishop was and receiving no answer, she was beginning to despair. She spotted a young policeman, standing smartly in his blue jersey and white shorts, his uniform topped off with his brown helmet – if anyone knew, it would surely be a policeman?

She didn't know whether to be excited or irritated when the policeman informed her that the Archbishop of Canterbury had left Nairobi and was on his way to give a speech at Fort Hall. Glad that she hadn't booked a hotel first, she waved down a taxi and spent the last of her money on chasing after the man of God.

Five thousand people had turned up for the Archbishop's speech and the enormity of her task in reaching him overwhelmed her. She knew he was going to Uganda after the speech so it was now or never. She started making her way through the crowds, praying all the way for the protection of God to surround her.

These Kenyans didn't look the same as the Africans she'd got used to in Mombasa. In Mombasa they always had a smile and generally seemed good-natured. Here, well this was something else. She felt their hostility towards her like a thousand stabs in the back, but she had a job to do and she mustn't fail. For surely the Archbishop would help them get supplies for the hospital, if only he knew about them? She couldn't get through the crowd, though. She knew they were deliberately blocking her, their elbows constantly jabbing her. Several spat at her feet and she started praying in earnest.

The loud-speaker was turned on and the Archbishop was announced, and she gave up. Slowly, she started edging her way out of the hostile crowd.

"I address you as friends; whether you are my friends or not, only God can tell." A hush fell over the crowd, for this man of God from England in his pompous attire was here to memorialize Kikuyu Loyalists who died during the Mau Mau uprising.

What was I thinking, God? Have I truly become the Crazy Woman of Mombasa? She knew what the colonials called her when they thought she couldn't hear. She was past caring about what people thought; she knew God had brought her here to help the people of Mombasa. *But coming to Nairobi? Chasing after an Archbishop with his army entourage? Idiot, sometimes I'm an idiot.*

Of course the taxi's gone! Now what? She skirted around the crowds, trying her best to stay unobserved. Maybe a policeman would give her a lift back to Nairobi? *Of course they don't want to give me a lift. Is this my punishment, God, for being reckless, to have to walk back?*

The short speech was over and the Archbishop was ushered away quickly. *What? Not staying to mingle with your congregation, shake their hands and offer them genuine thanks? Sorry, Lord, sorry. It's just I think it's going to be a long walk back.*

Before long, the road or rather, the heavily compacted dirt track, was full of people. If her feet hadn't already begun to throb she might have been more afraid. She was used to walking and fit, but still it took her over two-and-a-half hours to walk to Maragua. Matatus had gone by now and again, but although she'd waved like crazy none had stopped for her. Maybe she'd get lucky and find a taxi in Maragua?

As with every other day in Kenya, when the sun set it was at the same time and happened very quickly. One minute there was light and the next, darkness. With the dropping of the sun also came the cold, and Grace was now beyond reprimanding herself and starting to get extremely worried.

She walked everywhere at night in Mombasa, despite endless warnings, she believed beyond a doubt that God was with her wherever she went. But this? This was her own fault and she wondered if God might turn a blind eye to teach her a lesson. As she approached the streets of the small town the hairs on her neck and arms stood up and her mouth went dry. *I'm an idiot.*

She waved as a car came up behind her, but it didn't stop and carried on. She was walking slowly now as her heart thumped wildly. *Show me what to do, Father-God.*

There was a commotion, yells and a gunshot. Grace froze. Shapes ran towards her and she squeezed her shoulders inwards as if to make herself so thin that they would run around her without noticing her. The first few did. Then the tallest man Grace had ever seen came to a stop right in front of her. He yelled for the others to stop and see what was on the road. A crazy, white woman, ready for killing. Grace started praying the Lord's Prayer.

She understood a good amount of Swahili now and could converse with most Africans, but their conversation went over her head and she couldn't decipher it. Someone jabbed her in the shoulder with the butt of his rifle and fired questions at her. She knew she should answer him, but fear had run away with her tongue. A short man with a pox-filled face came and started yelling at her, and she began to shake.

Then someone else was speaking in a more hushed voice, quietly telling the short man in front of her something she couldn't hear, well almost couldn't hear, she caught the sound of two words – "Mrs God." She looked at him in shock, had he called her that? She peered through the darkness to see if she recognised him, but no, he definitely wasn't someone she knew.

"Where you from?" demanded the man.

Without hesitation. "Mombasa."

More whispering continued, then the pox faced man asked another question.

"Where you work?"

Without hesitation again, and without stopping to consider it wasn't the full truth she answered, "Native Civic Hospital."

More whispering, then a pause as the men observed her.

"You lucky, he know you, Mrs-God. Now go home." Without another word the gang sprinted past her down the road. When she couldn't hear them any more she breathed in deeply and nearly fainted.

Just then, Grace heard a vehicle approaching and spun around to see car headlights. She wasn't going to let this car pass her by. She stood in the middle of the road, legs apart, flapping her arms over her head as the car came to a screeching halt.

A Kenyan got out of the car and started yelling at her and waving his arms like mad to indicate she should move off the road.

"I need a lift to Nairobi, please."

The back door of the car opened and a white man got out.

"Are you English?" asked a very American drawl. Only then, did she realise that after hours of walking along the road she was concealed in dust, from head to foot.

"Yes, I am," she said in total relief, "could you give me a lift, please?"

"Of course, but I must say you will have to explain what on earth you are doing out here in the middle of nowhere."

"With pleasure."

He held the door open for her and Grace climbed into the back seat as he walked around the car and got in on the other side. Only with the bang of the door and the realisation that she was safe did Grace give in to tears and the shakes.

"Here, dear girl," said the man, handing her a white cloth. When she finally got herself back under control he said, "Robert Anderson, at your service." He held out his hand.

"Grace Clifton, pleased to meet you."

"So let's have your story little English lady, I'm very intrigued."

By the time the car reached Nairobi city centre, Robert had persuaded Grace to stay at the same hotel as him, absolutely insisting that it was his treat, she deserved it after her ordeal. They stopped at the station so she could fetch her bag and then pulled up outside what must have been the grandest building in Kenya.

"You're staying here?"

"We're staying here. Come along little Miss," he offered Grace his elbow, "let's get you checked in so you can wash that dirt off your face and I can see who it really is that I rescued on the road."

An hour later, after a soak in the bath and a change of clothes, Grace still felt like a pauper and was uncomfortable being totally surrounded by toffs, all of whom she was convinced were looking down their noses at her.

"Two gin and tonics, no ice," Robert ordered whilst helping Grace up onto a bar stool.

"Oh, just water for me, please."

"Rubbish, gal. You need fortifying after your run in with the Mau Mau."

"They might not have been Mau Mau."

"Of course they were, who else would be shooting guns and running around in gangs. Goodness, Grace, you could have been killed." Robert knocked back his drink and ordered another. "Do you know how many white people they've killed over the last few years? Too many, let me tell you."

"Do you know how many Africans the British have slaughtered over the last few years?"

"Goodness gracious, gal." Robert threw up his hands as if to surrender. "Don't shoot the guy who saved your ass!"

Grace laughed at his theatrics. "Actually, I think it was my feet you saved."

Robert put his hands down and looked at her feet. "Well they be mighty fine lookin' feet, and let me tell you I've seen some damn-awful looking feet in my time. Some feet do turn me green I feel so sick. So I'm happy to have saved yours. Now drink your gin, there's quinine in that there tonic, do you the world of good."

What was she to do? After all, he had rescued her, maybe not from death but definitely from an eight-hour walk. She took a drink. Three seconds later, she was coughing and spluttering all over the place.

"That's the most disgusting thing I've ever tasted."

"Two more please." Robert waved at the barman. "By the time you've finished your third you'll think it's the best thing in the world."

They were both still laughing when someone approached them.

"Grace?"

Grace turned around in her seat to look up at a fair-haired, blue-eyed stunner. "Christopher!" She jumped out of her seat and hugged him like he was a long lost friend. After a moment, the realisation that she was hugging someone she had merely had a few conversations with dawned on her and she pulled herself back sharply. "How are you? What are you doing in Nairobi? I thought you were working at the Aga Khan in Mombasa. Is your fiancée here? Oh my, I'm being so rude, let me introduce you. Christopher, this is Robert from San Diego, Robert, this is Christopher from London."

Christopher and Robert shook hands.

"Soo pleased to meet you, won't you join us?" Robert asked.

Christopher gave Grace an enquiring look.

"Oh yes, do join us."

Christopher pulled up a bar stool and sat down. "To answer your questions, I'm well, I work in Nairobi and my fiancée has decided to wait for me in England, the climate here didn't suit her. Does that answer all your questions?"

Grace went red. "I went to the Aga Khan to see you and they told me at the door that you weren't there. I thought they were lying and that you didn't want to see me."

"Why on earth wouldn't I want to see you?"

"I just assumed you had heard of my begging and you were staying out of the way."

"Begging?"

"It's a long story. Here, do you like gin and tonic? You can have mine, dreadful stuff."

Christopher took the glass. "Don't mind if I do, it's exactly what brought me in here tonight. Cheers."

"Cheers, darlin'," said Robert clinking their glasses together. "I do sooo love a gin drinker." His merry, drank too much, slur made them all laugh. "Bartender, three more drinks, please."

No amount of declining would persuade the jolly American that she didn't like gin, and in the end Grace found herself giving in and drinking.

During the evening, they found out that Robert's family were into fishing, especially canning fish, and that in his words, he was simply, totally and completely filthy rich. He recounted story after story where he'd got into trouble growing up and the three of them literally howled with laughter at his over-the-top descriptions of everything. He simply was larger than life, and became more so with each gin and tonic.

Not a hundred percent sure how it happened, both Grace and Christopher found themselves agreeing to go on a mini safari with Robert the next day. His planned travelling companions, against all Robert's warnings, had ice in their drinks the day before and both of them were paying the price now and unable to leave their rooms. Not wanting to go on a jolly-drive on his own, it made perfect sense that three near-strangers should spend the weekend together.

The next morning, after a small breakfast, Grace found herself sitting in the lobby wondering why on earth she'd agreed to go. She wouldn't be able to get back to work until Tuesday and they were expecting her on Monday. She had no appropriate clothes with her and no money left. She chewed her bottom lip and tried to sort out the shambles of her feelings. This was proving to be very difficult due to her throbbing headache, which had only been slightly alleviated by eating. She was drawn to Christopher in the same way she had been attracted to Milton, and that rather shocked her as he was engaged. She had just concluded that going on this safari was a dreadful idea and was standing up to make a bolt for the railway station, when Robert came striding towards her.

"Good morning, fair lady. How's that head of yours this morning?"

Grace groaned. "If I ask you to whisper does that answer your question?"

Robert laughed and flopped onto a chair next to her. "Have you seen Chris this morning? The Jeep is out front and we should get going soon."

"Umm, well, about that. I've realised that I need to be at work on Monday so I'm afraid I can't come with you. I was just waiting to say goodbye and thank you for everything."

"Stuff and nonsense, of course you're coming, it wouldn't be the same without you. Two men going off on their own, well it would simply *ruin* Chris's reputation. You wouldn't do that to him, would you?"

Grace chuckled. "Oh, I hadn't thought of it like that."

"That's settled then. I'll not hear of you pulling out, I've never met a woman so in need of a holiday in my life. This will do you the world of good; strengthen you up for your return to Mombasa."

Grace looked at Robert and was overcome with thankfulness for his generous nature.

"You're not going to cry, are you? I can't abide crying women, blubbering wrecks. I don't understand why they would want their faces to become contorted, swollen and blotchy. It is the most unbecoming thing in the whole world." He gave an exaggerated shiver.

Grace laughed, she couldn't help herself, Robert's flamboyant mannerisms were so cheering. "You must have got up very early this morning, to be packed and ready to go already."

"Yes, well, I had a little business to attend to."

"What was that?"

"If I tell you I might have to kill you," Robert said raising one eyebrow at her frank inquisitiveness.

"Oh, I'm sorry. I didn't mean to be rude."

Robert patted her knee. "Just messing with you. I did get up very early despite the gin and tonic drums that were beating in my head. I wanted to take some pictures, you see, before everyone was up and about."

Grace clasped her hands together in her lap, determined not to blurt out more questions.

Robert grinned at her. "I've been to the concentration camps."

"You have?" Grace was shocked. "Why?"

"I do a little reporting as a hobby. Yesterday morning, when I heard the Archbishop of Canterbury was going to Fort Hall to honour the memories of the Kikuyu loyalists who died in the Civil War, I thought, this is something I have to see. You know about five thousand people turned out to listen to him? Anyway, I stayed to watch him bless the cornerstone of the forthcoming

Anglican Church and then I was about to leave when I overheard some British soldiers talking."

Just then a rather white-looking Christopher turned up carrying a suitcase.

"Morning," he said without much enthusiasm and sat down in a wicker chair opposite them.

"You look worse than I feel," said Grace with a smile.

"Thanks! Do we think this safari is a good idea? Maybe we should just stay here?"

"Good grief, what is it with you English people? Stiff upper lip and all that means you should be ready to face anything today, right?"

"Not really," said Christopher.

Grace giggled.

"Well I'd certainly like it if you came, the pair of you, but I'll not force you to come with me. Jeez, I didn't know I was such bad company."

"Oh but you're not. You are perfectly delightful company, honestly."

"I agree with Grace, I had a marvellous time last night. Not laughed so much in years."

"Then you'll come?"

"Yes."

"Yes, I'd love to," said Grace putting her hand on Robert's arm to reinforce her statement.

"Right, we should be off then," said Robert, starting to stand.

"Please finish telling me about your early morning escapade first," said Grace. "What did you overhear?"

Robert settled back down. "That prisoners from the nearby detention camps would be doing the building." Robert peered at Grace waiting for her to understand what he was saying.

As the meaning dawned on her, Grace's mouth dropped open in shock. "No."

"Yes. Slave labour to build a church, and for a country that declared to the world that there should be no slavery in 1833. You'd think then, that by 1955 this just wouldn't be possible, wouldn't you?"

"I'm sure there has been a misunderstanding somewhere, we'd never use slave labour, especially to build a church. The Church of England would never sanction such a thing." Christopher was now sitting up fully straight, headache forgotten.

Robert fished in his pocket and pulled out a photograph that he passed to Christopher. "The men in this camp will be used to start work on it tomorrow." He handed the black and white picture over.

"Let me see," said Grace holding out her hand for the photograph. Chris passed it to her. Grace instantly filled up with emotion. "What can we do?"

"Nothing," said Christopher, clearly upset.

"We must be able to do something? Maybe we should write to the government?"

"They won't listen to us, Grace."

"The Washington Post wants the story. I've already wired them the main gist of things. I'll finish it off when I get home."

There was silence as the horror of the last three years of the Mau Mau Uprising encompassed them. The Mau Mau had killed a number of white families and been ruthless in their attacks; however, the British soldiers were killing thousands of Kenyans in retribution. It was, without question, shocking and unjust, and using prisoners to build a church just incomprehensible.

"Do you think it's safe to go on safari?" Grace asked.

"I have hired two outriders who will be carrying rifles when we do the safaris. I don't think anyone would risk attacking us." Robert looked at their solemn faces. "Come on, let's live a little dangerously. If Miss English, here, can take herself off walking the roads at night on her own, then I'm sure we'll be fine with an escort."

*****

The Sun was high in the sky as they drove through the gates of Tsavo Game Park. They were all excited, for all of them this was their first safari and they were full of joy as they scanned the horizon looking for animals. The Jeep's suspension bounced them over ruts and potholes and often lifted them right off their seats.

"I'll demand a refund if you break the bones in my posterior!" Robert warned the driver. The driver turned in his seat, his smile broad as he nodded, then turned back to look at the dirt track.

"Maybe he could drive a little slower?" said Grace, her head bobbing up and down.

Robert tapped the driver on his shoulder. "Slower. Drive slower."

Once more the driver grinned at them, nodded and carried on as before.

"Polepole," yelled Christopher. Instantly, the driver took his foot off the pedal slightly and slowed down.

"Oh, thank Heavens," said Grace as she finally stopped bouncing up and down. "I think I'm going to be black and blue by the time we get to the lodge."

"You and me both, darlin'," said Robert. "No idea at all, why I thought it would be fun to travel here in a Jeep."

Vast red-earthed plains stretched before them. Clusters of Baobab and Doum trees, patchy runs of grasses and thorny bushes broke up the redness, whilst the rolling hills in the distance formed a perfect backdrop. It was breath taking, and for a long time the passengers didn't talk as they drank in the beauty of the park.

They arrived at the lodge tired and thirsty and in need of a shower, so agreed to retire for a siesta and meet again at four, before setting off across the plains for a sun-downer at one of the watering holes.

Just as Grace was about to be led off by a receptionist, Robert called to her.

He tossed her a bag. "My travelling companion, Maisy, who couldn't join me on the safari, gave me these for you as she wouldn't be needing them. They'll be too big for you, but maybe you could use a belt or something. Anyway, hope they come in useful. It's a colour the flies aren't attracted to, apparently."

"Thank you," said Grace peeping inside the bag to see some beige coloured clothes.

Grace woke after a two-hour sleep feeling like a different person. The headache was gone and so were the drive-induced aches. She showered and felt like a princess as she wrapped the huge, soft towel around herself. Her thatched, round room had windows overlooking a small watering hole, and Grace watched as Elands gathered round to drink.

It was a peaceful, quiet environment and it was hard to believe this was part of the same country that homed the bustling, angry streets of Nairobi, and the smelly, poverty filled streets of Mombasa.

The clothes were too big for her, but as she didn't have anything appropriate to wear so she put them on. Luckily, she could weave her belt through the top of the trousers and pull it in tight to hold them up, and she tucked the massive shirt into the trousers. She pulled on a floppy, cotton hat and went to the mirror. She couldn't help chuckling when she looked at herself as she looked a bit like a stuffed scarecrow from the farms back home. She felt bad that Maisy was stuck in the hotel in Nairobi, but also glad to borrow her clothes.

Thinking of home led to a wave of homesickness and she sat on the bed fighting to hold back the tears. She played with William's ring, which hung around her neck on the silver chain that Mrs Reynolds had given her, wishing for the umpteenth time that it were a ring from Milton. *What am I doing here, Lord?*

Just then, there was a gentle knock on the door.

"Grace, are you ready? We're all set to go."

"Just coming, Chris." Grace gave the mirror a quick check to make sure her face was all right and then opened the door with a smile. "Let the evening adventure begin."

Christopher offered Grace his arm and the two of them hastened outside, where Robert was talking to the Lodge Manager.

"You're here, great. My good man here, tells me that we should see plenty of game tonight as they're in a bit of a drought season and everything makes its way to the watering hole." Robert climbed onto the lodge's open-sided Land Rover next to the driver, careful not to knock his huge Leica camera.

Christopher helped Grace up as two mlinzi climbed on the back with their rifles across their backs.

"Onwards and upwards," Robert declared thrusting his arm up and pointing ahead.

It took them well over an hour to reach the watering hole, and all along the way they had been vigilant, searching for game, but they were disappointed when all they saw were Eland and Warthogs.

The Land Rover came to a stop on what felt like a huge flat stone jutting out at the top of a hill. As they climbed off the Land Rover, Robert instantly raised his camera and started taking shots. As they looked at the valley below they could see a watering hole that appeared to be nothing much more than a pool in a hollowed out basin.

"Well, this is unimpressive," declared Robert. "They'd better have brought us gin for our sun-downer or I'm going to be totally peeved off."

The two mlinzi helped the driver empty the back of the Land Rover and in no time at all a table and three chairs had been set up on the ledge, complete with white tablecloth, crystal glasses and bone china plates.

"Champagne?" asked the driver, showing Robert a bottle.

"Things are looking up. Yes, my good man, please pour away."

A delicious feast was spread on the table beside them, and they were delightedly impressed to be receiving such wonderful food in the middle of nowhere. When the second bottle of champagne was empty, Robert demanded gin and tonics all round. When they confirmed that they only had champagne, he became most put out.

"Really, it's not good enough. Don't you have gin and tonic at the lodge?"

"Yes, bwana, there is some at the lodge and also on the other game drives."

"There are other drivers out? But we haven't seen another vehicle since we entered the park."

"Yes, bwana."

"Then call them."

"Bwana?"

"Call one of the other cars and ask them to bring us their gin and tonic."

"Yes, bwana."

The driver picked up the two-way radio and Robert came back to the table.

"Might as well have the last bottle of champagne while we wait," he said, popping open the third bottle.

The meal was jolly and fun and the three of them spent most of the time laughing, all sharing funny stories from their past, Robert of course having the most outrageous ones to tell.

It wasn't too long before the other driver pulled up next to the parked Land Rover. The guides shared a quick discussion and then the driver was given a cool box, which contained the gin and tonic.

"Yoo-hoo," called Robert, to the other safari-goers. "Why don't you come and join us?"

"No, thank you," said a man sounding very grumpy.

"We've come to see the wildlife," said a young lady, "we won't see anything around here with all the noise your group is making."

"Eh?" said Robert.

"Bye," called the passengers, "enjoy your drinks."

"Do you think they were being funny?" asked Robert, turning serious for a moment.

"Not as funny as you," said Grace as she burst out laughing.

As the sun sank over the hills, the driver lit a few candles and placed them in glass jars on the ground all around the table.

"Very romantic," said Robert, helping himself to another drink.

"No, thank you," said Grace when he went to fill her glass.

"Nor me," said Christopher putting his hand over the top of his glass.

Of course, the other group had been correct. The laughter of the three newly made friends was keeping all the animals away.

The next morning they were woken early by the lodge staff, and with a picnic breakfast they set off to watch the sun rise over the plains. Their headaches insisted on a no-talking morning, as they sat harbouring their own pains and regrets of too much alcohol. They stopped at the entrance to an open flat land and once again the driver set up their table and got everything ready for breakfast. Grace poured out glasses of fresh orange juice with a shaky hand. They nibbled on pieces of mango and banana and then sat still in wonder, as the first rays poured through the valley.

With the light came the realisation that the valley was full of animals drinking from the Voi River. Robert shot back to the Land Rover and grabbed his camera. Grace and Christopher stood up, too amazed to remain seated. Christopher came and stood behind Grace and put his hands on her shoulders. She turned to look up at him, smiling, her eyes glistening with joy, and Christopher caught his breath.

"Beautiful," he said.

"Isn't it though," said Grace turning around again. "I think it's the most beautiful thing I have ever seen."

They had a wonderful day and were blessed to see all the main types of game, including a family of lions, who played in the long grass as if putting on a show. After the evening meal, served at the lodge, they sat on the veranda to take in the glorious views of Tsavo at night.

"I'll never be able to thank you enough for this wonderful trip, I am quite simply bowled over by your generosity and kindness," said Grace, full of emotion.

"The pleasure's all mine. Can you imagine how bored I would have been without company?" said Robert. They all laughed because they knew it was true, Robert thrived on making people laugh.

"The funny thing is," said Robert, "the more I give away the more I seem to be given in return. And I don't mean financial reward, I mean joy."

"Oh, I understand that," said Grace. "The more I help at the hospital the more peace I seem to have. It's quite hard to describe, but it's very real."

"On that note, I'll be taking my leave until the morrow. I think I may have overdone the drinking in the last few days. Night."

"Night," said Grace standing to give Robert a hug.

"Night," said Christopher.

"Top bloke that," said Christopher once Robert had gone.

"Certainly is."

They sat in silence for a while, enjoying their guava juice as they stared at the open log fire in front of them.

"I've had a wonderful day, Grace."

"Yes, me too."

"I've really enjoyed your company."

It seemed as if Grace's heartbeat stopped as she waited for him to continue.

"Grace?"

She looked up at him.

"Grace, I… I can't help thinking, what if?"

"Life's too short for ifs and buts, Chris."

"But what if I had met you before Alice?"

"You didn't, and she is your fiancée."

"I don't think she'd be too upset if I broke it off."

Grace pushed her chair back and stood up. "Stop. Stop it right now. There are no ifs and buts, they bring only sadness, and life is too short." She turned around and practically ran to her room.

Throwing herself on the bed, Grace began to cry. Tears of loneliness and wishes that things could have been different enveloped her for a while. In the last few days, her feelings for Christopher had grown strong, but he wasn't free. If he had been then maybe things could have been different. But no matter how much she longed for his arms around her, there was no way she would allow herself to become the reason for someone else's sadness. As the tears subsided she found herself stroking William's ring. *You would have loved it here.* Then, as if a picture had been put in front of her, she saw William's letter in her mind.

I have this recurring dream that you are under a blazing sun watching animals move across a red

"Matthew 25:35." Grace got out of bed and splashed her face with some water. She buried her face for a moment in the softness of the towel and then went and knelt by her bed.

"Lord, I am here. I love you and I am willing to do your work. All I ask is that you guide me always. Show me the right path to walk upon and that is the way I shall go. I am your servant, your daughter, and your friend. You are all I need, only remain with me always, dear Lord, that I may be strengthened in you. Give me eyes to see the world as you see it, and give me a heart to love everyone, even as you do. Let me keep my eyes ever Heavenwards, for the things of this world are temporal and the things of God eternal. I choose you. In the name of our Lord Jesus Christ, Amen."

Chapter 20

Blessings in Disguise
February 1958

Homeless. Five years she had lived here in the small room in the attic and now she stood on the street with her suitcase wondering what on earth she was going to do. She picked up her case and started walking through Old Town towards the hospital. Where else could she go?

She couldn't blame Mrs Brinley, she hadn't paid any rent in three months and, as the landlady put it, she had bills to pay and wasn't a charity. She could have gone to the British Consulate, she was sure they would have loaned her the money to go home. Home? No, England wasn't home anymore, Mombasa was. She would just have to find another job and somewhere else to stay, and more importantly somewhere to sleep tonight.

She would need to make herself more disciplined and make sure she went to work this time. The trouble was the hospital was always calling to her spirit, someone always needed help and prayers and she knew that was where she belonged, going to work was a complete inconvenience to be honest.

The Civic had deteriorated in the last five years and looked worse than ever, in all fairness this was due in part to the fact that they were demolishing some of the buildings that had become unsafe.

Grace had been outraged at first, telling anyone who would listen that the place just needed some money to lift it up again. She'd been ignored. She was just that mad English woman running around with her crazy ideas and her constant begging.

When she'd first heard that the Maendeleo women's group had petitioned the British government for money for the hospital she had been over the moon. Then she'd been told the full plan, which was to build a maternity hospital on Kisauni Road, and she wasn't impressed. Would they fund that any better than the Civic? It was Dr Chopra who finally made her see that it was indeed a very good thing for the women of Mombasa and would hopefully prevent lots of unnecessary deaths.

She couldn't argue with that and had spent all her time helping with the changes.

Now she stood under the covered walkway listening to the rain pelt down onto the roof, water dripping off her body, and wondered where she could sleep. She decided that as they were knocking down one of the buildings anyway, she could sleep in there tonight and no one would be the wiser. She ignored the warning signs and went inside, finding a couple of mattresses in one of the rooms and sighing in relief that she wouldn't be on the concrete floor.

She was soaking and knew she should change her clothes, but she was mentally exhausted and so simply lay down on the mattress and closed her eyes. It was a shame that Bernice was on sabbatical in America, otherwise she could have spent a few nights with her. Grace drifted off to sleep thinking of the different Americans she had met in her life and wishing one of them was with her right now.

The next morning, the sound of workers talking woke her, and not wanting to be found she jumped up, picked up her case and quickly ran from the room and down the external walkway to the main building. As her hand reached out to open the door, the sound of walls crashing pounded the atmosphere and she shivered at her narrow escape.

"You look terrible," one of the Asian nurses said. "You should go home, Grace, you look like you're ill." Then her eyes fell on Grace's suitcase. "Are you leaving us?" Her face showed her sorrow.

"No, Jasmine. I am just temporarily without a residence."

"Go to the kitchen, cook will fill you up, make you feel better."

Grace smiled as Jasmine went on her way. Jasmine had been in Grace's head as a possibility of somewhere to live. That offer was obviously not coming. As she entered the kitchen the smell of cooking stew made her feel sick and she down quickly on a stool near the sink.

"You all right there, Mrs?" asked Abuya the cook.

"I've been better. I don't suppose there is a spare banana I could have, is there?"

Abuya went into the larder and came back out with a banana.

"Thank you," said Grace peeling the banana straight away.

"So where you going little white girl?"

Grace smiled as she looked at Abuya. In the five years she had been here she had never been able to stop the cook calling her little white girl. She must admit, even to herself, that at five foot one inch tall and skinny as a rake, she did appear to be extremely little.

"What's going on here?" asked Dr Singh, pointing at the case. "Don't tell me Mrs Brinley has thrown you out at last." He looked at Grace's face which confirmed the bad news. "So you're going home then?"

"This is my home," answered Grace.

Dr Singh pulled up a stool and sat down next to her. "Don't you have family you can go to, Grace?"

"All the family I have is you and the staff."

"And Oborneo."

"Yes of course, Oborneo and Wokabi."

"Does he know you're homeless?"

"Not yet."

"He'll want you to go and live with them, you know."

"I know he will, but I'll have to decline. They only have one bedroll for the pair of them as it is, and there is no space inside their hut for me."

"He won't be able to see you sleep on the street, Grace."

"Then I must find somewhere else to live, and quickly, my bed of last night is now lying under a pile of bricks."

"You slept in the old part of the hospital?"

"It was raining, I couldn't sleep outside."

"Oh dearie me, Grace, this is a very bad situation."

"I'm sure God has something in mind for me."

"Well He better had, because you're looking awful, and you'll be sleeping in the hospital as a patient if you don't take care," interjected Abuyu.

"You have a point there, she looks terrible." Dr Singh touched Grace's chin and tilted it upwards so he could look into her eyes. "You're definitely coming down with something."

"I think I have a cold coming on, I feel a bit hot and bothered."

Dr Singh instantly touched her forehead. "Come," he said standing up and picking up Grace's case. "We have two empty wards at the moment; you should sleep in one until you're feeling better."

Grace, normally argumentative about such things, simply nodded and got up. Dr Singh was immediately worried. Grace managed to get herself down the hallway and onto the bed before she began to feel faint. The last thing she remembered was Dr Singh looking worried.

For three days, Grace's body battled against malaria. The disease seemed to be winning, Grace's already fragile body becoming like a skeleton as she wasted away under endless perspiring. On the fourth day there was a slight improvement, and on the fifth, Dr Singh knew they had broken the back of the malaria and she was on the way to recovery.

Grace came around confused; she lay awake for a while before attempting to open her eyes, trying to work out where she was. It was the torrential rain bombarding the roof which reminded her that she was in Mombasa. At first, she was disappointed. She had been dreaming of farming with Milton in Ohio, the realisation that she hadn't married him and gone to America was too much and she started crying.

She became aware that a hand was stroking her face, and someone was hushing her and she felt obliged to stop crying and open her eyes. A tiny smile lit up her eyes when she saw Oborneo's face beaming down at her.

"Oh, Mrs God, you worry me to my grave."

"I'm sorry Oborneo. How long…"

"Five days," said another voice, and Grace looked across the room to see Dr Singh standing in the doorway, grinning from ear to ear. He came across the room, clipboard under his arm, shaking his head.

"I have to admit, I thought you wouldn't survive, quite a miracle if you ask me. When Mrs Brinley arrived with some medicine for you, I almost sent her away as I thought it was too late, but she was quite distraught so to calm her I told her I would give it to you."

Grace was surprised. "Mrs Brinley? But how did she know I was ill?"

Oborneo backed away from the bed slightly. "I didn't know who else to ask."

"Dear Oborneo." Grace reached out to grab his hand. "You will have to go straight back to her and say I send my humble thanks, and let her know I pulled through." Grace stopped for a moment and raised an eyebrow at Dr Singh. "Even against all odds, and a very pessimistic doctor."

Dr Singh started laughing.

"And what's so funny?" Grace tried sitting up a bit but both men rushed forward to prevent her.

"It is very nice to have you back again, Mrs God. I have missed your bossy voice." Dr Singh stepped back as Grace took a swipe at him.

"Don't you start with that, I am quite fed up with telling young Oborneo here to stop calling me that, I don't need you encouraging him. Anyway, you are particularly jolly today, what's going on?"

"Two miracles in one day, it is indeed quite a day to remember."

"What's happened?"

"I found you a job!" Dr Singh puffed out his chest with pride.

"That's very amiable of you," said Grace with a touch of sarcasm. "When are you planning to evict me from my sick bed? And will they wait that long?"

"Oh yes, your new boss is a very understanding, kind-hearted man, with noble standing and high moral ethics. You are very lucky, indeed, to have a job working for him."

"Sounds too good to be true. Is he a priest by any chance?"

"Indeed not, he is a very religious man however, and he won't tolerate things if you start bringing a multitude of strangers back to your room."

"Dr Singh! That's a terrible thing to imply, you know I never bring anyone back to my room. What on earth have you told this man, he must think me a terrible person if you have planted such ideas into his head."

Both Oborneo and Dr Singh burst out laughing.

"What the Dickens is so funny? I'm dreadfully sick you know, I don't think I can handle such stress." Grace put her hand on her chest and closed her eyes for good effect. The laughter stopped.

"Mrs Grace, he is pulling your arm."

Grace opened one eye and looked at Oborneo. "You mean he is pulling my leg."

"I don't think Dr Singh would pull your leg, Mrs Grace. If you were standing up you would fall down."

If Grace had had any energy she would have laughed. However, her chest felt caved in and she felt breathless, and all she wanted to do was go back to sleep.

29th March 1958

Grace stood in the doorway and looked at her room. Some people might not have thought it up to much, but for Grace it was paradise. A bed against the far wall, a desk and chair, and a small chest of drawers to her right – it was plain, simple, and all she needed. Her mother's Bible lay safely on her pillow, her dad's cardigan hung on the back of the chair, and an ebony cross (that Oborneo had made for her) hung on the wall.

When she had come around again, and Dr Singh explained that he was her new boss and that he'd managed to persuade the board he needed an administrator she'd been full of joy, still was. Not only would she get paid for being at the hospital, although a pittance, she'd also been given two rooms. One room to sleep in, and another to work in. She was literally so happy she thought she might burst. She shut the door to her bedroom and turned around to face her new study.

Two huge desks had appeared the previous day, along with a couple of chairs, some filing cabinets and a typewriter. There were several boxes of Dr Singh's paperwork and a note stuck on the top wishing her good luck.

Grace was surrounded by sheets of Dr Singh's notes, when he stuck his head around the corner.

"You ready? The big unveiling is about to happen."

Grace got up from the floor, where she had been trying to get the paperwork into date order, and brushed the dust off her dress. "Do you think her highness will mind if I turn up in a dirty dress?"

"Tut, tut, not very gracious of you, you don't live up to your name, do you?"

"Well really, if the lady truly cared about people don't you think she would do more?"

"Grace Clifton, you are becoming a bitter old woman. The Governor's wife does tremendous good for the country, I don't know where we would be without her; we certainly wouldn't be opening a new maternity hospital that's for sure. Now are you coming or not?"

Grace was still mulling over the fact she'd just been told she was getting old, but nodded and followed him out of the hospital. The other staff members were in the gardens waiting for them, they were excited about the new building in Kisauni Road, and Grace was charged with feelings of remorse. *Maybe she was becoming bitter?*

The new hospital building did look grand and Grace knew it was much needed. Her real fear was that once the unveiling had been done all interest in the hospital would diminish. Still, as she watched the Maendeleo ladies bustle around with a sense of achievement she almost envied them for a moment. Rich, upper-class ladies volunteering their spare hours to do good works, and then retiring to their colonial homes to order their black servants around, without another thought for the people they avowed to help. For a moment, Grace wondered what her life would be like if she could switch the caring for others persona on and off.

The press took pictures as the Lady Mary Baring cut the ribbon and declared the hospital open, although in actual fact it had never be shut, but that was another point. The Civic was no more, it was now the Coast Provincial General Hospital, and hurrah for that. Maybe now it had a new name they would be able to hold on to some equipment. You never know, the roaming gangs might care enough for their fellow people to leave the x-ray machines behind, after all, with their dangerous pursuits they might need them themselves one day. Well, one could wish.

So far, any piece of hospital equipment installed had mysteriously disappeared within weeks of arriving. Everyone blamed the Mau Mau, but honestly, there were so many coastal tribes fighting for dominance that it could have been anyone. Anyone that is, who cared more for the money they would get from re-selling the equipment than they did about people.

There was a lot of clapping and cheering and Grace was pulled out of her grumpy musings. She started looking around for Oborneo and Wokabi who were sure to be here somewhere, probably near the food tables. She glanced around for Dr Singh and spotted him heartily shaking the Lady Baring's hand. Grace smiled and went in search of the food.

"Oh, Mrs Grace," said Oborneo, his mouth full of food, "what a marble this day is."

"You mean, what a marvel this food is," said Grace laughing.

"Grace, you must come home with us after the celebrations here, and have evening food with us," said Wokabi.

"I'd love to, thank you."

Grace picked up a plate and accepted a slice of cake from a young Kenyan woman who was grinning as wide as could be. "This is sultana cake, which I make this morning," she declared with great pride.

"Thank you," said Grace, "it looks delicious."

Grace moved away from the table and stood in the throng of people wondering if anyone would notice if she slipped off to carry on working.

"Is it good?"

Grace looked up to see Mr Lakviar, the chemist. "Well it's not the best I've ever had, but it is perfectly edible, you should try a slice."

"Oh, no thank you," he answered tapping his rather rotund stomach, "I'm watching what I eat at the moment, health reasons you know. So, what do you think of this, then?" He circled his arm to indicate everything.

"The hospital, or the do-gooders?"

"Both," he answered with a shrug.

"The hospital is good. The idea to split it and leave eight wards in the old part was good common sense. Will the equipment stay in place? We'll have to see. As for the Maendeleo ya Wanawale (Swahili for Women's Progress) Association, I'm not sure teaching young ladies to bake English cakes is what is needed by the local women. Can you see them baking cakes once they are left on their own? They essentially need help learning how to farm so they can grow food to feed their families. These Colonial women try hard, I'll give them that and they seem genuinely sympathetic, but they'll never understand the African woman's needs. Serving tea in the afternoon in china cups is about as useful as an empty bucket when you need to build a house."

Grace chomped into her cake to stop herself from rambling on any more.

A few hours later, Grace made her way through the Old Town and across the island to the Native Quarter. The sun was setting and the island becoming more alive, as the cool wind rolled in heralding the evening's slight drop in temperature. Her peers pronounced her insane when they found out she walked into the Native Quarter on her own. But what did they know? She was beginning to know many of the Swahili people by name and was greeted with smiles from most of them.

Being at the bottom of the poor list, Oborneo and Wokabi had only recently built a small, round mud hut in the Native Quarter. Wokabi had been given a job as a cleaner at Woolworths, after Grace had pleaded her case, and since then with the small amount of money she got paid they had changed their lives. With the money they had been able to buy a knife for cutting twigs and sticks, and string to tie them together. They'd also fed their neighbours a big meal after they helped the young couple pack the frames with mud. Now, with Oborneo coming to help her in the hospital, they considered themselves extremely blessed and told everyone who would listen, that God gave them everything. Including a second bedroll, Wokabi's first purchase after the hut had been built, for them to sleep on.

With new pots for cooking and money to buy food, they considered themselves very blessed.

They were sitting on up-turned fruit boxes outside their hut as Grace approached. They jumped up and with big smiles, beckoned her to come and sit on Oborneo's box. Oborneo sat crossed-legged on the floor once Grace sat down.

A small fire burned in a hole in front of them, around which were placed several large stones. Balancing on the stones were two black pots, Grace could smell the goat stew and her stomach rumbled making both Oborneo and Wokabi laugh.

"Karibu," said Wokabi pouring some ugali (maize flour) into the pot with the boiling water and stirring.

"It smells good," said Grace.

"We added spices from the Arab markets, you were right, it changes the taste very much," said Oborneo.

As Wokabi mixed the ugali into the water waiting for it to be absorbed, they talked about the day and the changes at the hospital.

When they finished eating, Wokabi and Grace went down to the sea to wash the pots. When they returned they asked her about England and Grace reminisced about home and told them about her upbringing.

"I hope, when our sons are grown, that they can go to school to learn, as you did," said Wokabi.

Grace looked at her in surprise. "Wokabi, are you…"

"Yes!" declared Oborneo jumping up. "I," he thumped his chest, "I'm going to have sons."

Both Grace and Wokabi also jumped up.

"Oh," said Grace, throwing her arms around Wokabi, "I am so happy for you."

"And me? You are happy for me?"

Grace turned around and threw her arms around Oborneo. "Yes, I am very happy for you. Although, you do know it might be a girl."

"I have asked God for a boy, I am sure now a boy is coming."

Grace smiled at him and he threw his arms around her again. "Mrs Grace, you are my family, you are of my heart."

Grace felt tears spring to her eyes as she gave him one last squeeze and then pushed him away. "I must be getting back to the hospital now."

"I walk you," said Oborneo.

"Asante sana," (thank you very much) answered Grace.

"Karibu," (you're welcome) answered Oborneo.

"Asante sana for the lovely meal, Wokabi."

"Karibu," she answered, her smile showing big white teeth.

1960

State of emergency ends. Britain announces plans to prepare Kenya for majority African rule. Grace read the headlines of the paper three times before she could finally stop holding her breath. Praise God, was all that was in her head. She looked over at Oborneo who smiled back at her.

"Maybe our land can begin to heal now," said Oborneo.

"I think there is still much to be done before there is real peace, but praise God, this is such good news."

"Will the British leave now?"

Grace looked at Oborneo, who was watching her under hooded eyes. She knew that he held her in great esteem, but that still didn't stop the overwhelming desire that the British would go.

"I believe this is the first step of handing Kenya back to the people, so yes, I think the British will leave."

Oborneo's smile said it all and although Grace was filled with joy for the Kenyan people, she was also sad that she herself might also be made to leave. Still, no matter how sad that might make her it was insignificant in comparison to the thousands of Kenyans who had been murdered by the British army. It was a disgrace and she wasn't particularly proud of being British anymore.

Chapter 21

You Can't Out Give God
21st August 1961

Bernice had been ill for days by the time Grace arrived. Shocked to see Bernice's normal golden skin a sickly yellow and to hear her rasping, Grace dropped to her knees by her friend's bed.

"I'll go to the church and ask for help. You need to be in the hospital." Grace grabbed Bernice's hand and wrapped hers around it.

Bernice shook her head. "Spiritual," she croaked.

"What?"

"Witch doctor was here, I've been ill ever since. Pray for me, Grace."

Grace didn't believe in the power of Witch doctors, or of the presence of evil spirits the way that Bernice did, but she did believe in the power of prayer and so she closed her eyes and prayed in earnest. Time slowed as words poured from her. Unsure of the power of spiritual warfare, Grace did, however, know the Bible inside and out and before she knew it she was quoting verses from Ephesians.

The more she prayed Bible verses the more 'awake' she became. Something was happening inside her and heat was radiating from her. Becoming sure the Holy Spirit was with them, Grace placed her hands on Bernice and spoke positive words of complete healing. It was a miracle; there was no other way to describe it. From the moment she put her hands on Bernice, she started to recover. The yellow in her skin began to fade, and although still pale, her normal mocha colour returned. Her breathing also instantly settled, and the wracking of her chest ceased as Bernice's whole body seemed to sigh in relief.

"Thank you," whispered Bernice before she dropped into exhausted sleep.

Grace stood for a moment looking at Bernice as she slept, in awe of God's greatness but also full of questions. Why had Bernice fallen ill? Did Witch Doctors really have some sort of evil power? If they did, why did God allow it? She sank into a chair for a moment, lost and confused as to why the world was full of such evil and such sadness. She was nearly fifty and yet she was still extremely distressed every time someone did something wicked. She shook her head, she just couldn't understand why people acted the way they did.

"Oh Lord, if only we could go back to the Garden of Eden, back to innocence and peace." Then as an afterthought, Grace added, "But with clothes on, I'm not too sure fig leaves would suit me."

"Grace."

Grace was awake in an instant and by Bernice's bed. "How are you feeling?"

"Like myself again."

"That's good. You certainly look better today, your cheeks have colour in them again. Would you like a cup of tea?"

Bernice smiled. "How many years have you been here, Grace? Yet still so very English."

"I take it that's a yes."

When Grace went into the kitchen to put some water on to boil, Bernice got up and went for a wash. A short time later, they were sitting at the kitchen table drinking lemon tea.

"I prayed for you to come, you know."

"Really?"

"I just knew God would use you to help me and that He would create some reason for you to trek all the way out here to see me."

"Well, there was some news and I felt compelled to come and share it with you as I know your radio isn't working."

"What is it?"

"Yesterday, Jomo Kenyatta was freed and is assuming presidency, it looks like independence is coming."

"Praise the Lord for that! Please God let that be an end to the killing."

"Amen to that."

They were silent for a moment; both lost in their own thoughts, and after a while they both spoke at the same time.

"You need to go home," said Grace.

"I've decided I'm going home," said Bernice.

They looked at each other and laughed.

"I'm glad," said Grace, "I don't think your Church should have let you come to Kenya on your own."

"To be honest, they did everything they could to stop me, but I was convinced that God wanted me as a missionary here, and I do believe I have spread the Gospel to quite a few homes."

"I know that you have, but Bernice, what would have happened to you if I hadn't have come yesterday? You might have died in your bed with no one with you." Grace shuddered at the thought.

"I would never die alone, God is always with me."

"You looked very alone when I arrived, and very ill."

"And yet here we are," Bernice raised her arms, "alive and well."

Grace chewed her bottom lip, trying to get her thoughts in order. "Why did the Witch Doctor come to your house?"

Bernice took a big breath and leaned back in her chair. "I have been trying to persuade the women that female genital mutilation is wrong. A few families who have accepted Jesus into their lives were beginning to see how cruel it is, one mother refused to take her two daughters up to Kisii as usual, knowing it was the season for this to happen."

"So that's why he came to see you, to warn you off?"

"He said he had cursed me and that I was going to die."

"Why didn't you come straight to me?"

"Because from the moment he spat at me I began to feel ill. Within a few minutes of him leaving I was feeling faint, I had just enough energy to take myself to my bed."

They went silent again for a while. The morning sun was pouring through the small kitchen window and the temperature was rising, it felt good, like a warm blanket after a cold night. A dog barked nearby and some men could be heard talking as they walked down the dirt track that passed Bernice's small home.

"I've heard that they collect snake venom and this is what they spit at people to make them ill," said Grace, reaching out to hold Bernice's hand.

Bernice gripped Grace's hand back in a reassuring hold. "I'm fine now. However, I do want to go back to Washington. I don't think there is much more I can do here. At home I will campaign for more missionaries to come. It might be difficult now if there is to be an African government; they may not want foreigners at all anymore, we'll have to wait and see. Do you think you will be asked to leave?"

"I hope not, but I don't know. Kenya has been a British Protectorate since 1920, I'm sure the Africans can't wait to see the back of us."

Bernice frowned at Grace's tone. "They've done lots of good as well, Grace, you know that right?" Grace didn't answer. "Seriously, Grace, the British have built churches, schools, power plants, waterways, the roads, and hospitals – your hospital for goodness sake."

"It just doesn't feel like enough. You know how the Africans live; do you think their lives have changed for the better because the British were here?"

"Yes, of course I do. Don't paint everyone with the same brush. Anyway, look at you. You've poured your entire being into helping these people, and you're British."

"I don't feel as if I've accomplished much at all. People die at the hospital every day."

"And you are there, praying for them to be accepted into Heaven. Grace you daft thing, there is no greater thing that anyone could do."

12th December 1963

The noise was deafening. Cheering, singing, chanting, stamping. Throngs of people were swaying, jumping, and waving their arms in the air. It was joyous and amazing and would be a day that Grace would never forget. It was the day Kenya received independence from Britain.

Grace stood on the hospital veranda and smiled as she watched Mombasa celebrate a day that was long overdue. Tribal and family groups danced along the street, the Dogos with their nose rings, the Embu with their grass skirts and monkey headdresses, and the Kikuyu men with their bodies adorned with strings of beads. The crowd as one bounced to the chanting, arms in the air, broad smiles by one and all. When her legs grew tired from standing, Grace returned to her room. She tried to do some work but was unable to. The infectious joy of the country infiltrated every part of the day, and went right through the night to the next day.

Lying awake on her bed listening to the drums and the chanting as the sun began to rise the next day, Grace wondered what would happen next. She had read Kenyatta's book 'Facing Mount Kenya' and felt sure that he was an honourable man who would lead the country in the right direction. But what was to become of her life? Would she be able to stay? Should she stay?

The town was finally becoming quiet and Grace was just dropping off to sleep when a nurse knocked on her door.

"Mrs Grace."

Grace roused herself. "Yes."

"Please come, there is a man asking for you."

Beyond tired, but also curious, Grace got out of bed and threw her dress on, slipped her feet into her shoes and opened the door.

"Who wants me?"

The nurse threw her a worried look. "Aluoch."

"I don't recognise that name, should I know him?"

The nurse just looked at Grace with wide eyes. "Come," she said.

Instead of leading the way to one of the wards, the nurse led Grace towards the uninhabited part of the old building. "In there." The nurse pointed towards a dark room before turning and running back to the main part of the hospital.

A man suddenly appeared in the doorway, making Grace jump. "Mrs-God?"

Grace gulped and nodded.

"Come." It was a command she couldn't refuse and she followed the man into the room. Once her eyes had become used to the dim light, Grace could make out a small boy lying on the floor. She could hear him moaning quietly.

"What's wrong with him?" Grace asked.

"Snake bite. You fix him."

"I can't, we need a doctor and quickly before the poison seeps through his blood. Do you know what type of snake bit him?"

"Cobra."

"Nooo. We have to get him some anti-venom immediately or he will die. Quick, pick him up."

"No."

Grace turned to look at the man properly for the first time. He was taller than average and lean. His eyes were bloodshot and his skin covered completely in scars. Her eyes travelled to his hand, which held a machete.

She took a step back. "You know he will die without medicine?"

"I watch you for long time, Mrs-God."

"Oh," Grace didn't know what else to say.

"I saved you in Nairobi on speech-day. You walk right into Mau Mau path. Aluoch," he stopped to thump his chest, "save you."

"You were the man who told him I was Mrs-God?"

"Yes. I saved your life, now you save his," he pointed to the boy.

"Let me fetch the doctor, we have had medicine delivered this week, you are lucky, I'm sure we will have some anti-venom left."

"No."

"Why not?" said Grace getting distressed as time was running out.

"Police look for us. You fix him, Mrs-God, just you."

"I can't, I need the medicine, let me see if the doctor will let me have it without coming back with me."

Aluoch swung his machete. "No."

The boy started rasping, his ability to draw breath becoming harder. Grace sank onto the floor beside the boy. *Oh Lord,* she cried in her spirit, *please help us.* Without any real expectation that the prayer would be answered, she started to pray aloud. She started with the Lord's Prayer and then launched into a cry for mercy and for a miracle. As she prayed, she could hear the boy's breathing becoming more laboured. She opened her eyes and looked at him. He was such a young lad. Then the memory of laying hands on Bernice came to her and she reached over and placed a hand on his chest.

"Dear Father-God, in your mercy and by your grace, please draw the venom from his body and let him live, that your name may be glorified."

The boy coughed and spluttered so hard that his body jerked upright into a sitting position. He coughed and seemed to be choking. Grace wrapped her arms around him and continued to pray.

Another cough brought a pile of blood shooting from his mouth. Grace stroked his head and continued to pray. Then as suddenly as it had started, the coughing stopped, and he lay back in her arms. For a moment, Grace thought he had died as his breathing had become so still, then he opened his eyes and looked up into hers. Dark brown pools of gratefulness stared up at her.

Grace looked up at Aluoch, not too sure what to say.

"Odinga?" Aluoch said.

"Ndiyo baba," the boy answered.

Aluoch let his head fall backwards and a sound came from him that pierced the air. When the cry stopped, Aluoch leant down and none too gently pushed Grace out of the way so that he could pick up his son. Without looking back, he ran out of the room.

Grace started crying. "Father-God you are wonderful beyond words, and so mysterious."

When Grace told Oborneo what had happened he had been furious with the nurse and would have admonished her for eternity if Grace hadn't told him to stop.

"She shouldn't have taken you to him," Oborneo said with fists clenched. "He is a known killer; no one knows how many people he has killed. I can't believe that God saved his son, he deserves to die."

"Oborneo! That is a terrible thing to say."

"If he had killed your family, you would think so too."

Grace paused for a moment. "I suppose I might, but God works in mysterious ways and we don't know what the outcome of last night will be. Maybe God will change his ways? Who knows? I shall pray for his soul and for the safety of his son, Odinga."

Three weeks later, near the end of a long day, Grace was sitting at her desk typing a letter when a shadow fell over the typewriter. She looked up and instantly caught her breath in surprise when she saw Christopher smiling down at her. With a surge of joy she jumped up and into his arms. After a quick, very tight hug, she pulled herself away and looked up into his handsome sun-kissed face.

"What are you doing here?"

"I was about to fly back to England when this impulse to see you overwhelmed me, so I changed my flight plans and here I am."

"Why?"

"So direct, Grace, it is good to see you haven't changed."

"Not even after, what is it, six or seven years?"

"Eight."

Grace was aware that they were both standing, gawking at each other.

"Sorry, I don't mean to be rude, please take a seat, can I get you a drink?"

"No thank you. I have a taxi waiting outside for us. Will you come and have dinner with me, Grace?"

"I never say no to a free meal," Grace laughed, then abruptly stopped. "Sorry, I don't mean to assume you will pay, it's just everyone around here knows I never have any money."

Christopher smiled and his eyes twinkled. "It would be my pleasure to buy you dinner."

"Thank you. Just give me two minutes please, to wash some of the day's dust off me." Grace disappeared into her room and re-emerged a couple of minutes later complete with washed face and a clean dress. For the first time in years, she felt uncomfortable with the fact that her dress was years old and threadbare. Still, it was all she had so it would have to do. It was clean and comfortable, what more did she need?

The taxi drove them off the island and along the north side of the coast to the hotel where Christopher was staying. He had booked them a table at the beach side restaurant and offered her his arm as they walked through the hotel. Now, Grace was mortified she didn't own anything more fitting than her shift style dress and kept her eyes straight ahead to avoid the glances from the other guests.

"I wish you hadn't brought me here," she whispered after the waiter left them at the table.

"Why not?"

"I don't fit in. I feel like a pauper in their immaculate world."

"You're a beautiful person, Grace, and I am sure that's all anyone will see."

The waiter came back with the menus.

"Do you think if I order too much food they will allow me to take it home with me if I don't eat it?"

Christopher threw back his head and laughed. "Order whatever you want."

Over dinner, they exchanged news and talked like long lost friends.

"So, you haven't mentioned your wife yet, how is…" Grace chased around her brain for the name.

"I never married Alice."

Grace's eyes searched Christopher's eyes.

"What happened?" she asked softly.

"When my initial time was up I decided I wasn't ready to go back to England so I extended my contract. I've been working in Nairobi ever since. Alice wasn't too pleased and called off the engagement."

"Oh, I'm sorry." Grace didn't feel sorry, she felt rather irritated. The engagement had been broken for years but he had only come to see her now, when he was about to leave the country?

"Come back to England with me."

"What? Why on earth would I do that?"

Christopher chuckled and took a drink of wine. "Two reasons. One, Kenya has its independence and I don't think we are welcome any more. And two, I have never stopped thinking about you, and with your permission I would like to get to know you better. We can hardly do that if we are in different countries."

"Then stay here. Get a job in the Aga Khan. I'm sure they would have you."

"No, my time in Kenya is over." He went quiet, looking into his glass. "I have seen horrors which I wish to forget. I'll not forget them so long as I am here." He looked up at her and gave a cheeky grin. "I have found a position in a small practice in Hampshire, I am truly looking forward to having nothing more to deal with than broken bones from bike falls and a few complaints of gall-stones. Bring on the quiet life!"

Grace smiled back at him, but the smile didn't reach her eyes. "This is my home, I'm not leaving."

Christopher reached across the table and grabbed her hand. "Why not? You're living in a tiny room in a hospital surrounded by strangers. Leave it, Grace. Come and start a new life with me in England."

Grace pulled back her hand and studied his face for a moment. "This is where God wants me, I know this as well as I know the lines on my hands. This is home, this is where I am needed."

"Grace if you married me you could have so much more. I'm quite well off you know, I own property as well as having a well-paid job. I could surround you in comfort for the rest of your life. Don't sacrifice your last years here, let me love you and take care of you."

"I have given my life to God, to serve Him and the people of Mombasa."

"Then He asks too much of you, Grace. You have given years already, please come home with me."

"You don't understand. He has given me so much more than I have given Him. What have I given up? Things that are temporal and pass by, clothes, money, fancy foods," Grace spread her hand over their empty plates. "He has given me so much more. I can't begin to explain the joy that floods my body each time someone new gives their life to Christ. And peace, such peace, in knowing I am in the right place doing the right thing. I know where I am going when I leave Mombasa, and it's not to England."

"You mean Heaven."

"I do. I know that's where I am going as clearly as I know I am sitting at this table with you."

"He wouldn't stop you going to Heaven just because you married me Grace."

"No, he wouldn't. But I'm sorry, Chris, I am not going to marry you, nor go back to England."

"Somehow, I knew you wouldn't, that's why it has taken me years to come and see you. But I just couldn't leave the country without trying once. You see, you turned and looked at me one day, with those beautiful sparkly eyes of yours, and in that moment you melted my heart."

Grace didn't know what else to say. "I'm sorry."

"Goodness, there is nothing to be sorry about, it was hardly your fault. I'm awfully glad I came to see you though. Knowing that you are happy and content with your life will enable me to move on."

Chapter 22

Unexpected Blessings
February 1993

Grace did her morning rounds with unusual slowness. She felt weary and drained and every bit her age of eighty-one. Her eyes still smiled at people and her love poured from her in her prayers with patients who wanted them, but as she made her way back to her room, her heart felt heavy.

Sitting at her desk, she picked up the tiny white envelope with the Kenyan stamp and scraggly handwriting and with uncertainty etched on her face took the letter out. She had read it and put it back in the envelope a hundred times since it arrived three days ago but she was still unsure how she felt. She read it again.

> *My Dearest Grace,*
> *We have space for you here at the convent.*
> *Let us take care of you and come and be with us.*
> *We will send you a train ticket as soon as you are ready.*
> *I am full of joy at the thought of seeing you again.*
> *Your sister in Christ*
> *Mary-Beth*

Folding the paper carefully, she slid it back into the envelope and then dropped her head to pray.

"Father-God please have mercy on me and hear my prayers. I hope that I have served you well these last few years, but I am tired in my bones and in my spirit and long to rest in the cool airs north of Nairobi. Yet I am forlorn that I should be leaving here too soon. Lord I ask Thee, please give me a sign that I am no longer needed here and that your work will carry on when I am gone. Let your blessing be upon the people who need you, show them your love and give them your word so that they may know you for themselves. This I ask in the precious name of our Lord Jesus Christ. Amen."

Slowly lifting her head out of prayer, Grace looked up and got a shock when she saw a young woman standing in the doorway.

"Can I help you?" she asked, her surprise making her voice a bit sharp.

"I am looking for someone called Grace," the woman replied.

Grace stood up. "Well then you have found her, how can I help you?"

The young English woman hesitated in the doorway for just a moment before stepping into the office.

"I don't really have anything to offer, but I feel compelled to come and ask you if there is anything I can do for you."

Grace looked at the woman with a slight smile. "Take a seat, and tell me why you feel like that."

After they had sat down at the desk, Grace waited for the woman to speak.

"My name is Tracy, and I live just north of Mombasa with my husband and four young boys. I am very sad that I only heard about you yesterday, for my husband has been sacked and we are waiting for our plane tickets so that we can return to the UK, therefore I don't have any time to give you." The woman paused and looked Grace directly in her eyes before carrying on.

"All our savings were in the Trade Bank of Kenya, which you probably know closed on 15th April due to the bank manager running away with all the money. I therefore don't have any money to give you. In fact, we are only managing ourselves because our friends are bringing us food." The young woman looked at Grace with the love of God written all over her face.

"Still, without time or money to offer you, I felt the need to come and ask – is there anything I can do for you?"

Grace was having an internal discussion with God.

Oh, but you do have a sense of humour, don't you? I ask for help and here you send me a woman, who seems pleasant enough, but nevertheless has nothing to offer. Really? Grace felt the Lord reply, *Nothing?* And in that moment into Grace's mind came the picture of letters in her A3 folder. She looked at the woman, who sat patiently waiting for an answer, then got up and went across the room to the other desk. She rummaged around the papers for a while until she found her writing folder. She picked it up and went back to the desk where she sat down once more.

"We ran out of Bibles nearly seven years ago. I have written numerous letters to different organisations, but no one is responding any more. If you could write some letters for us, telling them of our need for Bibles and trackers, in both English and Swahili, then that would be helpful."

Tracy reached out and accepted the folder. "I can certainly do that for you," she answered. "I have to get back to the boys now, but I will bring back your folder before we leave Mombasa."

"Thank you."

Grace watched the young English woman walk away and instantly knew that something had happened.

"Have you answered my prayers already?" she asked. A sudden burst of joy filled her spirit. In that moment, she didn't understand why or how but she knew that God was happy for her to retire. She started sorting through huge piles of papers, something she had been meaning to do, for, well years.

"Give me joy in my heart, keep me praising. Give me joy in my heart, I pray. Give me joy in my heart, keep me praising. Keep me praising till the break of day."

"Sing hosanna, sing hosanna, sing hosanna to the King of Kings."

Grace turned around and smiled at Oborneo who was singing in the doorway. "It's a good day, Oborneo."

"It is indeed. But is there a particular reason why today is so good?"

"I am reminded that God knows what we need even before we ask, and my heart is full of joy."

"Praise be to God."

"Praise be to God."

The two of them spent the afternoon singing and working and it came as a shock when the light began to dim and they knew 6 pm had arrived.

"Come and join us for dinner, Grace?" Oborneo asked getting ready to leave.

"Not today, but thank you. I will come soon though."

"Okay, Grace. Goodnight."

"Goodnight, Oborneo."

That night as Grace did her rounds to pray with the patients, joy seeped from her spirit and touched those who listened to her words, poured out to the Father in love. No one jumped out of bed, miraculously healed, but everyone's pain seemed to fade and they slept with the peace of babes.

Not sure what was coming, Grace found herself fidgety for the next few days, and every time she heard steps she looked up eagerly to see who was coming. When nothing seemed to be happening, her joy faded a little. Maybe she had been wrong about the woman?

Twenty days later, Grace was resigned to the fact that her own longing for rest had made her believe God was talking to her, yet although she had got it wrong she knew she was too tired to go on.

"I am going to accept their offer," Grace declared.

Oborneo took his glasses off and put them on the table. "I'm glad. We will all miss you, but it is time for you to live the last part of your life."

"I *live* here."

"No Grace, you used to live here, now you just work here. Until a few weeks ago – when it briefly reappeared, the joy from your eyes had been gone and I see your exhaustion. It is time for you to start a new life."

There was no arguing with the man who knew her, almost as well as God.

"You'll write and tell me all that is happening?"

"Yes, I will write."

"Then I shall answer Mary-Beth's letter today and ask her to send me a train ticket when she feels the time is right."

"Good, write it now and I will post it for you on the way home."

"You have a stamp?"

"No, but Mary Umbungo is working at the Post Office today, and I'm sure she will give me a stamp."

"How is Mary? And how is that niece of hers?"

"Both Mary and her niece are fine. Rose's employers are leaving Mombasa but they have found her another job with a missionary family, so she will be okay."

"Mary must be relieved, I'm glad."

When Oborneo left, taking the quickly written letter, Grace decided to go to her tree. She walked across the cool yard and sat down on the tiny bench under the palm tree. She had taken her mother's Bible with her and having a moment of fancy, she closed her eyes and opened the Bible at random.

As her eyes fell across the words written on the page open in front of her, a tender sweet joy filled her and tears started to flow.

For I was hungry, and you fed me: I was thirsty, and you gave me a drink: I was a stranger, and you invited me in.

This verse had repeatedly been given to Grace, over the last forty years, by different people and in various ways. It had become part of her strength and lay like a shield around her spirit, protecting her from doubt and weariness.

"I love you Father-God, I love you. I pour my heart out to you and thank you for your mercies, which are new every morning. Thank you for your unending patience and for the guidance of your Holy Spirit. I would not be here now without you, Father, and I leave with a heavy heart. All I ask is that you continue to bless Oborneo and others so that your word may bear fruit."

Grace slept peacefully that night, trusting in a Father who she knew had never let her down before, and would not fail to answer her prayers of today, in His time and according to His good will.

Friday started off like any other day. She stood in the kitchens and argued for half an hour with the chef over the hygiene of the pots, then she had taken her Bible and done her rounds of the wards. Little Gasira was actually eating when she came to her bedside, and Grace smiled at the tiny girl with thankfulness in her heart. Her mother, Kioni, sprang to her feet as Grace approached.

"She's strong," she said, grinning widely.

"She is indeed, very strong. Did you manage to get some honey?"

"Yes, Mrs-Grace. I got honey from the baker, he said I can work for him when Gasira is better, to pay him back."

"That's good, and who knows, if you work hard he might keep you on and pay you?" Kioni burst into a grin, her big brown eyes full of joy.

"Grace, Grace?" Grace looked up in surprise as Oborneo came rushing into the ward. "There you are, quick, come see. You're not going to believe it."

"I'll come back later," she said to Kioni.

As soon as she reached the doorway Oborneo grabbed her arm and practically dragged her along the hallway.

"Oborneo, you're worrying me. What on earth has happened?"

"You'll see," said Oborneo, not letting go of her arm or slowing the pace.

As they rounded the doorway and came into her rooms Grace was met by boxes. Loads of boxes. Big and small, littered all over the office floor and on every surface.

"What is it?" she asked in a hushed voice.

"Bibles," declared Oborneo. "Hundreds of Bibles!"

They spent the next hour cutting open all the boxes, which revealed Bibles in both English and Swahili, and a mountain of trackers to hand out. They sorted the boxes into a bit of an order and managed to clear some floor space by piling them on top of each other. They had only just finished when Tracy turned up.

"Hello," she said from the doorway. "We've got our flight tickets and leave next week so I wanted to bring these back to you."

Both Grace and Oborneo just stood and looked at her for a full minute.

Eventually, Grace asked, "Who are you?"

A bit surprised, Tracy answered, "I'm just a mother and a housewife."

Grace came to her quickly and took her by the elbow. "Look," she said pointing to all the boxes.

Tracy just looked puzzled.

"It's Bibles," said Grace, hardly able to contain her excitement. "What on earth did you write in those letters?"

After the initial excitement, the two women sat down at the desk and dived into conversation. Grace briefly explained when and how she had arrived in Mombasa and why she had stayed, and Tracy told a bit of her own story about how she had become a Christian three years previously.

"I just prayed before I wrote," she explained. "Then when I was posting each letter I asked God to take them on the wings of His angels and deliver them quickly and safely to the person in each organisation who made the decision. Also, that as soon as the letters arrived on their desks, their decision to send Bibles would be swift and they would come under God's protection."

"It only took twenty-one days for them to arrive; do you know that is a miracle in and of itself? Normally, Bibles are shipped to us by sea and take three months, everyone who has sent us Bibles and trackers this time have all sent them by air. And there are so many in Swahili, which is such a blessing. But probably the most amazing thing is that we didn't have to pay any chi (bribe) money to get them out of customs."

"God is good," answered Tracy.

"He is indeed, and I would be interested to follow your walk in Christ."

"I am sure it won't be a tiny bit as wonderful as yours," Tracy answered slightly embarrassed.

"Everyone's walk is wonderful, if only they would open their eyes and see." They talked for about an hour until Tracy had to leave. Before she left, she showed Grace a picture of her sons that she always carried with her.

"These are my joy," she said showing the picture.

"I am sure they will be a blessing to you," replied Grace.

Oborneo and Grace walked Tracy to the hospital door.

"I wish for you a happy retirement in the convent," said Tracy.

"And I will pray that your steps are ever on God's path," replied Grace.

They watched Tracy drive away in her white Beetle and then returned to their treasure that had just arrived on the wings of Angels.

Chapter 23

Until We Meet Again
May 1995

One small suitcase, battered and tied with string, stood next to her on the floor as Grace took one last look at the room, which had been 'home' for the last thirty-seven out of forty-two years that she had been on the island. She was surprised she didn't feel emotional but put it down to the fact that she was eighty-three and just downright tired.

"Ready, *Mrs-God*?" Oborneo asked quietly. Grace nodded and Oborneo bent down and picked up the suitcase. She followed him down the corridor and a sudden lump came to her throat as she realised this would be the last time she walked along this cool pathway. Oborneo led her through to the main entrance of the hospital and Grace took a deep breath when she saw that all the staff had come to wave her off.

Nurses, doctors, cooks, cleaners and even patients either shook her hand or hugged her tight.

"Bless you," she repeated over and over again.

Oborneo pulled open the taxi door and the driver put the case in the boot. As the car pulled away from the hospital, Grace turned around in the seat and waved to everyone through the window until they rounded a corner and the hospital was out of sight. She slowly turned around and for a moment felt lost, feeling as if her purpose for living was fading behind her.

"Grace?"

She looked up at Oborneo who was unashamedly crying.

"Don't cry, we'll meet again in Heaven."

"I have something for you," said Oborneo and opened his hand to reveal a little gold ring with a tiny sapphire. Grace began to shake, her chin wobbled and then tears streamed down her cheeks.

"Where on earth did you find it?" Grace asked picking up William's ring with trembling hands.

"Do you remember, Aluoch from the street gang?"

"The man whose son was bitten by a snake?"

"Yes, him. Well he asked to do something for you and I remarked saying getting your ring back would be good. Of course, I never thought he would manage to get it but apparently, he made it his mission to repay you. It took him five years but eventually he came back to me and gave me the ring."

Grace looked at Oborneo in surprise. "You've had it all this time, why didn't you give it to me back then?"

"Because as soon as you needed to get medicine for someone you would have gone straight back to that crook and sold it again. I decided to keep it until such a time when you wouldn't need to sell it." Tears were still flowing down Grace's cheeks and Oborneo took out a white hankie and passed it to her.

"Thank you, for this," Grace said lifting the handkerchief, "and for the ring. I am more touched than I could ever put into words."

"You are most welcome." They rode the last ten minutes to the station in silence – with their goodbyes already expressed there seemed no more need for words. As the taxi pulled up outside the train station a sudden cry went out. Grace looked up as the taxi door opened to see a huge crowd of people. They erupted into song and the noise made shivers run down Grace's spine.

'Oh Jesus I have promised' echoed throughout the station. Women, men and children sang the hymn with joy and moved in unison whilst swinging their arms and swaying their hips. Tears of joy poured from Grace's eyes as she walked along and hugged everyone she could.

"Mrs Milliopawa, oh my Lord, it is so good to see you," said Grace smiling.

"Good to see you too, Mrs-God. Blessings be bountiful on you."

"Thank you." The walk through the crowd was almost unbearable, she had such joy that they should have come to see her, and such sorrow that she was leaving them.

Waiting on the platform were Wokabi and the children. Grace's heart flutters with a moment of doubt she was doing the right thing. Then all of them, Oborneo, Wokabi and the children were hugging her and crying and she was overwhelmed by their love.

Finally, Oborneo got her onto the train and put her suitcase behind her seat.

"You write me, Mrs-God," said Oborneo openly sobbing.

"I promise." Oborneo made a hasty retreat from the carriage as the guard blew his whistle. Grace pulled down the window and hung out of the train waving like crazy.

"We'll never forget you, Grace," Oborneo cried as the train chugged forward.

"Until we meet again, my dearest friend," Grace called back.

The End

Thank you so much for reading Grace in Mombasa, and for helping to support Barnabas Outreach.

If you enjoyed Grace's story could I please encourage you to leave me a review from your place of purchase? Without reviews a book never succeeds and I would really appreciate your endorsement. Many thanks.

You can also find me on Facebook if you would like to know more about me or this book and Barnabas Outreach. https://www.facebook.com/groups/292316321513651

Or my web page is: www.tntraynor.uk

About the author

I became a Christian in 1990, at the age of thirty, whilst living in Kenya. It was a time of great learning and excitement for me as I gave myself fully to the Lord and became extremely hungry for his Word.

The Lord spoke extremely clearly to me and several things happened that I put down to the miraculous workings of God.

In April 1993 Paul (my husband at that time) was baptised in the Indian Ocean on Easter Sunday morning at 7 am as the sun was rising over horizon. On the 16th April 1993 the Trade Bank of Kenya closed its doors due to illegal activities. All our savings, from the past three and a half years were in the Trade Bank, we never received a penny of our money back. Three days later Paul went into work to be told he was fired.

Our flat that we had rented out in the UK was repossessed as the tenants didn't pay the rent and the agency looking after it never took care of the matter.

So by the end of April 1993 we were technically homeless and broke, with four young boys to look after. The house we lived in, in Mombasa, was ours only until Paul found another job, we were also given our flights home. During the following weeks friends delivered baskets of food to keep us going, things were extremely dismal.

It was at this time that someone told me about an English, Christian lady who worked at the Coast General Hospital (the government run free hospital), who spent her days evangelising. I went to visit her the same day. Her name was Moira Smith. I told her I had no time and no money and yet I felt compelled to come and ask if there was anything I could do for her. She asked me to write some letters, to replenish the stock of Bibles and trackers, (that had run out seven years previously) which I did. Several weeks later I went back to say goodbye and return her folder and was full of joy to see that tons of Bibles had miraculously arrived.

Before we left Mombasa we 'sold' all our possessions (including the car) to an American missionary, whose church had said they would wire the payment to our UK account – the money never arrived. Dawn (an American missionary) said she would sell the things for what she could and send the money to us. After a very brief discussion, Paul and I decided that these things should be given to Dawn as a gift for her work and told her to keep them.

Stripped bare of all our earthly possessions we left Kenya and went to Botswana with only a few suitcases of clothes and a few toys for the boys. Of course, that it is outwards…. On the inside, we left with the Holy Spirit in our hearts, worth more than all the gold and silver in the world.

The biggest lesson I learnt whilst in Mombasa, is that you can't out give God. The more I gave to Him and to others, the more I received. On the odd occasion this was possessions but mostly it was love, security and peace.

Through several experiences I have learnt that bricks and mortar are temporal and not worth striving to hold on to, whilst 'giving' brings a joy and riches beyond measure.

About Moira Smith

The lady behind the inspiration behind Grace

Moira Smith was born in 1912, in England. On 25th July 1953, aged 41, she boarded the ship SS Uganda and set sail for Mombasa, Kenya.

On the next page is the Captain's shipping log of the SS Uganda that shows that Moira had a one way ticket to Mombasa.

She spent her years on the island helping people who came to the Mombasa Coast General Hospital, in any way that she could – and by taking every opportunity to spread the gospel.

She never got to retire in the convent. She died in the hospital, in the mid 1990s, where her last action was to give away the medicine that people brought in for her, to the other patients.

Moira's ashes are buried in the compound of St Peter's Church, Nyali, Kenya. An attempt to find living relatives was made, but none were found.

I pray that this story sells well as I am giving 50% of all monies received to Barnabas Outreach Trust Mombasa, to continue Moira's work in helping Kenyan people.

Name of Ship "Strathia" Page 2. Date of Departure 25th July 19[illegible]

Steamship Line—P. & O. Where Bound INDIA

NAMES AND DESCRIPTIONS OF **BRITISH** PASSENGERS EMBARKED AT THE PORT OF LONDON

Port	Names of Passengers	Class	Adults	Children	Address	Occupation	Country of Residence
[illegible]	NICHOLAS, Kate Mary Gordon	[illegible]	[illegible]		63, Foster Road, Portsmouth	Southend [illegible]	Kenya
"	SAUNDERS, Mary Janes	"	34		—do—	Housewife	"
"	NICHOLAS, Christine Elizabeth	"		6	—do—	[illegible]	"
"	NICHOLAS, Susan Patricia Ann	"		4	—do—	[illegible]	"
"	SAUNDERS, Carol Jean Mary	"		[illegible]	—do—	[illegible]	"
[illegible]	RICE, Elizabeth	"	38		122, N. Frederick St., Glasgow	Housewife	N. Rhodesia
"	RICE, Peter	"	16		—do—	Engineer	"
"	RICE, Patrick	"	13		—do—	[illegible]	"
"	RICE, Elizabeth Mary	"		8	—do—	[illegible]	"
[illegible]	RUDOLF, Alan William Vande	"	24		Halifax, [illegible] Rd., [illegible]	[illegible]	[illegible]
[illegible]	BULLE, James Alfred	[illegible] 30			68, Parma Crescent, S.W.11	[illegible]	Kenya
"	JONES, Edith Florence	"	35		—do—	Housewife	"
[illegible]	DONOGHUE, Maureen Ashley	"		20	[illegible]	[illegible]	[illegible]
"	STRATHAM, George Ashley	"	21		[illegible]	Engineer	"
"	STRATHAM, Ida Helen Catherine	"	20		—do—	Housewife	"
[illegible]	STUART, Walter	"	42		[illegible] Cottage, [illegible], Glos.	[illegible]	[illegible]
"	STUART, Elsie Mildred	"	35		—do—	Housewife	"
[illegible]	WELLINGTON, Thomas	"	29		[illegible] Avenue, [illegible]	Waiter	[illegible]
"	WELLINGTON, Pauline	"		2	—do—	[illegible]	"
[illegible]	CHATTERJEE, [illegible]	"	34		c/o Col. Harrod, [illegible]	[illegible]	[illegible]
"	[illegible], Kate Mary Hannah	"	32		[illegible], Str[illegible], Herts.	[illegible]	"
"	[illegible], Abdul [illegible]	[illegible]	27		[illegible] Hall, [illegible]	Student	"
[illegible]	SCOTLAND, John Fraser	"	24		[illegible] Lodge, [illegible] Rd.	[illegible]	[illegible]
[illegible]	SATOW, Myra	"		21	[illegible], S.E.5	[illegible]	Lagos
[illegible]	LEDWIDGE, Ida Marguerite	"		28	The George Inn, [illegible]	[illegible]	W. Africa
"	SMITH, Lawrence Herbert Reynold	"	28		[illegible], [illegible]	Col. [illegible]	[illegible]
[illegible]	SMITH, Terence Jack	"	11		4, [illegible] Cottages, [illegible]	[illegible]	S. Rhodesia
[illegible]	[illegible], Maurice	"	33		[illegible]	Eng.	[illegible]
[illegible]	SIMPSON, Douglas Wade	[illegible] 30			[illegible] Cottage, [illegible]	[illegible]	[illegible]
"	SIMPSON, Mary Louise	"	26		—do—	Housewife	"
"	SIMPSON, Angela Joanne	"		2	—do—	[illegible]	"
[illegible]	TITMUSS, Sheila Alison Elizabeth	"		25	[illegible], The Road End, [illegible]	Teacher	[illegible]
[illegible]	SMITH, Sidney Frank	"	41		[illegible] House, [illegible]	Clerk	[illegible]
"	SMITH, Kathleen Elizabeth	"	35		—do—	Housewife	"
"	SMITH, [illegible] Audrey	"		3	—do—	[illegible]	"
[illegible]	TRIBE, Bruce Frederick	"	32		c/o [illegible] Agent, Cleveland [illegible]	Engr.	[illegible]

The Mombasa Project

For the last twelve years, the Mombasa project, headed up by Sean & Joyce McIntyre, has been making a difference in one of the poorest areas of Mombasa, Kenya. Their work involves preaching, teaching and caring as they seek to meet the spiritual and practical needs of the local people.

Some of the activities that they're involved in are:

Teaching & Discipleship

Sean and Joyce are passionate about seeing revival and transformation. Through New Life Church, which they planted in 2002, they are seeking to provide an alternative to the syncretism (the mixing of traditional beliefs with Christian teaching) and false teaching (such as the prosperity Gospel) which has become so prevalent in Africa.

The church provides discipleship and solid biblical teaching in a caring community of believers.

Empowering Women

The Women of Bokole, are hardworking and committed to their families. However, they often lack the resources needed to take care of their children and a disproportionate number of them suffer from difficult and often abusive marriages. Together with Sean & Joyce we have started a project called Women of Hope.

Working through the church, Women of Hope gives women an interest free micro loan (usually £80 -£100). This loan provides them with the capital to start a small business which will support their families. By loaning, rather than giving the money, we encourage financial responsibility and the same money can be used to help more than one person. Participants can even receive another loan to expand their business even further.

Sponsoring children

In the next twelve months, we plan to open a playgroup enabling children in Bokole to have several hours of fun and stimulating activities and providing some basic food to supplement their otherwise meagre diet.

In 2016 we will be launching a child sponsorship programme both for the children in the playgroup and also to contribute towards primary and secondary education for children in low income families.

If you would like to support the project without buying the book, you can send cheques to **Barnabas Outreach Trust** - 6 Heatherside Road, Epsom, Surrey. KT19 9QU. UK.

Or visit their website to donate: http://www.barnabasuk.org

Barnabas update from Sean McIntyre

Endorsement

My wife and I only recently returned to the United kingdom after spending seventeen years of our life living and working in Mombasa. Reading Tracy's book brought so many memories flooding back; some of them my own and others shared with me by paternal grandmother. Some Seventy years ago, my grandmother travelled to Mombasa by ship with my then 2 year old father and his siblings. She was to be reunited with her husband but found on arrival that he had abandoned her and so she worked for their passage home by teaching in the convent, whilst living in the White Castle Hotel. The hotel still stands today and is only a stones throw from Nkrumah Road which is mentioned in the book. Much has changed but much is still the same and I can readily identify with the frustration and heartache experienced by the poor, in hospitals that are ill equipped to provide adequate healthcare, a problem only compounded by corruption. Now living in England but still overseeing the work we established in kenya, we still enjoy a regular plate of ugali and sukumaweeki.

The story of Grace captures the experience of many others who, though quite ordinary by themselves, find that the love of God propels them towards quite extraordinary endeavours. Tracy is the author of Grace's story but the inspiration was Moira Smith and the author of her story was none other than God himself, described in the Bible as the 'author and finisher of our faith'. I commend Tracy's book *"Grace in Mombasa"* to you in the hope that, inspired by the story of Grace and Moira, you will become hungry for a story of your own and that you will turn to the great author of all our lives. He already has a story prepared for you!

What We Do...

We have been working in Mombasa for seventeen years, where we have been able with God's help to start a church in one of the poorest areas of Mombasa, called Bokole. We're not a large charitable organisation but we mostly work through friendships we have built with the local people and especially the women, which means that whatever money we raise goes directly to meet the needs of people in Bokole who we personally know. We have established a small group of ladies called 'Women of Hope' who have started their own businesses, using micro-loans from a self-managed fund. Simple activities like selling food to factory workers or second-hand clothes in the market helps to put food on the table and take care of their children. The women also meet regularly to support, pray for and encourage one another. We currently support a number of children by sponsoring their education and in the last couple of years we have helped two women suffering with breast cancer. In 2010 we acquired a 1.3 acre plot and built a church building and presently we're building a small structure for the Sunday School and other activities. Our dream would be to one day establish a small school and clinic on the site as well.

I sincerely hope that this book raises money to help build the church and clinic.

For my research, I would like to thank…

Information about the Manchester Blitz – The Manchester Evening News website
Lord Haw Haw – You Tube posts
GI's in Burtonwood – www.newton-le-willows.com
Picture inspiration – The Imperial War Museum
www.iwm.org.uk

History facts about WW2 – BBC archives www.bbc.co.uk

Maps of Manchester – Manchester University
www.luna.manchester.ac.uk

Lancashire Infantry Museum
http://www.lancashireinfantrymuseum.org.uk/world-war-ii-1/

Burtonwood photos
http://www.historicaviationmilitary.com/burtonwoodhome.html

The Decolonization of Christianity in Colonial Kenya by Amanda Ruth Ford

FACTS

During the **Manchester Christmas** Blitz, 770 people were killed and thousands were injured. The fire was the worst ever seen in Britain outside of the Great Fire of London in 1666.

Burtonwood was given to the US army in 1942. By the end of the war 18,000 servicemen were stationed there. During the Second World War, RAF Burtonwood served as the largest airfield in Europe – playing a crucial role in how the war developed. The presence of GIs in Manchester's nightlife was vibrant. From 1942 to 1945 over a million American service personnel were stationed in Britain, and around 100,000 of them were Afro-Americans GIs. From Burtonwood airbase they would travel into Manchester to taste the nightlife. This threatened to cause some problems as the US armed forces were segregated; the US army authorities pressurised the British government to put restrictions of where black servicemen could go, but the British government decided there should be no restrictions on what were then called 'coloured' troops. The popularity of the jitterbug was down to the GIs; although already known in the UK the GIs helped the craze reach its height around 1945.

Once a year the Burtonwood site celebrates the past, with a nostalgia weekend.

The **Vulcan Foundry** was instrumental to the start of the railway age. Newton Le Willows, to this day, still houses the oldest waiting room in the world, at Earlstown station.

1st Loyals, Lancashire Infantry. Repeated German counter-attacks culminated on 16th February 1944, in a massive thrust by three divisions down the Rome-Anzio Raod, with the object of splitting the beach-head and driving its defenders into the sea. In the direct path of this assault, 1st Loyals occupied the final line of defence around the vital Fly-over Bridge and along Wigan Street. On the 18th and 19th February, the enemy launched repeated and heavy assaults on this position, but despite mounting casualties the Loyals fought back valiantly and held their ground until, on the afternoon of the 19th, they were able to mount a successful counter-attack. This was the turning point of the battle and, although there was much hard fighting over the next few weeks, by the end of May 1st Loyals were advancing on Rome, which was captured on 4th June 1944.

GI Brides. Neither the British nor the American government made it easy for British women to marry GI's, but despite this around 70,000 weddings took place during WW2. For brides who did manage to marry their GIs the road ahead was difficult, especially the immigration and transportation issues. Not all marriages were happy-ever-after either, in fact a lot of them ended in divorce when the 'dream' faded and reality sunk in. The grass is rarely greener on the other side.

World War II fatality statistics vary, with estimates of total deaths ranging from 50 million to more than 80 million. The higher figure of over 80 million includes deaths from war-related disease and famine. Civilians killed totalled 50 to 55 million, including 19 to 28 million from war-related disease and famine.

Archbishop of Canterbury, Geoffry Fishen went to Fort Hall, Kenyan in 1955 to memorialize the Kikuyu loyalists who had died during the Mau Mau uprising. At the end of his short speech he blessed the foundational stone of the forthcoming Anglican Church. Labour for this project was to be provided by inmates in the nearby British run detention camp. Despite the importance of the occasion – that no less than the head of the Anglican church was seen to be participating in forced labour during a civil war – the ceremony has only been recorded in history twice, the first a small snippet in the series *The British Empire in Colour,* and it also makes a brief appearance in Daniel Branch's work *Defeating the Mau Mau, creating Kenya.*

Elephantiasis. Lymphatic filariasis, commonly known as elephantiasis, is a neglected tropical disease. Infection occurs when filarial parasites are transmitted to humans through mosquitoes. Infection is usually acquired in childhood causing hidden damage to the lymphatic system. The painful and profoundly disfiguring visible manifestations of the disease, lymphoedema, elephantiasis and scrotal swelling occur later in life and can lead to permanent disability. These patients are not only physically disabled, but suffer mental, social and financial losses contributing to stigma and poverty. Elephantiasis is caused by infection with parasites classified as nematodes (roundworms). Mosquitoes are infected with microfilariae by ingesting blood when biting an infected host. Microfilariae mature into infective larvae within the mosquito. When infected mosquitoes bite people, mature parasite larvae are deposited on the skin from where they can enter the body. The larvae then migrate to the lymphatic vessels where they develop into adult worms, thus continuing a cycle of transmission.

Malaria. About 90% of all malaria deaths in the world today occur in Africa south of the Sahara. At least a million people die from malaria each year. 70% of the deaths are of children under 5. Put another way, 7 jumbo jets full of children disappear because of malaria every day. **Quinine** is a bitter compound that comes from the bark of the cinchona tree. The tree is most commonly found in South America, Central America, the islands of the Caribbean, and parts of the western coast of Africa. Quinine was originally developed as a medicine to fight malaria. It was crucial in reducing the death rate of workers building the Panama Canal in the early 20[th]century.

Mau Mau. In 2013 the British Government announced that it would pay compensation totalling £20 million to more than 5,000 Kenyan citizens who were abused during the Mau Mau Uprising. The Mau Mau uprising convinced the British of the need for reform in Kenya and the wheels were set in motion for the transition to independence. On 12th December 1963 Kenya became an independent nation. Queen Elizabeth II remained the nation's Head of State until the following year when it became a republic. Up to date, it is uncertain how the name Mau Mau came about, however, most Kenyans believe it is the Swahili of Mzungo Aende Ulaya, Mwafrika Apate Uhuru – which means white people go back to your land, let the African be free.

The meaning behind the Kenyan Flag.
The black stripe represents the indigenous black population, who have always inhabited Kenya. The red stripe represents the blood shed during the fight for independence. The green stripe stands for the beautiful and fertile landscape and natural wealth of the country. The small white stripes in-between the main stripes stands for peace and unity, whilst the warrior shield from the Maasai tribe symbolizes the defence of freedom.

Swahili to English

Wazungu	White Man
Jambo	Hello
Harabi	Hello or How are you
Mlinzi	Guard
Pole pole	Slowly
Bwana	Sir
Ugali	Maize
Sukuma wiki	A green leaf vegetable, like Spring Greens
Chi money	A bribe

Other Books in this series

If you'd like to know more about my books please check out my web.

http://www.tntraynor.uk

You can also find me on Facebook.

https://www.facebook.com/groups/292316321513651

Or Twitter: @tracy_traynor

If you enjoyed this book you might also enjoy one of my other books in this series.
https://www.amazon.com/gp/product/B087JRY8FS

MULTI AWARD WINNING SERIES

WOMEN OF COURAGE

Inspired by the life of Moira Smith 1912 - 1985

Inspired by the Welsh Revival 1904 - 1905

A 2020 Love Story

A story of hope 1958

Standalone Stories with a theme of courage and love

Coming in 2022

The last book in the Women of Courage Series

Set in 1664, Brianna's faith is such that when she prays for people they are healed. Stories about her miraculous healings put her under the eye of the witch hunter Black Wolf, and a chase across England begins.

If you would like to receive updates by receiving my email newsletter, please sign up at SendFox https://sendfox.com/tntraynor

In my newsletter will be updates about my books, book competitions, a book review from me and ebooks that are on offer or free by other authors. The newsletter is only quarterly, so only 4 a year ☺ no spam or sharing of details.

Thank you for reading, I value your support, for without readers there would be no point in writing – and I do so love to write!

Lots of blessings to you,

Tracy

Made in the USA
Las Vegas, NV
23 June 2023

73793656R10184